DUNE MASTER
A
FRANK HERBERT
BIBLIOGRAPHY

Meckler's Bibliographies on Science Fiction, Fantasy, and Horror

1. PKD: A Philip K. Dick Bibliography, Revised Edition
   Daniel J. H. Levack and Steven Owen Godersky
   ISBN 0-88736-096-3 1988 CIP

2. DUNE MASTER: A Frank Herbert Bibliography
   Daniel J. H. Levack and Mark Willard
   ISBN 0-88736-099-8 1988 CIP

3. GOTHIC FICTION: A Master List of Twentieth Century
   Criticism and Research
   Frederick S. Frank
   ISBN 0-88736-218-4 1988 CIP

DUNE MASTER
A
FRANK HERBERT
BIBLIOGRAPHY

Compiled by
Daniel J H Levack

with
Annotations
by
Mark Willard

Meckler

FIRST EDITION   # 16649538

Library of Congress Cataloging-in-Publication Data

Levack, Daniel J. H.
    Dune master.

    (Meckler's bibliographies on science fiction, fantasy,
and horror; 2)
    Bibliography: p.
    Includes index.
    1. Herbert, Frank--Bibliography. 2. Science fiction,
American--Bibliography. I. Willard, Mark. II. Title. III. Series.
Z8398.27.L48   1988   016.813'54   87-25034
[PS3558.E63]
ISBN 0-88736-099-8 (alk. paper)

British Library Cataloguing in Publication Data

Levack, Daniel J. H.
    Dune master: a Frank Herbert bibliography
    (Meckler's bibliographies on science fiction, fantasy, and
    horror; 2).
    1. Herbert, Frank—Bibliography
    I. Title II. Willard, Mark
    016.813'54   Z8398.2/

    ISBN 088736-099-8

Meckler Corporation, 11 Ferry Lane West, Westport, CT 06880.
Meckler Ltd., Grosvenor Gardens House, Grosvenor Gardens,
    London SW1W 0BS.

Printed on acid free paper.

Manufactured in the United States of America.

To
Erin and Daniel Levack

—Daniel J H Levack

To
Mona Clee
and
Bill and Hannah Willard
Wife, Parents, and Support System

—Mark Willard

Contents

Introduction

This Bibliography attempts to cite all the published works of Frank Herbert through early 1987. Such foreign- and English-language publications as fictional and non-fictional works, verse and prose, films and sound recordings, are included. Published letters, interviews and book reviews are not included. The work is not complete, however. Specifically, foreign-language citations are far from complete, and foreign-language book editions are cited more extensively than are foreign-language story appearances because of the more elusive nature of the story appearances (at least in the United States). Also, although 20 of Herbert's newspaper articles are cited, there are probably many more. (Herbert worked as a newspaperman for many years.) Nonetheless, the net result is a Frank Herbert Bibliography more extensive than any previously published and probably close to complete in English-language appearances (except for newspaper articles) through early 1987.

A number of additional features attempt to make the Bibliography both useful and entertaining. Annotations by Mark Willard are included. Physical descriptions are given for the majority of hardcover books and for paper-backs where there was something unusual about the edition. Pictures of various citations are included in the Appendix. A dagger (†) next to the descriptive entry signifies the inclusion of an illustration. Series and connected stories are separately listed as are Herbert's pseudonym appearances and collaborations.

Also, checklists of Herbert's fiction, non-fiction, verse and other media appearances are included for reference and all of his work is cross-indexed in chronological order. A periodical checklist and a representative secondary Bibliography are included to round out the presentation.

Each citation that has been physically examined is marked with a "*" at the end of the citation. Errors in the details of the citation are possible, but this assures that the cited item itself exists.

For a new printing of a book to appear as a new citation it was required that something about the edition other than a new statement of printing be changed; e.g., the cover, book number, price, title or some other element must have changed. When the only change was an additional statement such as "second printing" or lack of a first edition statement, then this is noted by the phrase "Reprinted 1977,1979" or as appropriate, under the affected citation. No doubt a number of these simple reprintings have been omitted.

The NON-BOOK APPEARANCES section contains all works by Herbert that did not appear between their own covers. It includes fiction, non-fiction, verse, a film and sound recordings. Anything not marked as non-fiction or verse is fiction.

For a citation to be included in the NON-BOOK APPEARANCES section it had to represent a new choice to publish the cited work. Consequently, only the first printing of anthologies or collections is given; paperback editions of hardcover editions and reprints are not separately cited or normally even mentioned. There are two exceptions to this rule. First, if the reprints do not include the cited work, that will be mentioned. (It is not uncommon for paperback reprints of hardcover anthologies to drop some stories.) Second, foreign-language translations of anthologies and collections are included since there is nothing automatic about foreign-language editions and they thus represent a new choice to publish the cited work (often the first or only appearance in a given language). However, reprints of these foreign-language anthologies and collections are not separately cited.

In the physical description of states of an edition anything in quotes will actually be found printed in the item cited, with the convention that a double slash (//) within a quote means that the text drops to a new line (a single slash (/) simply means that there is a slash in the text quoted).

Within the body of the Bibliography an all upper case title represents a book, a title with both upper and lower case characters represents a periodical and a title enclosed in quotes represents a story (i.e., anything, including a novel, that appeared in a periodical or in an anthology). For all entries except periodicals the lack of the word "paper" implies a hardbound edition. The format for entries is the following:

a. hardbound books: TITLE, EDITOR (if appropriate), PUBLISHER, PLACE OF PUBLICATION (PRICE), YEAR OF PUBLICATION.
b. paperbound books: TITLE, EDITOR (if appropriate), PUBLISHER, BOOK NUMBER (PRICE), YEAR OF PUBLICATION, "paper".
c. periodicals: TITLE, DATE (sometimes also or instead a Volume and Number and/or a whole issue number).

The extensive Bibliography that Charles E Yenter of Tacoma, Washington had been compiling for many years formed the starting point for this Bibliography. The extensive collection of Frank Herbert's manuscripts, correspondence and books in the Special Collections Section of the California State University, Fullerton, Library added a great deal more. The Special Collections Librarian, Linda Herman, was particularly helpful in allowing access to, and explaining, the available material. A description of parts of that collection is included in a separate section of this Bibliography including a large number of unpublished manuscripts. However, the bulk of the information found its way into the main body of the Bibliography. This collection was particularly helpful for finding newspaper articles, manuscript titles, some word counts and for providing hints which then led to further information. For example, a piece of correspondence suggested that Frank Herbert had written some poetry that was published, and associated the name Jory Sherman with it. When Jory Sherman was finally contacted he was able to provide enough information that Tom Whitmore could, after extensive searching, actually find the five short poems that Frank Herbert had published in 1960 in San Francisco. Another important source was the book FRANK HERBERT by Timothy O'Reilly (an excellent look at Herbert's main themes and their implementation) which provided three additional newspaper articles and a non-fiction article. Additionally, Beverly Herbert saw a very early version of this work and provided some very useful information which was incorporated. Further help was obtained from Roy Prosterman for films; from L W Curry, Charles N Brown and Tom Whitmore for physical state descriptions and; from Brian Herbert for bibliographic information and leads to other people. Manuscript titles are generally from the California State, Fullerton, collection. Word counts are sometimes from that collection, but mostly from Norm Metcalf's THE INDEX OF SCIENCE FICTION MAGAZINES 1951-1965.

Additions and corrections to the Bibliography are desired and welcome, as are comments on format and content. All such can be sent to:

Daniel J H Levack
7745 Jason Avenue
Canoga Park, California 91304
USA

—Daniel J.H. Levack

Annotator's Introduction

When I began the project of annotating Frank Herbert's writings I thought myself reasonably familiar with his work; after all, I considered him one of my favorite authors. This included a small element of geographical bias; I especially enjoyed and appreciated his occasional tales set in the American Northwest, the area from which I hail. I looked forward to the task being interesting, informative and rewarding. I was correct on all counts, but I had not counted on quite how informative. After a brief survey of Dan Levack's working Bibliography I was surprised to discover that Herbert's writings were more extensive and varied than I had imagined. Additionally, I was startled to be reminded that among the Herbert books I had read were a number that I had not liked very much. While I struggled to reconcile my schizoid perception of Herbert as a favorite writer with the overlooked circumstance that I had found a number of his works disappointing or even disagreeable, I forged ahead with rescanning the familiar books and reading the unfamiliar ones.

I was gratified to rediscover a number of stories first read at an age when I was paying no particular attention to details like the author's name, but which had left particularly strong impressions. I also located critical works about Herbert, in particular Timothy O'Reilly's excellent volume (see the WORKS ABOUT FRANK HERBERT section), which illuminated and rendered more accessible a great deal of Herbert's work. The critical texts provided many reasons for my reactions to various works, both positive and negative, and over the course of the project my attitude toward all of Herbert's works changed considerably in the direction of increased apprehension and appreciation.

Viewed simply as entertainment, some or much of Herbert's writing does fall short of masterful execution. Despite his reputation for building a monumentally realistic world in DUNE, the settings of many of his books are sketchy and unconvincing and a number of books exhibit a sparseness in the human dimensions--the realistic complexity or believability of characters and their backgrounds--as well as curious plot manipulations and cryptic (to the uninitiated) thematic concerns. Herbert's "superhuman" or hyperconscious intellects such as Leto II, the God-Emperor, think and behave unlike ordinary people, and the reader has little means of following their rationale. Originally, I was put off by these lacks or complications; I now find them more than compensated for by the stimulation of new ideas and perspectives, broader viewpoints, more vigorous, comprehensive and challenging approaches to life and our universe. Herbert's primary purpose did not always seem to be entertainment (though he certainly achieved this and more in most of his works); rather, entertainment was his camouflage for sneaking up on the reader with mind-altering questions.

Herbert is certainly, as David Miller says (see the WORKS ABOUT FRANK HERBERT section), "an author who follows the same metaphysical questions in sequential books". Herbert re-explores a whole gallery of topics, metaphysical and otherwise, approaching them from different perspectives and in various permutations. These can be ranked on several levels. Some of them include:

- Serial incarnations of the same person, and the effect that awareness of their predecessors will have on latter individuals in the series: police head Max Allgood in EYES OF HEISENBERG, the Duncan Idahos in later Dune volumes and the Tegas/Bacit entity of "Murder Will In";
- Immortality (and/or absolute prescience) leading to ennui: a factor in THE HEAVEN MAKERS, THE EYES OF HEISENBERG, GOD-EMPEROR OF DUNE, the "Ship" series and others;
- Verbal interchanges in which momentous outcomes hang on the character of a gesture or the inflection of a word;
- The value of a back cross, the periodic confrontation and/or commingling of an advanced strain of mentality or of physical humanity with an "essential primitive" or representative of its earlier states: this is one aspect of the serial Duncans in the Dune series, of Raja Flattery/Thomas in THE JESUS INCIDENT and the colonists awakened from hybernation at the end of THE LAZARUS EFFECT, as well as Jorj X McKie in THE DOSADI EXPERIMENT;
- A secret controlling female infrasociety with exceptionally long-term goals: that of the Nathians in THE GOD MAKERS, leading up to the far more developed Bene Gesserit society in DUNE (reportedly based on Herbert's 10 maternal aunts!).

These reiterations of specific situations or general plot facets contribute to the repeated re-investigations of larger-scale concerns, a few of which are the following:

- Synergistic phenomena, interactions where the sum is greater than the parts;
- The functional meaning of various abstractions, such as "peace" or "consciousness";
- A fascination with altered states of perception, especially hyperconsciousness (in most of Herbert's books, particularly DESTINATION: VOID, and including the non-fiction book/film script THRESHOLD about the Blue Angels flying team);
- Awareness of the "jungle telegraph"--the reading of body language and nonverbal cues that might be carried to a degree of refinement at which adepts might divine more information (including truth and falsehood) from a person's unspoken signals than from their actual words;
- Characters acting under immense pressure, frequently achieving hyperconsciousness as an alternative to succumbing to that pressure;
- Conviction of a need for awareness and foresight on a species level (often through heightened or broadened consciousness), and an awareness of the long-range consequences of actions.

Sometimes the re-examination of a particular mix of concerns was a matter of scale, story versus novel. "The Gone Dogs" foreshadows THE WHITE PLAGUE in dealing with the broadcast of a genetically tailored virus; the material and characterizations treated in "Songs Of A Sentient Flute" were reworked in augmented fashion in THE JESUS INCIDENT. In the extreme example, rather than writing a different book, Herbert produced three published versions of DESTINATION: VOID.

These first two general orders of concerns are interwoven with still larger-scale enveloping motifs that permeate the whole body of Herbert's work. I came to think of these overriding concerns as "the three C's": *crisis, consciousness* and *communication. Crisis* encompasses the human range of reaction to crisis situations, comprehension (or lack of it) of how they originated and the fact that human mindsets often seem to produce situations making crisis inevitable. *Consciousness* and hyperconsciousness, and the persistent goal of Herbert's characters of attaining a higher or expanded mode of consciousness, crop up again and again. *Communication* from the individual to the interspecies levels, especially communication of broad concepts and modes of thought and as a path to expanded consciousness, figures persistently as a means of coping with crisis.

A last recurring and reverberating imagery is that of the *ocean.* Oceanic imagery figures in many more of Herbert's works than those actually set in or on oceans and ocean worlds. In an interview discussing his original research on sand dunes, Herbert remarked that "sand is just a slow-motion wave, when you've got enough wind" and the deserts of DUNE are "an ocean without water". The precognitive talents figuring prominently in DUNE are also described largely through ocean imagery; Paul's prescience is compared to the glimpses a rider in a tiny coracle on a wave-tossed sea can get of more distant wave-crests and what lies beyond them.

The oceanic themes and imagery encompass all the motifs mentioned above; waves, tides and currents are metaphors for the cycles of calm and crisis in the affairs of human societies. Likewise, consciousness and communication can enable a perception of a reality as broad and as subtly unified as the world's seas.

When less than fully integrated, or when Herbert's exploration of them ranged into more experimental areas, these themes could interfere with the reader's apprehension or enjoyment of the book. This is best seen in the cases of some of the books I was unhappy with, and what Herbert was actually doing in them.

HELLSTROM'S HIVE, which I read soon after its publication and found very disquieting, confuses us by its character casting. Antipathetic villains and bunglers struggle ineptly through the roles where the reader strains to detect sympathetic individuals of heroic stature. The Hive dwellers are repulsive, inhuman monsters that conduct themselves in such a fashion in opposition to those villains and bunglers that they must be, whether or not the reader consciously registers it, the book's heroes. Readers who don't or can't perceive that their perceptions are being toyed with are likely to finish the novel dissatisfied and unsettled.

In THE SANTAROGA BARRIER the reader is presented with an alternative form of human community and asked: Is it utopia? or Is it an aberration? Herbert is not going to tell us, or even give us reason to lean one way or another, because he wants us to *think* about it and make up our own minds. Enough pros and cons have been demonstrated that the main character's choice at the book's end is not necessarily the choice the reader can empathize with.

Other books are ambitiously conceived but perhaps not fully realized. THE JESUS INCIDENT and THE LAZARUS EFFECT are fitted with *deus ex machina* endings, appropriate enough for novels concerning a supercomputer that has become God, but puzzling to the reader. These novels also have a complex thematic structure, but they don't resonate at quite the same levels, or simply aren't as fully integrated and developed as in Herbert's greater successes. There are too many characters, too busily occupying the stage, for any to attain memorable status. The characters and the world Pandora come across as being set up for their roles rather than those roles and the books' events springing naturally and inevitably from the natures of the setting and characters, as they did in DUNE.

These and other works can be unsatisfactory to the reader looking simply for entertainment because at the end one is left with no signpost;

Herbert provides no resolution of the questions raised, just a poke in the consciousness. Certain things have been brought to our attention and we are left, somewhat uncomfortably, to think them over. This was an intended result; Herbert remarked that he hoped to stimulate hyperconsciousness or other forms of expanded perception in his readers, by writing about those topics. Herbert created truly "interactive texts" that demand far more of a reader than simply choosing between two or more supplied alternatives.

So much has been written about DUNE that it might be foolish for me to attempt any detailed commentary here. Instead, I'd like to mention a discovery, illuminating to me, about the first three books of the series. Herbert has frequently been quoted to the effect that portions of the last two books of the Dune trilogy were written before the first book was finished. He has even specifically stated that parts of CHILDREN OF DUNE and DUNE MESSIAH were already written before he completed DUNE; in fact, he has said different things at different times on the subject, some of them apparently contradictory. The two statements above do not mean quite the same thing, and both can lead to a false apprehension of how to approach the first three Dune books.

As I interpret the available information, the three books of the original trilogy referred to in the first instance are "Dune World" and "Prophet of Dune" (serialized separately nearly a year apart in Analog, but combined, with additional material, into one volume for publication as DUNE), and DUNE MESSIAH. CHILDREN OF DUNE was the fourth volume, or the first afterthought to the originally planned trilogy, conceived and quite probably begun while the first three books were being written, but whose completion was much delayed by other demands on Herbert's time. The apparent confusion may stem from the fact that two trilogies are being discussed; the Dune trilogy as conceived and begun and the revised trilogy as published and completed. Of course it became far, far simpler for Herbert to refer to the trilogy-as-published than to preface each statement with a disclaimer about the trilogy-as-conceived.

This may seem a small detail, but it's especially pertinent to analysis and apprehension of the books in question. CHILDREN and succeeding volumes were influenced by new ideas to which Herbert had been exposed and new directions his writing had taken in the interim, and are distanced thematically and treatment-wise from DUNE/DUNE MESSIAH.

Additionally, there is a quite noticeable difference between DUNE and anything else Herbert wrote. O'Reilly describes CHILDREN OF DUNE as "perhaps too full of ideas forced together *without the brilliant layering technique of DUNE*" (my emphasis). DUNE had a formidable number of themes and levels, which Herbert had to keep in mind simultaneously at each stage in the book's construction. Herbert acknowledged that DUNE was "a book that really drained me"; he was mentally and physically exhausted after completing it. Can one help but suspect that after finishing DUNE, he decided--consciously or unconsciously--that it was neither necessary nor good for his health to work at quite that level of effort again?

DUNE recounted the triumph of a hero; this was certainly a great factor in the book's success, but it was only a part of Herbert's aims. Many readers who found DUNE a marvelously enjoyable book were startled and dissatisfied by the second and third volumes in the series. As in HELLSTROM'S HIVE and THE SANTAROGA BARRIER, Herbert had deliberately led them in an unexpected direction and stimulated them to think about something they were perhaps resistant to considering--if they grasped it at all.

In dealing with mythic resonances, Herbert invites readers to look at the harmful as well as the beneficent sides of favorite myths. Perhaps the most dangerously misleading tenet of the myth Herbert deliberately evoked so strongly in DUNE is that, after the climactic victorious effort, there really can be a sustained fadeout of "happily ever after". The traditional practice in fiction (and perhaps in science fiction more than some other areas) is to end the narrative there, both because what happens later will most likely be anticlimax and from disinclination on the writer's part to challenge such a powerful mythic structure. Herbert said that in DUNE MESSIAH he wished to show how he believed a person of heroic stature, however well motivated, attracts a power structure; an ideology and a bureaucracy take shape around them and assume an almost pre-ordained pattern, like iron filings aligned by a magnet. The bureaucrats and followers adulate their hero because he has enabled them to establish a new, *their*, status quo. Inexorably the new power structure renders its hero less and less effective and finally impotent. Many readers found this finale in which the hero did not remain triumphant deeply disappointing, and so did editor John W Campbell Jr, who declined to serialize DUNE MESSIAH in Analog as he had the two previous segments. Herbert was making extraordinary demands on the reader again; one wonders how many who read the book absorbed Herbert's "pot of message" and how many simply balked and grouched?

Hollywood certainly found Herbert's subtexts unacceptable. Despite his wholehearted support of the Dune movie, and although he was satisfied with many facets of the film, Herbert was not pleased with some of the film-makers' changes such as the ending depicting Paul as a rainmaking god and the deletion of "Chani's good [concluding] line". (In addition, rather than attempting to depict the superbly honed fighting skills and survival capacity of the Fremen, the movie shoehorned in on an incongruous "superweapon" which required the characters to utter peculiar shouts at climactic moments.) Herbert was also unhappy that the movie was too short because of studio policy/bureaucracy; he hoped it might appear someday as a television miniseries with the cut scenes restored.

The segmentation of the original Dune "trilogy" into the two volumes of DUNE and DUNE MESSIAH perhaps diluted its overall intended effect (i.e., had all three of the originally planned "books" been published as one massive volume, reader apprehension of Herbert's message might have been greater); but on the other hand it would surely not have enjoyed such success. (It was highly unlikely then simply for commercial reasons, anyway. DUNE met with rejection from a good number of prospective publishers because of its complexity--which, like the features of most groundbreaking works, grows less remarkable to us with time--and simply due to its length, which necessitated a high, for that time, hardcover price of more than $5.00. In considering DUNE's impact it is easy to overlook, more than 20 years after the event, that it was one of the first very long and complex science fiction novels set in an invented world of such rich background.)

CHILDREN OF DUNE follows the successor to a hero, an individual of potentially similar statute but radically different outlook, who judges that the hero before him erred and fell short. Leto II acts drastically upon unusual standards, and since he is "pre-born" and hyper-human from the onset, he never has the chance to engage the reader's empathy in the way that Paul Atreides did. GOD EMPEROR OF DUNE takes the second Leto still further from his, and our, bases and examines the course of humanity being shaped by an individual who has forsaken humanity. GOD EMPEROR stands somewhat apart from the rest of the series; HERETICS OF DUNE, CHAPTER HOUSE DUNE and the planned seventh book would have formed another trilogy of sorts within the longer sequence.

DUNE and other Herbert bestsellers have inevitably overshadowed some very worthy works. Out-of-genre books by writers perceived as genre authors often end up "orphan children", falling between readerships. SOUL CATCHER seems an undeservedly neglected work, probably because it is not science fiction. In it all Herbert's major and many minor themes are present in full force.

THE WHITE PLAGUE, as well as being one of my personal favorites, is an example of Herbert's "verbal fencing" and multilevel dialogue at its best (unlike previous books where this often came across as strained or over-dramatized); the continuing three-way Herity-John-Father Michael interchange rings more true to life and at the same time more complex and deep, more convincing than other character confrontations where every word is loaded with multiple meanings. One senses that portions of WHITE PLAGUE are perhaps layered as intricately as DUNE, although the novel's end unravels more like CHILDREN OF DUNE.

Many of Herbert's short stories, as well as being more straightforwardly entertainment-oriented, manage to feature the same themes extrapolated in his novels: "Try To Remember", "Come To The Party", "Murder Will In", "The Tactful Saboteur", "Seed Stock" and many others deal briefly and succinctly with communication, crisis, consciousness, the values of a broad adaptability, and in fact nearly all of the topics mentioned earlier in connection with the novels.

While I've said that many of Herbert's works are less than perfect as stories because the ideas, the "bones" show through, in Herbert's works, unlike others of which one might make a similar criticism, a tremendous vitality and excitement communicates itself. Later and "lesser" of Herbert's books are stocked with a groundwork of concepts that might have placed them nearly on a level with DUNE; it seems to be largely the treatment that differs, and the degree of realization of the other story elements. Now, to me, the excitement of the concepts affords a reading pleasure distinct from, and perhaps as great as, that derived from the integration and polish of one of Herbert's books' narratives and the development of its characters.

Herbert had ulterior purposes in the content, style and structure of his writing; he used fiction both to entertain and as a means of conveying concepts that would have had a much more limited readership if phrased in conventional expository form. In much of his fiction the ideas lie very close to the surface, hardly masked by fictional technique. His non-fiction essays are especially meaty and idea-dense, sometimes so much so as to make slow and demanding reading. Many of his works could be called, in effect, essays or expositions not *disguised* as, but *phrased* in fictional form.

As well as being a frequently masterful storyteller, Frank Herbert had important things to say about the situation of the human species and about the ways in which we perceive that situation; fiction was his most visible chosen means of disseminating these ideas. Immersion in Frank Herbert's works and exposure to the scope of his ideas and craft certainly has had and will continue to have a grassroots effect on my own writing and, indeed, my world view.

While the preparation of bibliographic annotations may seem a dry business, it had its moments of excitement. Some of these related to the physical works themselves: finally locating copies of the somewhat elusive NEW WORLD OR NO WORLD and THRESHOLD in the same bookstore in Corvallis, Oregon (and then finding four more copies of NEW WORLD on the shelves of Powell's in Portland!), and obtaining access to older and rarer items. (There were also those that got away. I was not able to examine any newspaper articles with Herbert's byline; and have never seen a copy of TOMORROW, AND TOMORROW, AND TOMORROW, which seems to be a textbook for a university science fiction course; SURVIVAL AND THE ATOM or several short works. Hence a few, hopefully minor, writings of Herbert's have meager or no annotations herein.) In addition there was the intellectual excitement of discovery and apprehension, when a work that had been opaque became clearer or when I seemed to have achieved integration of some idea or admonition presented by Herbert with the workings of the world around me.

This work was begun for Underwood-Miller and completed for Meckler. Work on the annotations was frequently set aside in favor of many and notable pressing distractions. The project eventually spanned four years during which, in the midst of repeated drastic changes in my situation (moving from Idaho, to Texas, to Los Angeles, to San Francisco, getting married and switching jobs with each change of scene), I was periodically re-immersed in the world of Frank Herbert's writings, returning after rumination on his concepts and with new viewpoints afforded by my new experiences in the interims.

In the intermittent course of this project I was able to meet Frank Herbert at three booksignings and a lecture, for a combined total of about five minutes of conversation. I took no initiative so far as trying to involve him in the process of annotating his works, or simply trying to get to know him; at each event I was one of dozens or hundreds of people whose claim on his attention was equally large (or small) and I felt it would be an intrusion on his time and energy. I trusted that opportunity would arise later when I might be introduced to him on a different footing, perhaps after the publication of this book. My mistake; and I was startled and saddened by his death for many more reasons than the simple fact that there would be no more books from him.

There were many works in progress or planned. There was to be at least one more DUNE book, as well as a shorter "prequel" novella or novelette set in the same universe. Another volume in the "Ship" series was in progress. Herbert wanted to see his own screenplay for SOUL CATCHER produced and "do it right", with the tragic ending unchanged. He also hoped to travel to the Himalayas to examine and document the East-West culture clash ongoing in that region.

A few words on the actual annotations: I took cues from the annotators of previous volumes in this series (from Underwood-Miller) while just as often diverging from their approach. Thus, in some cases the annotation is a fairly straightforward summary of the story; in many I have tried to convey something of the mood/atmosphere/treatment of the work as I perceived it. While I usually tried for objectivity, opinions and value judgments have inevitably crept in, even if not deliberately included.

I tended to assume that the reader or user of this volume would be more familiar with, or perhaps more interested in, Herbert's works than the average. That made it no less of a problem, however, to try to tailor an entry both for the individual who might wish to be aware of a story in order to read it, and for someone else who might not care whether or not I gave away the story's climax and in fact might not want to go to the trouble of tracking down the item to discover how it ended. Many situations tended toward a sort of uneasy compromise where the best I could attempt was to keep the plot summaries from lapsing into coyness.

In the case of series or connected stories, the most detailed description of the common background will be found in the annotation for the first in the series by the series' chronology (usually the first-published story or book) with a few exceptions, such as "A Matter of Traces" which is the first Jorj X McKie story but one in which he and the Bureau of Sabotage are featured in a very minor role. Other than actual series works, I've tried to indicate when enjoyment or apprehension of one item might be enhanced by awareness of another.

Thanks are due to a number of people whose help ranged from active assistance to supportive tolerance. Some are thanked in my dedication. Thanks are also particularly due to Ken Craven and Willie Siros at the

Humanities Research Center (aka the Harry Ransom Center) at the University of Texas at Austin, for facilitating access to the Lee Huddleston Science Fiction Collection and the LW Currey Science Fiction and Fantasy Collection. Many thanks are also due to Tim Underwood, Chuck Miller and, of course, Dan Levack.

--Mark Willard

Books

Abbreviations:

Ed - edited

No - Number

sr# - serial in # parts

Vol - Volume

1. **THE BEST OF FRANK HERBERT**
   Edited by Angus Wells.
   The aim of this anthology (and others in the series edited by Angus Wells) was to present "representative stories in chronological order." The book excerpts have additional introductions by Wells, who selected them.
   Contents: Introduction; Looking For Something?; Nightmare Blues; Dragon In The Sea (Excerpt); Cease Fire; Egg And Ashes; The Mary Celeste Move; Committee Of The Whole; Dune (Excerpt); By The Book; The Primatives; The Heaven Makers (Excerpt); The Being Machine; Seed Stock; Bibliography.
   † a. ＿＿＿, Sidgwick & Jackson, London (£4.40), 1975.
   Bound in blue paper boards with silver lettering on the spine. No date on the title page. "First published in Great Britain in 1975 // by Sidgwick and Jackson Limited" on the copyright page.
   † b. (as THE BEST OF FRANK HERBERT: 1952-1964), Sphere: 4523 (55p), 1976, paper.*
   Contains only the first six stories plus the introduction and the bibliography. "Published by Sphere Books 1976" on the copyright page.
   † c. (as THE BEST OF FRANK HERBERT: 1965-1970), Sphere: 4528 (55p), 1976, paper.*
   Contains only the last seven stories plus the introduction and the bibliography. "Published by Sphere Books 1976" on the copyright page.
   d. (as THE BEST OF FRANK HERBERT: 1952-1964), Sphere: 4534 (75p), 1977, paper.
   Contains only the first six stories. Reprinted May 1979.
   e. (as THE BEST OF FRANK HERBERT: 1965-1970), Sphere: 4535 (75p), 1977, paper.
   Contains only the last seven stories. Reprinted May 1979.
   f. ＿＿＿, Sphere (£1.75), 1982, paper.

THE BEST OF FRANK HERBERT: 1952-1964
See THE BEST OF FRANK HERBERT.

THE BEST OF FRANK HERBERT: 1965-1970
See THE BEST OF FRANK HERBERT.

2. **THE BOOK OF FRANK HERBERT**
   Contents: Seed Stock; The Nothing; Rat Race; Gambling Device; Looking For Something?; The Gone Dogs; Passage For Piano; Encounter In A Lonely Place; Operation Syndrome; Occupation Force.
   † a. ＿＿＿, DAW: 39 ($0.95), 1973, paper.*
   Also numbered UQ1039. "FIRST PRINTING, JANUARY 1973" on the copyright page. Reprinted.
   b. (HERRSCHER DER ERDE) [German], Pabel: Terra Taschenbuch, 1974, paper.
   Translator: Eduard Lukschandl.
   c. ＿＿＿, Panther: 04644 (60 p), 1977, paper.*
   "First published in Great Britain in 1977 // by Panther Books Ltd" on copyright page. Reprinted July 1978.
   d. ＿＿＿, DAW: UW1301 ($1.50), 1977, paper.*
   Reprinted.
   e. ＿＿＿, Berkley: 04527 ($2.25), 1981, paper.*
   "Berkley edition   May 1981" on copyright page.
   f. ＿＿＿, Berkley: 07464 ($2.75), 1984, paper.*

† *A dagger indicates that an illustration of the item described appears in the appendix beginning on page 155 below.*

3.   CHAPTER HOUSE DUNE
     The sixth Dune novel.
     This is a direct sequel to and continues the events set in motion at the
     conclusion of HERETICS OF DUNE. (See that annotation for some detail
     pertinent to this novel.)
     Darwe Odrade is now Mother Superior of the Bene Gesserit, held
     somewhat in awe since she has as her primary "other memory" that of
     her near-legendary predecessor Taraza. Dune has been destroyed, the
     renowned Bashar Miles Teg perishing there. All the resources of the
     Bene Gesserit are channeled into resistance of the Honored Matre
     onslaught. The Order has pulled back all it can salvage to the refuge of
     its baseworld Chapterhouse, behind a massive screen of guardian no-
     ships. Losses in worlds, lives and all other measures are stupendous.
     Hidden on Chapterhouse, Odrade has at least some breathing space to
     develop her subtle weapons against the overwhelming numbers, might
     and ferocity of her Order's implacable foes.
     Odrade's resources include: a lone sandworm saved from Dune's
     destruction; Murbella, a captured Honored Matre bonded with the latest
     Duncan Idaho ghola, and Duncan himself, housed in the grounded no-
     ship which carried the worm; Sheeana, the Rakian waif and sometime
     priestess able to control Dune's sandworms and the focus of a cult in
     what remains of the old Empire; and a new ghola of the Bashar Teg.
     Besides engineering resistance to the Honored Matres, Odrade bears the
     mundane but vital task of maintaining her Order's confidence, con-
     tinuing the routine duties of training of acolytes, plantings and
     harvests, and the greater Bene Gesserit husbandry of the human race.
     One of Odrade's greatest personal resources is Chapterhouse itself.
     It is a planet painstakingly adapted and tended over 1500 years of
     occupancy to serve as the Order's heart; a pastoral world of leaf-
     dappled orchards, fresh grassy meadows and pastures; hives of bees and
     herds of cattle. Its cities are pleasant but functional; the whole is as
     near as possible an ecological closed circle preserved by minute
     planning and agencies such as Weather Control, which even hold or
     advance the seasons.
     Odrade's advisors, councillors and friends who share her tasks if
     not her supreme responsibility include Bellonda, the heavyset, florid,
     phlegmatic Mentat-Archivist (of a strain preserved and valued by the
     Order for its natural viciousness), and elderly snowy-haired Tamalane.
     Odrade's council, at times, seems to her constrained by age and by
     ultra-orthodox thinking as well as the dedication, which Odrade cannot
     entirely share, to the Bene Gesserit ideal of confined emotions, but
     potential additions such as Sheeana are too much of unknown quantities
     for this time of crisis.
     The Honored Matres, ranged against the Bene Gesserit-Bene
     Tleilax alliance, have ravaged world after world of the Old Empire's
     center. Dozens of Bene Gesserit keeps and millions upon millions of the
     ordinary citizenry who looked to them for protection have been
     obliterated. Most recently the Bene Gesserit library and training-school
     world of Lampadas has been destroyed, with Miles Teg's trainee the
     Bashar Burzmali perishing in that defeat. The Honored Matres are
     searching relentlessly for Chapterhouse, frustrated by captured Reverend
     Mothers who choose to die rather than reveal its location.
     Reverend Mother Lucilla is the only Bene Gesserit to have
     survived Lampadas' destruction. On Honored Matre-occupied Gammu she
     has managed to make contact briefly with a society of Jews living in
     utmost secrecy and known as such only to the Bene Gesserit. Rebecca,
     a "wild Reverend Mother" of the Jewish sect, shares the memory-load
     of the Lampadas Horde--millions of memory-lives of the Sisterhood on

that world--before Lucilla is of necessity surrendered to the Honored Matres. The sect's Rabbi, despite his people's commitment to the Bene Gesserit, is skeptical of this uneasy melding of influences and fearful of potential disagreements with his faith's tenets in the vast information and new perspectives Rebecca has thus gained.

On the Spacing Guild's baseworld of Junction, where the Honored Matres have settled in force, Lucilla has repeated captive audiences with Dama, the Great Honored Matre. Lucilla's life rides from moment to moment on the paranoid, hyperaggressive Honored Matre tempera-ment as she learns what she can and explores subtle manipulations using Voice. There is no way to carry her discoveries back to her sisters.

The Honored Matres make use of an artificial spice substitute, the source of the orange flecks that swim in their eyes when they burst into anger or violence which is carried out with blindingly swift reflexes. They tend towards lean muscularity, generally wearing capes and leotards. Their strongest motivations seem to be power, the desire to take, control and subordinate, as well as xenophobia and fear of the stranger. Their nature as adrenaline addicts delighting in challenge, excitement, danger and crisis overlies a severely conservative mental stance.

Evidence is mounting that the Honored Matres' return from the Scattering was not only out of desire to possess the natural melange sources but that they were fleeing some nemesis encountered or developed out in the Scattering, more powerful and deadly than themselves.

Futars are creatures associated with the Honored Matres, man-like hybrids of human and feline, savage hunting beings with moderately low intelligence. Although some are kept as captives or pets of a sort by the Honored Matres (who seem both fascinated by and fearful of them), they appear to have been developed as a weapon--but are capable of killing only upon the correct command from a Futar Handler.

The Tleilaxu have fared worse at the hands of the invaders than the Bene Gesserit; all their worlds have gone the way of Dune. The only surviving Tleilaxu master is Scytale, a guest/captive in a section of the same no-ship that houses Idaho and Murbella. The elfin Scytale has only his knowledge of the still mostly-secret Tleilaxu sciences as bargaining material, but hopes to endure until the situation can be altered to his advantage.

Prior to the Tleilaxu erasure, the Bene Gesserit had obtained at least functional knowledge of the Tleilaxu axolotl "tanks." The first ghola produced (actually a clone whose memories Odrade hopes to restore ghola-style) is the Bashar Miles Teg, who must now grow from childhood at a natural pace. Darwe Odrade--Teg's daughter--is in the position of mother-figure and surrogate to the winning, inquisitive child. Odrade has high hopes riding on Teg's Atreides "wild card" tendencies but the Order as a whole is wary and fearful because of the haphazardly reported events of Teg's last days, most notably his mystery-shrouded "acceleration" on Gammu. Odrade also holds the hope that in the Atreides lineage, if nowhere else, the ability to perceive no-ships may finally crop up.

The Bene Gesserit are fearful of the flaws and unpredictable creativity of the Atreides genes as a whole. The line has been one of their most powerful tools but has also produced the premature Kwisatz Haderach Paul Muad'dib, the God-Emperor and his long oppression, and the Scattering. This caution and fear carry over even to the familiars of the Atreides line, the Bene Gesserit remembering Paul's mother

Jessica and her defiance of the Order when they consider Duncan Idaho.

Idaho and Murbella, not having genes from the Siona Atreides strain, are held inside the grounded no-ship to shield them, and thus Chapterhouse, from the perceptions of prescients. They are confined, though not unhappily, in an even greater degree by their mutual interdependence through the sexual and emotional bonding resulting from the interaction of Murbella's Honored Matre sexual-addiction skills and Duncan's Tleilaxu programming. Murbella's adaptation to Bene Gesserit instruction and Duncan's unknown potentials are of great concern to the Sisterhood; thus the couple's every moment, in every room and corridor of their housing, is monitored constantly by comeyes and observers. Even the pair's most casual and most intimate moments are colored by awareness of the watchers recording and analyzing every nuance of word, gesture, expression and action.

Murbella is undergoing rigorous accelerated training in Bene Gesserit lore, with the aim of making her a Reverend Mother. For her the contrast between Bene Gesserit and Honored Matre training has been a heady experience. She hungers for the knowledge and the latencies being awakened in her even though attainment of full Reverend Mother status cannot help but estrange her from her beloved Duncan.

Duncan Idaho's first intense sexual encounter and bonding with Murbella unexplainably awakens, in addition to his original-life memories, memory of the many, many serial lives of his ghola existences serving the God-Emperor. Unlike the compartmentalized Other Memories of the Bene Gesserit, these are to him as the continuous flow of one immensely long existence. In this incarnation, cumulatively, he is mentat, truthsayer, philosopher and more; all this makes him potentially more valuable but equally as dangerous to the Sisterhood. Fellow Mentat Bellonda is particularly hostile to the idea of preserving the ghola and his unknown potentials.

The sandworm brought from Dune has been allowed to metamorphosize into sandtrout in a zone of Chapterhouse where the Rakian desert is being recreated. The sandtrout thrive and Chapterhouse is undergoing noticeable climatic change, with surrounding areas being evacuated as the desert grows. New worms, and spice, are slow to appear.

Sheeana awaits these signs that the full transplantation of the Rakian ecology has been accomplished at the Desert Watch station, passing the time with sculpture and sexual self-indulgence shocking to the more staid Bene Gesserit, although one of her duties is polishing males trained by Duncan Idaho in erotic-bonding techniques to be sent out to plague the Honored Matres. As much as Idaho and Murbella, Sheeana is chafing under the controls of the Sisterhood, wishing to create her own statement of her life. The originally planned bonding of Sheeana to Idaho was short-circuited by his encounter with Murbella, but a fascination is still present. She and Duncan converse in Atreides sign language when opportunity arises, discussing means of escape and rebellion against Darwe Odrade and the Order.

At last the pressure of the Honored Matre onslaught and imminent discovery of Chapterhouse leaves no time for the Teg ghola-child to mature to full adult stature. When awakened to his full memory, by Sheeana's sexual technique rather than the calculated-pain-and-shock method by which the old Bashar restored Duncan to his original memory, the Bashar Teg is still housed in a child body, speaking in a piping voice. An acolyte is assigned to be his "horse," carrying him on her back.

Dortjulia, an exiled Reverend Mother on a backwater world, has been contacted by Futar Handlers and is also able to open a line of contact with Honored Matres. Through these channels Odrade can begin negotiations while laying the groundwork for Teg-planned military strikes against Honored Matre-occupied Gammu and Junction. Murbella's passage through the spice agony and into full Reverend Mothership must also be hastened.

For Odrade the culmination of all her planning is adaptation to inevitable but hardly congenial change, with the cruel climactic alterations to her beloved Chapterhouse as well as necessary radical adaptations for her Order. For Murbella, a unique bridge between the opposing sides, the price of change is breakage of her special bonding with Duncan Idaho. But for other principals the climactic changes offer an escape from the constraints of untenable situations into a broader uncertainty.

a. _____, Gollancz, London (£8.95), 1985.*
Bound in maroon paper boards with gold lettering on the spine. 1985 on the title page. "First published in Great Britain 1985 // by Victor Gollancz Ltd" on the copyright page. Jacket by Peter Goodfellow.

b. (as CHAPTERHOUSE: DUNE), Putnam, New York ($17.95), 1985.*
Bound in a three-piece case with light tan front and rear paper boards and with a light salmon/rust colored cloth on the spine. Gold lettering on the spine. No date on the title page. "1 2 3 4 5 6 7 8 9 10" on the copyright page. Jacket by John Schoenherr. There are minor textual differences between the British and the American editions since they were copyedited independently.

c. (as CHAPTERHOUSE: DUNE), Putnam, New York ($100.00), 1985.*
Special boxed and signed edition of 750 copies. Bound in maroon cloth with gold lettering on the spine. The slipcase is in maroon cloth. Issued without a dust jacket. No date on the title page. "1 2 3 4 5 6 7 8 9 10" on the copyright page. There is a color frontispiece, from the jacket of the Putnam trade edition ("b" above), by John Schoenherr. The limitation page is the first sheet after the front free endpaper. It reads: "Of the first edition of // CHAPTERHOUSE: DUNE // 750 specially printed and bound copies // have been signed by the author // and numbered. // Number _____". The copy the compiler saw was signed on the half-title page facing the copyright page. The limited editions of most of the other Herbert titles that the compiler saw were signed on the limitation page.

d. _____, NEL: 05886 (£2.95), 1986, paper.

e. (as CHAPTERHOUSE: DUNE), Berkley: 09214 ($7.95), 1986, paper.*
"Berkley trade paperback edition / October 1986" on the copyright page.

CHAPTERHOUSE: DUNE
See CHAPTER HOUSE DUNE.

4. CHILDREN OF DUNE
("Children Of Dune", Analog, sr4, January 1976)
Working title "Arrakis".
The third Dune novel.
Nine years have passed since Emperor Paul Maud'dib Atreides walked blind into the desert. This time, however, Paul's sister Alia has acted as regent for Paul and Chani's twins, Leto II and Ghanima, assisted by Paul's widow Irulan, Alia's husband the ghola/mentat Duncan Idaho, and Stilgar, Fremen naib and Paul's Minister of State.

Alia and the twins are all "pre-born," i.e., awakened in the womb to full consciousness and to the collective memories and personalities of their entire ancestry with no chance to have formed discrete personalities of their own to contain and order this shattering experience. The Bene Gesserit Sisterhood fears pre-borns because of their potential to become Abomination, possessed by the (usually malign) ego and intellect of some ancestor.

Alia has in fact lost that internal struggle for balance. Desperate for aid against the clamoring ancestor-lives that threatened to overwhelm her, she allied with and is now possessed by the one strongest within her: her grandfather the Baron Harkonnen. Leto and Ghanima are aware of Alia's state. They have successfully resisted Abomination thus far and have restricted their intake of the melange spice, fearing that heavy use such as Alia's might be a factor tipping the balance toward possession.

As regent Alia has assumed the religious mantle and power roles that her brother Paul shunned. Neither she nor the Baron within her intend to abdicate the regency. Alia knows that House Corrino, the deposed former Emperor's line, desires a return to power and Irulan's sister Wensicia is scheming to place her son Farad'n on the throne. Prince Farad'n is a sensitive, intelligent individual whose mother and her aide, the Saradaukar Bashar Tyekanik, are coaching him into ambition for the emperorship. Without the prince's knowledge, these two have trained specially augmented Laza Tigers to assassinate the Atreides twins when a suitable opportunity presents itself in the wilds of Dune. Since the twins are an impediment to Alia she is in tacit support of the Corrino aims. A number of other factions desire an Atreides-Corrino confrontation, principally the Bene Gesserit Order, which hopes to arbitrate the clash when it comes and regain control of their derailed human genetic program.

The ecological transformation of Dune has gathered momentum until it is nearly out of control, rapidly approaching the point where the sandworms and the natural spice-producing systems will be unable to survive the relative "moistness" even in the regions that are still desert. Alia and her priesthood have chosen to ignore and deny this trend and its potential for catastrophic curtailment of the spice supply necessary to Spacing Guild navigation; the resulting shutdown of interworld transport would barbarize the Empire.

Yet another problem for Alia is the Preacher, a wandering mystic who speaks heresies to the townspeople and decries Alia's rule of the church. The Preacher is blind, guided by a cocksure young boy; many believe him to be Paul Muad'dib returned.

The most immediate threat to Alia is Paul's mother Jessica, newly returned from Caladan where she had retired with the former Atreides Warmaster Gurney Halleck. Jessica has come at urgings from the Bene Gesserit, largely to determine if Alia and the twins are, or are likely to become, Abominations.

Alia's condition is immediately evident to Jessica at their meeting at the spaceport. Jessica is saddened and horrified, and a bitter opponent of the thing her daughter has become. She is unsure of the state of Leto and Ghanima, both cautious of and fearful for them. In interviews with the nine-year-old twins Jessica is startlingly reminded that their vast inner memory-stores include Paul's memories and her own. Leto and Ghanima are much more than children, precociously mature and with stores of insight and "other-life" experiences available to few adults.

Alia has ordered Duncan Idaho to investigate the Preacher. The wandering mystic, however, has been secretly taken to Salusa Secundus, the world of the Corrino's exile, to interpret a dream that Prince Farad'n had. The mystic pronounces the dream significant but refuses to reveal its import; he declares Farad'n in need of intensive instruction in the details and subtleties of power. The Corrinos are offered, through the Preacher, command of Duncan Idaho; Idaho is directed to abduct and deliver the Lady Jessica to them. Alia has also urged Idaho to dispose of Jessica. Duncan is by now aware of Alia's possessed state and full of grief for the woman he loved; he also knows that Alia has taken as a companion Javid, a political aspirant from an obscure, archaic Fremen tribe. He is inclined to fall back on whatever loyalty he discovers he has toward the Preacher.

The open break between Jessica and Alia occurs during a public audience where an attempt is made on Jessica's life. This is also the occasion for the growing tensions between traditional desert and "urbanized" Fremen to erupt into hostilities. Jessica escapes, to be kidnapped by Idaho and conveyed to Salusa Secundus. There Jessica undertakes to instruct Farad'n in Bene Gesserit disciplines in exchange for the banishment of Farad'n's plotting mother; the prince agrees.

The Laza Tiger attack on Leto and Ghanima is unsuccessful, though Ghanima is wounded. However, the tiger incident is Leto's opportunity to launch upon a long-planned private strategy, his vision of a so-called Golden Path, the best way to ensure the long-term survival of humankind. So that Leto may work unhindered, Ghanima hypnotizes herself to believe that the tigers killed him. Returning to Sietch Tabr with news of her brother's death, Ghanima is persuaded by Alia and Irulan to accept betrothal to Farad'n.

Alia believes, and rightly, that Ghanima will revenge Leto by killing the Corrino at the first chance, neatly removing both obstacles to Alia's consolidation of power. Alia has also, in disguise, observed the Preacher at one of his appearances and learned that he is indeed her brother Paul. She is filled with dismay and despair but gives orders for the Preacher's death. Unable to combat her malign possession or seek help against it, she is yet more determined upon the course she has fallen into. She is coming to physically resemble the old Baron, as his habits influence her lifestyle.

Leto, alone, travels into the desert intending to take refuge at the tabu sietch of Jacurutu, once the home of a tribe of Fremen water-stealers who preyed on other Fremen. Instead Leto is captured by smugglers utilizing the abandoned sietch as a base. His captors are led by Namri, father of Javid, and Gurney Halleck. This pair has been commissioned by Jessica to test Leto for his ability to avoid Abomination; instant death is the cost of failure to satisfy them. Namri, in particular, is a harsh judge who declares that his tests will teach Leto to deal with his own powers even though Leto has presumed himself, with his immense memory-knowledge reservoirs, beyond judgment or schooling by the ordinary humans around him.

Leto is fed massive overdoses of spice essence, and in the trances achieves an improved integration of his ancestral personalities. He has in a sense avoided possession but cannot convince Gurney Halleck of this; in addition Namri is secretly loyal to Alia and intends to kill Leto in the end no matter what transpires. Leto escapes from Sabiha, Namri's niece, to forge deeper into the desert to Shuloch sietch, a place yet more secret than Jacurutu.

Shuloch is the home of descendants of the survivors of the original Jacurutu tribe, who now live by selling sandtrout and sandworms offplanet to factions who hope to establish the spice cycle on other worlds. They have also co-opted the Preacher, who uses Shuloch as his base. Leto overcomes Muriz, Shuloch's leader and father of the Preacher's guide, to force his temporary acceptance into the place.

At Shuloch Leto takes an irreversible step along his Golden Path. At the edge of the reservoirs he captures sandtrout, the immature water-stealing polyp stage of the sandworm, and induces them to cover him as a second skin. Control of his internal biochemistry allows him to survive the insinuation of sandtrout cilia through his pores; he and the sandworm forerunners are bonded into a symbiosis that can last for thousands of years. The sandtrout skin is like a living, growing armor that can never be removed. That Leto is no longer entirely human, and will grow less so, is one of the prices of the future he has wholly committed himself to.

With the juggernaut strength and speed endowed by his metamorphosis, Leto is single-handedly able to destroy enough water-trapping and storage facilities to temporarily reverse his debilitating greening of Dune. His course also requires him to tear down Alia's religion and the legend of his father on which it is built, cutting the threads of other visions. Leto and Ghanima, Fremen born and raised, have settled upon a harsh choice among evils. Their choice will mean many generations of oppressive social order for humanity culminating in the Kralizec "typhoon struggle," the race's fragmentation and rebirth into a state infinitely less susceptible to extinction.

Meanwhile, under Jessica's instruction, Farad'n has become more Bene Gesserit than Corrino. Duncan Idaho, his loyalties spent, has resigned from Atreides service and returned to Dune, to goad Stilgar into an awakening to the old traditions. Leto confronts the Preacher, who is now only a vision-haunted shell of Paul Atreides and must yield to Leto's greater conviction. On the occasion of Farad'n and Ghanima's official betrothal, Leto accompanies the Preacher to Arrakeen to draw out Alia for a confrontation by which Leto may seize the Emperorship and make concrete his Golden Path.

† a. _____, Putnam, New York ($8.95), 1976.*
Bound in rust-colored cloth with gold lettering on the spine. States nothing about printing or edition on the copyright page. Subsequent printings explicitly state the fact with a statement such as "Second Impression" or "Tenth Impression". Reprinted many times. There were 7,500 copies of the first printing.

b. _____, Science Fiction Book Club, Garden City, 1976.*
No date on the title page. No indication of printing or edition on the copyright page. Date code at lower margin of page 409. The date codes "H17" and "L04" were seen. The jacket carries the code 3108.

† c. _____, Gollancz, London (£3.95), 1976.*
Bound in buff-colored paper boards with gold lettering on the spine. "1976" on the title page. No indication of printing or edition on the copyright page. Reprinted.

d. _____, Berkley: 03310 ($1.95), 1977, paper.*
First printing is dated February but actually came out in April. "Berkley Medallion Edition, FEBRUARY, 1977" on the copyright page. Reprinted.

† e. (KINDEREN VAN DUIN) [Dutch], Meulenhoff: SF 116, 1977, paper.

f. (   ) [Japanese], Hayakawa Shobo, 1977, paper(?).

g. (   ) [Spanish], Acervo, Barcelona, 1977. Hardcover(?).

h. (I FIGLI DI DUNE) [Italian], Nord, Milan (L4500), 1977.
Cosmo Oro 27. Translator: G P Cossato & S Sandrelli.

i. _____, NEL: 03427 (£1.25), 1978, paper.
Reprinted December 1978.

j.　(DIE KINDER DES WÜSTENPLANETEN) [German], Heyne: 3615 (DM 7.80), 1978, paper.
　　Translator: Ronald M. Hahn.
k.　(LES ENFANTS DE DUNE) [French], Laffont (48.00F), 1978, paper(?).
l.　_____, Berkley: 04075 ($2.25), 1979, paper.
m.　_____, Berkley: 04383 ($2.50), 1980(?), paper.*
n.　_____, NEL: 05075 (£1.50), 1980, paper.
o.　_____, NEL: 05307 (£1.75), 1981, paper.
p.　_____, Berkley: 05315 ($6.95), 1982, paper.*
　　Trade paperback in size. "Berkley trade paperback edition / April 1982" on the copyright page.
q.　_____, Berkley: 05472 ($2.75), 1982, paper.
r.　_____, Berkley: 07179 ($3.50), 1984, paper.*
s.　_____, Berkley: 07499 ($3.95), 1984, paper.*
t.　_____, NEL, 1986, paper.

5.　DESTINATION: VOID
　　("Do I Wake Or Dream?", Galaxy, August 1965)
　　Working titles "When Shall I Wake?", "Many Brave Hearts".
　　The voidship Earthling is launched from Moonbase with a twofold mission. Its ostensible purpose is to establish a colony in the Tau Ceti system; toward this end its holds are stocked with 3,000 colonists plus plant and animal specimens in "hybernation" (a state of ultra-hibernation). The ship will be manned by an umbilicus crew of six until it leaves the Solar System. Then the crew will join their fellows in hybernation and the vessel will be run solely by the Organic Mental Core (OMC), an artificially maintained human brain specially trained to operate the ship's massive, sophisticated computer systems.

　　In fact, the voidship's primary and secret purpose is the development of a super-conscious controllable artificial intelligence. Prior experiments in this field have backfired badly on Earth; one supercomputer constructed on an island in Puget Sound awoke, killed all in the vicinity, and vanished in the destruction of most of the island. Now, for safety's sake, the program is being carried on at the maximum possible distance from Earth. The crew, including those awake and those in hybernation, are expendable clones. The umbilicus crew are a painstakingly assembled group loaded with subconscious compulsions designed to goad them along the proper courses when the ship is disabled by a series of programmed malfunctions and disasters. The Earthling is the seventh attempt along these lines; six previous voidships and clone crews of thousands have failed and been obliterated by the project's built-in safeguards.

　　Before the ship has traveled even a quarter of the way across the Solar System, the OMC and its two backups have gone insane and have to be disconnected. The crew cannot handle for long the strain of doing the massively complicated computations that keep the ship running as it steadily increases its acceleration. Three of the umbilicus crew have been killed by the malfunctioning OMCs. Those that remain are Bernard Bickel, an aggressive, drivingly intellectual computer expert; Raja Flattery, the haughty, self-contained chaplain-psychiatrist; and Gerrill Timberlake, the compassionate, intuitive life-systems engineer. They awaken one backup crew member from hybernation: medicine, ecology and computer-math expert Prudence Weygand.

　　Bickel has access to the computer only through a jury-rigged master board intended to monitor the OMC's performance. An attempt to build an additional gate to the computer backfires and becomes the new, uniquely limited means of input. Bickel, Weygand, Timberlake and

Flattery interact along the lines of their conditioning (some of their qualities have been accentuated, others developed but held in check throughout their Moonbase training), and are prodded by Moonbase Control director Morgan Hempstead into do-or-die efforts to awaken the computer itself to a state of consciousness that will replace the OMC function. Their efforts are both hampered and spurred by emergencies and continuing (programmed) malfunctions: the artificial gravity shifts, the ship's roboxes and other machinery go wild and disaster strikes one support system after another.

The crew's human minds are being driven closer to their maximum capabilities under huge stress; they turn to mathematics, mind-expanding drugs, radically new viewpoints and metaphysical angst in attempting to build a mechanism that will constantly inhabit the heightened states of consciousness that they can reach only at their momentary peaks. Bickel has no blueprint for consciousness; he must design systems into the computer's functioning that will produce an analogue of the attributes of consciousness, in hopes of striking on the real thing. Each contributes to the juggling of unknowns in their own fashion; a means is designed by which all their mental processes can be constantly fed into the computer--Bickel's drive and intelligence, Weygand's feeling and mastery of complexly interconnected systems, Timberlake's humaneness and Flattery's religious conscience.

Flattery is the crew member designed as the failsafe of the whole project; if the end result appears to be an entity that will run amok, he can signal the vessel's destruction. He alone has known all along that the colonization mission was a sham; Tau Ceti has no habitable planets. When the computer achieves a quantum shift in its state of being, after Bickel's attempted transfer of his own consciousness to it, Flattery pushes the destruct button: this proves the last key ingredient that gives the awakened computer-consciousness an orienting sense of its own identity and potential death. The newly created supercomputer is a godlike entity, hyperaware and with nearly omnipotent capabilities; it names itself Ship and announces a new mission for the crew and the colonists once they have been established on a Ship-created Edenic world. They must learn how to WorShip the entity that their creation has become.

The story is a deep and detailed exploration of the nature, attributes and components of consciousness, through the efforts and interactions of the characters. The magazine version, "Do I Wake Or Dream?", was revised and expanded into DESTINATION: VOID. Herbert later re-revised and further expanded this second version; in the latest version's afterword, he describes it as containing "significant additions, rewritten portions, changes in character development, and certain deletions." The mathematics and psychiatric components were updated to coincide with current theories; the revision was also substantially influenced by Herbert's reading, in the interim, of Mary Shelley's FRANKENSTEIN. This is evident in numerous chapter-heading quotes as well as in the book's religious and mythic themes. (Chapter breaks present in the magazine version were eliminated from the first book version and restored in the second, along with the introduction of chapter-heading quotes from Shelley, the characters and others.)

† a.   ____, Berkley: F1249 ($0.50), 1966, paper.*
      "BERKLEY MEDALLION EDITION, JUNE, 1966" on the copyright page.
  b.   ____, Penguin: 2689 (4/6), 1967, paper.
  c.   ____, Berkley: S1864 ($0.75), 1970, paper.*
      Also numbered 01864 on the spine. Reprinted.

d. (EIN CYBORG FÄLLT AUS) [German], Lichtenberg, Munich (DM 11.00), 1971.
   Translator: Thomas Schluck.

e. (EIN CYBORG FÄLLT AUS) [German], Recounte, 1971, paper(?).
   Translator: Thomas Schlück. Published in Switzerland.

f. (EIN CYBORG FÄLLT AUS) [German], Heyne: 3384, 1974, paper.
   Translator: Thomas Schlück.

g. _____, Berkley: 03030 ($0.95), 1975, paper.

†h. _____, Berkley: 03428 ($1.50), 1977, paper.

i. _____, Penguin: 2689 (60p), 1977, paper.

†j. _____, Berkley: 03922 ($1.95), 1978, paper.*
   Revised. "Revised Berkley Edition, DECEMBER, 1978" on the copyright page. An "Epilogue" has been added explaining the revisions.

k. _____, Berkley: 04366 ($2.25), 1978(?), paper.*

l. _____, Berkley: 06263 ($2.95), 1983(?), paper.*

m. _____, Berkley: 07465 ($2.95), 1984, paper.*

6. **DIRECT DESCENT**
   ("Pack Rat Planet", Astounding, December 1954 plus previously unpublished material)
   A very short novel in a very heavily illustrated edition.
   This volume consists of the 1954 story "Pack Rat Planet" together with the longer and previously unpublished story "Direct Descent". The setting for both is the Galactic Library, an Earth hollowed out into a vast storehouse for records and information, with a giant gravitronic unit in the planet's center compensating for the lost mass. The institution is governed by the Library Code, which among other things dictates freedom of access to the Library's information (tapes, randomly selected to ensure impartiality, are constantly broadcast over the Library's 500-channel network to all worlds of the Galactic Union), *and* absolute obedience to all rules and directives of the government of the Galactic Union currently in power. The stories examine two instances when these directives seem incompatible, as tyrants offended by the Library's broadcasts seek to control or shut down the facility. "Direct Descent" takes place 30 generations after "Pack Rat Planet".
   In "Pack Rat Planet" the Earth has become the repository of the Galactic Library, with nearly all its subsurface hollowed out into levels of squares 100 kilometers on a side, containing a vast wealth of records. A giant gravitronic unit in the planet's center compensates for the lost mass. Information in the Library is freely and constantly available to all; tapes are continually broadcast over a huge network to all the worlds, randomly selected to ensure impartiality. Everyone who lives on Earth is employed by the Library in one capacity or another. Unsympathetic factions on other worlds refer to the personnel of the Library as "Pack Rats" and regard the Library world itself as a gigantic, untidy pack rat's nest of useless and worthless trivia.
   Library worker Vincent Coogan is recalled from an information gathering trip to confer with Library Director Caldwell Patterson. A new government of the Galactic Union has been irritated by certain items in the random Library broadcasts and is sending an official censor, who will also consider whether or not to close down or destroy the Library entirely. Coogan is young and vigorous, and greatly disturbed by the much older Patterson's insistence on adhering to the Library Code, which mandates that the Library must first and foremost obey all rules and directives of the government in power. Another Library worker and a friend of Coogan's, Toris Sil-Chan, is preparing a faction of library personnel for armed resistance.

The new government's hatchetman and censor is Pchak, a chillingly brutal individual who immediately kills Patterson and installs Coogan
as Director. Coogan finds his attitudes and priorities altered by the new
situation. While fencing with Pchak and diverting him with Library
records of weapons, gladiatorial combats, and histories and methods of
warfare, Coogan outrages the Sil-Chan faction by insisting on compliance with the Library Code, even to the extent of suppressing Sil-
Chan's rebellion before it comes to Pchak's notice. To this end Coogan
rigs a switch that, if thrown, will cancel the gravitronic compensation
and send every unattached item and person on Earth drifting into
space. Coogan's hope is that the new Grand Regent, Leader Adams, may
be unseated before he learns of Pchak's noncompliance with his orders
and before harm comes to the Library.

"Direct Descent" follows Sooma Sil-Chan, 30-times-removed
grandson of the Toris Sil-Chan featured in "Pack Rat Planet", to which
this is a sequel. Sil-Chan is Chief Accountant of the Library. He is
summoned by Director Patterson Tchung, who reveals an urgent problem
threatening the Galactic Archives: for the past two weeks, accountants
sent by the government have been conducting a ruthless audit of the
Library, with a War Monitor vessel parked in orbit around Earth
enforcing their authority. The government has been incensed by one of
the Library's random broadcasts, a play poking fun at an imaginary set
of rulers whose name is unfortunately similar to that of the present
head of state: Supreme Imperator Hobart of the Myrmid Enclave. His
accountants have been ordered to find reason to shut down the Library;
they have already halted the dispatch of information-collection ships.

Tchung reveals to Sil-Chan the Dornbaker Account, a massive
ongoing expenditure that has been an integrated fixture of the Library's
finances for so long as to be overlooked by the accounting office in
normal business. Somehow it has accrued to such a stupendous sum that
it could bankrupt the whole government if "Dornbaker" demanded
payment. It cannot be hidden from Hobart's accountants for much
longer.

Sil-Chan discovers that the Dornbaker Account is principally the
cost of maintaining the gravometric balances necessary to keep stable a
cone-shaped chunk of Old Terra *not* hollowed out for Library use, the
large end of which is an island in the southern hemisphere. Procedures
growing out of centuries of routine have kept this island and its
inhabitants--Clan Dornbaker and related groups--from intruding upon
the attention of Library personnel. The island is also the last refuge of
the *Sequoia gigantica* trees, for which there is a tremendous added
expense for climate control.

Sil-Chan is Director Tchung's choice to investigate the island and
discover whether or not it might be used against the Myrmid government and its accountants. Tchung's decision seems to hinge partly on
Sil-Chan's youth and unmarried state; the Chief Accountant has been
single-mindedly dedicated in pursuit of his duties, using sex-suppressant
drugs to avoid distractions. While Sil-Chan visits the island, Tchung will
stall Ser Perlig Ambroso, the chief government auditor.

Sil-Chan crash-lands on Free Island Dornbaker and is dragged
from the wreck by David and Hepzebah, nephew and niece of the
island's Paternomer (PN), or clan leader. Sil-Chan finds Hepzebah
powerfully attractive; the PN is absent for two days on a hunting trip
and before that time is up Sil-Chan and Hepzebah are trothed. Upon
returning, the PN is informed of the Library's situation and confers
with his Merlin, a wizened, canny advisor. Although the clan members
live a relatively primitive, tribal existence they are familiar with
Galactic society. More than that, via the massive Dornbaker Account

debt, the PN is the sovereign ruler/owner of Earth. Unveiling a communications command center, he calls for a general assembly of the Galactic Union. Perlig Ambroso and Tchung arrive on the island. As the assembly progresses, Sil-Chan is alarmed by the PN's bid for personal power and takes his own steps to salvage the situation. Revealed at the end are the nature of the island's mass, the reasons for its and the Dornbaker Account's existences, and the motives behind Sil-Chan's manipulation by both Tchung and the PN.

a.   _____, Ace: 14897 ($6.95), 1980, paper.*
      Trade paperback in size. Heavily illustrated by Garcia. "First Ace printing: October 1980 // 2 4 6 8 0 9 7 5 3 1" on the copyright page.

b.   _____, Ace: 14903 ($1.95), 1981, paper.*
      "First Ace printing: October 1980 // First Mass Market Printing: October 1981 // 2 4 6 8 0 9 7 5 3 1" on the copyright page.

c.   _____, NEL: 05406 (£2.25), 1982, paper.

d.   _____, Berkley: 08186 ($2.95), 1985, paper.*
      "Berkley edition/October 1985" on copyright page.

7.   **THE DOSADI EXPERIMENT**
("The Dosadi Experiment", Galaxy, sr4, May 1977)
Jorj X McKie, of the Bureau of Sabotage, is assigned to investigate a rumored secret project holding the potential of crisis for its instigators, its participants and the Consentiency at large. (See "The Tactful Saboteur" and WHIPPING STAR for background on McKie, the Bureau and the Consentiency. Following events in WHIPPING STAR, a strong emotional bond has persisted between McKie and the Caleban, Fannie Mae. McKie has been unable to form any satisfactory emotional relationships with other humans and, while accepting, finds both perplexing and awesome the overwhelming love displayed toward him by this cryptic, multiphase being of godlike powers.)

The architects of the incipient crisis situation are the Running Phylum of the Gowachin race. The Gowachin frog-people are the least assimilated of the Consentiency's many races, a secretive species with a drive toward savage testing, evidenced by their weeding and killing of their own tads and by their complex and bloody legal system. Their "Dosadi Experiment" is rumored to involve an entire world and its population, and to conceal their evidently shameful actions the Gowachin may be prepared to obliterate the planet.

McKie's squat build and gnarled physiognomy lend him the semblance of a grouchy grandfather toad; to the Gowachin he has the fear-inspiring semblance of their oldest deity, the Giver of Law. McKie has been initiated as a Legum of the Gowachin legal process and is licensed to practice in the court arena where law is "religiously fluid", all grounds temporary, and "to be a Legum is to know where to place your feet". Each new decision in the court arena replaces all precedents and the losing Legum forfeits his life, as may practically anyone else-- witnesses, judges or spectators.

At the shrine of Holy Running McKie interviews old Aritch, High Magister of the Running Phylum. Also present is Ceylang, a member of the volatile Wreave species, who is being inducted into the convoluted Gowachin legal system (to offend or injure one Wreave is to incite vendetta with the vastly extended Wreave triad-families encompassing practically the whole race).

Dosadi, Aritch says, was set up as a psychological experiment but has gotten out of hand. Dosadi is a poison planet on which a population of humans and Gowachin has been marooned, isolated by a "god wall" energy barrier. The Gowachin experimenters oversee Dosadi with the aid of the vast powers of a contracted Caleban, who provides the "god wall", jumpdoor transportation to and from Dosadi and epiphanic communication with selected Dosadi leaders.

Dosadi is a crucible where the victors in the harsh struggle for sustenance then carry on into the single city's physical and political battles for power. Hundreds of millions of humans and Gowachin are now overcrowded into a barely habitable zone and Chu, the city located in a river canyon. Above the towers and warrens of Chu the desperate inhabitants of the poisonous Rim seek entry into the city's relative security and plenty. Dosadi's society is militaristic, a warlord system. The experiment's designers counted on the pressures of extreme negative conditions and intense competition to push both races toward their full mental and physical potentials, but their scenario has yielded beings viciously competitive, harsh, ruthless, hyperperceptive and hyperreactive beyond expectations. Both humans and Gowachin on Dosadi are vastly more *effective* than the inhabitants of the Consentiency outside and the leaders, at least, have enough clues to know that they are part of a manufactured situation. They are increasingly hungry not only for escape from Dosadi but for revenge on their unknown manipulators.

The wily Aritch makes Dosadi an issue in Gowachin law. McKie, as the investigating Legum, is obligated to visit the planet via jumpdoor and observe the situation firsthand. McKie suspects the Gowachin of hoping that his visit will spark some event giving them a tenable excuse to sterilize the world.

As McKie embarks upon his investigations, minor bureaucrat Keila Jedrik on Dosadi leaves her relatively secure niche in the tense, tightly monitored power hierarchy of Chu and sets in motion a long-planned strategy to make her own bid for warlord power. Her principal opponent is Broey, a Gowachin and current Elector, head of the warlord system. In their fortified headquarters in the heart of Chu, the principal worry of Broey and his human aides Gar and Tria is trouble between factions; deep divisions exist between the Rim-born and city natives and increasingly between Gowachin and human. Jedrik's goals, however, aim beyond Broey and Dosadi's politics; she means to break out of the god wall and the world itself.

Arriving on Dosadi, McKie learns that Fannie Mae is the Caleban contracted to "play God" for the Dosadi experiment; she is bound to continue by the peculiar and stringent Caleban ethical code. McKie is swiftly picked up by Jedrik's forces. Keila Jedrik is again taken aback at how inconsequential, by Dosadi standards, the "best" of the culture beyond the god wall are; even McKie seems naive, obvious, slow, dull and transparent. McKie himself is dismayed at the degree of cold brutality he must assimilate if he hopes to survive Dosadi.

McKie and Jedrik are able to make accommodations, despite their heated power-political, emotional and sexual interchanges. McKie learns that in addition to her military and political infrastructure, Jedrik has resources such as Pcharky, an aged Gowachin living in an energy cage of his own design, one of a caste of body-changers able to carry out ego transfers. In fact, one of the principal fears of Dosadi's natives is body-switching "travelers" from the universe outside. As well as a psychological testing ground, Dosadi appears to be in use as a body farm; superb physical specimens of the Dosadi-born ensure extended lives with enhanced physical capabilities for an unknown elite back in the Consentiency.

Attempting to utilize Pcharky for a body transfer, McKie and Jedrik confront a basic, fearsome level of the racial unconscious and instead of switching bodies find their identities merged; they share consciousness at whatever degree desired and are able to exchange bodies at will. They escape Dosadi with Fannie Mae's assistance. McKie can then put to use his newly Dosadi-honed capabilities to carry the matter to the Gowachin court arena, where the Wreave Ceylang is opposing Legum. He hopes to bring about the revelation and punishment of hitherto unguessed-at controlling levels of Gowachin society and of the "shadow rulers" of the Consentiency at large.

† a. _____, Berkley/Putnam, New York ($8.95), 1977.*
Bound in dark gray cloth with gold lettering on the spine. No indication of printing or edition on the copyright page. No date on the title page. Subsequent printings explicitly state the fact with a statement such as "Third Impression". Some copies had a banner wrapped around the outside of the dust jacket which was about 1.9 inches high. The banner was yellow and had printed on the front and back "FRANK HERBERT'S // FIRST NOVEL SINCE THE BEST SELLING // CHILDREN OF DUNE". Reprinted.

b. (   ) [French], Laffont, 1977, paper(?).
c. (ESPERIMENTO DOSADI) [Italian], Nord, Milan (L2500), 1977. Cosmo Argento 86. Translator: R Rambelli.
d. _____, Gollancz, London (L4.95), 1978. Reprinted.
† e. _____, Berkley: 03834 ($2.25), 1978, paper.*
"Berkley Edition, OCTOBER, 1978" on the copyright page. Reprinted.
f. (   ) [Japanese], 1978, paper(?).
g. _____, Encounters Book Club (British), London, 1979.
h. (HET DOSADI EXPERIMENT) [Dutch], Centripress, 1979, paper(?).
i. _____, Orbit: 8035 (L1.00), 1979, paper.
j. (DAS DOSADI-EXPERIMENT) [German], Heyne: 3699 (DM 5.80), 1980, paper.
Translator: Walter Brumm.
k. _____, Berkley: 05158 ($2.50), 1981, paper.
l. _____, Berkley: 05514 ($2.75), 1982, paper.*
m. _____, Berkley: 06236 ($2.95), 1983(?), paper.*
n. _____, Berkley: 08525 ($3.50), 1985, paper.*
o. _____, Berkley: 10244 ($3.95), 1986, paper.*

8.   THE DRAGON IN THE SEA
("Under Pressure", Astounding, sr3, November 1955)
In the early 21st century the United States and its allies are ensnarled in a grinding war with the Eastern Powers (EP) that has dragged on for 16 years. Atomic weapons have been used and some areas, including Britain, are radioactive ruins, but at present the conflict is a cold war fought on espionage, propaganda and sabotage fronts.

The United States' oil supplies are running low and the Navy has taken to pirating oil from secret wells drilled underseas in EP waters. This stratagem is running into hitches, however; through a combination of enemy sabotage (suspected due to sleeper agents) and crippling casualties from insanity among the crews of the oil-gathering subtugs, the last 20 missions to bring back oil have ended in failure. As secret as the failures have been kept, they are still affecting morale, already low because of the huge stresses of undersea warfare and the strangling, intensive security under which everyone operates. The two most powerful departments, Security and the Bureau of Psychology (BuPsych or BP), decide to collaborate to produce the needed success. They select the subtug whose crew, from their psychological profiles and past records, has the highest-rated chances. They also replace that sub's psychotic radio officer, the only casualty from its last voyage, with an agent of their own: Ensign John Ramsey, who is both an electronics officer and a trained psychologist and BuPsych operative. Ramsey's threefold mission is to function as a member of the subtug crew, uncover the sleeper agent, if any, and discover the roots of the stresses that are making sailors crack up in the undersea environment.

Members of BuPsych regard themselves as manipulators of the common men around them; at the initial conference the tall, freckled Ramsey and his blind chief Oberhausen use their masterful grasp of psychology and ability to read nonverbal cues to manipulate the Security and Navy people at the meeting. They expect that the crew of the selected subtug, the Fenian Ram, will be as transparent and as easily handled when Ramsey sets to work in the field.

The sub is launched from a base in Georgia, along a 160-mile underground canal into the Gulf of Mexico; the oil field that is its destination is on the Russian continental shelf, in Arctic waters off the western coast of Novaya Zemlya. The Ram is equipped with a collapsible plastic barge, or slug, which will be a mile long and carry a hundred million barrels of oil when filled. Ramsey's fellow crew members on the mission are the patriarchal Captain Sparrow, Lt Commander Les Bonnett and Joe (Jose) Garcia.

The sub's progress across the Atlantic is beset with a series of problems and crises. The corpse of a murdered Security man is discovered in the reactor-room access tunnel; a broadcasting device that will call down EP ships upon them is activated; the crew must avoid enemy patrols and wolfpacks as they approach enemy waters, diving to 8,000 feet to escape pursuers; radioactive icebergs come floating down from the north and radioactive currents run past the bombed-out British Isles; and the Ram sustains reactor-room damage from a battering by sonic search bombs.

From the first Ramsey finds the sub a hotbed of tensions. The atomic power plant which is the heart and lifeblood of the subtug is also a constant danger as its radioactivity threatens to rise above safe levels. At first Ramsey's actions lead the others to suspect him as the sleeper/saboteur; when some intimations of his true mission leak out a different sort of suspicion is generated. Ramsey discovers that the crew has made complex mental adaptations that allow them to function well in the stressful environment, but in his opinion the adaptations are insane in themselves and will inevitably lead to crisis unless he can provoke a defusing confrontation with Captain Sparrow at a noncritical moment. But Ramsey undergoes his own crises of nerves, and unwillingly finds himself, with Bonnett and Garcia, looking to Sparrow as an infallible father figure. The subtug microcosm's every moment and every incident are unavoidably monitored and magnified, in the same fashion that the men's vampire gauges monitor their bloodstreams and adjust the sub's atmosphere accordingly.

The Novaya Zemlya well is successfully reached, but the situation is yet more tense as the Fenian Ram fights its way back through undersea currents hampered by the oil-filled slug. The sleeper agent in the crew has a chance at expiation in the emergency of the sub's balky reactor's full-scale flareup, and Ramsey comes to understand both his crewmates' ways of coping and some of his own motivations and flaws.

In 1958 a flexible undersea oil barge based on the idea of the Fenian Ram's "slug" was designed by a British firm; the inventors christened it the "Dracone" (dragon) barge in acknowledgment of Herbert's book as the idea source.

† a. _____, Doubleday, Garden City ($2.95), 1956.*

"First Edition" on the copyright page, "1956" on the title page. Bound in textured black paper boards with yellow lettering and

Doubleday colophon on the spine. The edges are not stained. No date code. Jacket by Mel Hunter.

b. _____, Science Fiction Book Club, Garden City, 1956.*
Bound in black paper boards with yellow lettering and Doubleday colophon on the spine. Top edges stained yellow. No date on the title page, no indication of printing or edition on the copyright page. No date code (date codes started in Doubleday and Science Fiction Book Club books in 1958).

c. (as 21ST CENTURY SUB), Avon: T-146 ($0.35), 1956, paper.*

d. (ATOM-U-BOOT S 1881) [German], Utopia-Kriminal: 26, 1958, paper.*
Translator: Helmut and Edith Bittner.

e. (21-SEIKI SENSUIKAN) [Japanese], Hayakawa Shobo: 3006 (¥180), 1958, paper.
Translator: Yasukuni Takahashi.

f. (SMG "RAM" 2000) [Italian], Urania: 194 (L150), 1959, paper.
Translator: H Brinis.

g. _____, Gollancz, London (13/6), 1960.*

h. _____, Science Fiction Book Club (British), London, 1961.

i. (as 21ST CENTURY SUB), Avon: G1092 ($0.50), 1961, paper.*

† j. _____, Penguin: 1886 (3/6), 1963, paper.*

k. _____, Avon: S290 ($0.60), 1967, paper.*

l. (ATOM-U-BOOT S 1881) [German], Heyne: 3091 (DM 2.40), 1967, paper.*
Translator: Wulf H Bergner. Reprinted in 1971 and 1978.

m. _____, NEL: 2483 (5/-), 1969, paper.*

n. _____, Avon: V2330 ($0.75), 1970, paper.*

o. _____, NEL: 3001 (30p), 1971, paper.*
Reprinted August 1973, July 1974 and October 1974.

p. (LE MONSTRE SOUS LA MER) [French], Albin Michel: 6, 1972, paper.

q. (DE DRAAK IN DE ZEE) [Dutch], Luitingh, 1973, paper.
Translator: Jan Koesen.

r. (as UNDER PRESSURE), Ballantine: 23835 ($1.25), 1974, paper.*
Reprinted in 1974.

s. (as UNDER PRESSURE), Ballantine: 24494 ($1.50), 1974, paper.*

t. (as UNDER PRESSURE), Ballantine: 25597 ($1.50), 1976, paper.*

u. (as UNDER PRESSURE), Ballantine: 27540 ($1.75), 1977, paper.*

v. (as UNDER PRESSURE), Ballantine: 28011 ($1.95), 1978, paper.

w. _____, NEL: 04547 (85p), 1979, paper.

x. _____, Gregg Press, Boston ($13.95), 1980.*
Introduction by Peter Nicholls. Bound in tan cloth with red lettering on the spine and front cover. "1980" on the title page. "First Printing, October, 1980" on the copyright page. Issued without a dust jacket.

y. (as UNDER PRESSURE), Ballantine: 29829 ($5.95), 1981, paper.*
Trade paperback in size. "First Trade Edition: October 1981 // 10 9 8 7 6 5 4 3 2 1" on the copyright page.

z. (as UNDER PRESSURE), Ballantine: 29859 ($2.50), 1981, paper.*

9. DUNE
("Dune World", Analog, sr3, December 1963; "The Prophet Of Dune", Analog, sr5, January 1965)
Revised for book publication. Working title "Muad'Dib".
Won the 1966 Hugo for Best Novel.
Won the 1967 Nebula for Best Novel.
The first Dune novel.

Imperial power politics require the Great House of Atreides, headed by Duke Leto Atreides, to relinquish its generations-long fief of Caladan and relocate to take up rulership of the harsh desert planet Arrakis, better known as Dune. Other Atreides family members are Leto's 15-year-old son Paul and Leto's concubine and Paul's mother, the Lady Jessica.

The exchange of planetary fiefs bears the aspect of a reward from Emperor Shaddam IV. Arrakis' departing overlords are House Harkonnen, the Atreides' most bitter enemies in the inter-Great-House intrigues, and Arrakis is the only source of the fantastically valuable spice melange.

Arrakis/Dune is a dry, hot world of incredibly vast and harsh deserts, stark wastelands and violent coriolis storms. Melange is harvested from the deserts; only a few know it to be a byproduct of the complicated life cycle of the native sandworms, enormous predators that cruise swiftly through the sand, capable of devouring anything from a single man to massive spice-harvesting machinery. Dune's population and government centers are clustered around the slightly more temperate north pole, in sheltered basins behind the Shield Wall and other mountainous outcrops. The equatorial and southern zones are desert wastelands.

Melange is both a life-prolonging geriatric and, in larger doses, enables sensitive individuals to enter a prescient state where they may glimpse possible futures. In its concentrated liquor or essence forms the spice is essential to certain rituals of the Bene Gesserit order and is the Spacing Guild's key to navigation of their vessels between worlds. Melange is addictive; once it has been consumed in large doses stopping is fatal. All-blue eyes are the sign of a heavy spice diet, both iris and whites becoming impregnated with translucent pigment.

Jessica is a member of the Bene Gesserit sisterhood, an order devoted to the mental arts and conscious mastery of all muscular systems and internal processes, including the use of one's voice as an instrument of control or attack, and the secret manipulation of human genetic lines. Some Bene Gesserit Reverend Mothers are truthsayers able to function as lie-detectors and serve the Imperium and Great Houses in these and other capacities.

Paul has received instruction from his mother in many of her sisterhood's disciplines of mind and body control. Paul was born through Jessica's defiance of Bene Gesserit directives: to further the centuries-long human breeding program aimed at the creation of a superbeing termed the *Kwisatz Haderach,* Jessica was instructed to conceive a daughter with Leto. Instead she bore Paul, the son she knew the Duke hoped for. There is a possibility that Paul may be a latent Kwisatz Haderach. He has passed a grueling ordeal test administered by the Emperor's truthsayer, Reverend Mother Gaius Helen Mohiam, but she is reluctant to believe that Paul can be the Bene Gesserit's end product achieved early.

Among the Atreides retainers who have contributed to Paul's training and education are Mentat Assassin Thufir Hawat; the dashing Weapons Master Duncan Idaho; grizzled, battered warrior and troubadour Warmaster Gurney Halleck; and the Suk doctor, Wellington Yueh.

While the Atreides have been obliged to give up Caladan, the Harkonnens have retired to their power-base world, the drab, grim Giedi Prime. House Harkonnen's head is the gluttonous, cruel Baron Vladimir Harkonnen. His nephew "Beast" Rabban served as the brutal governor of Arrakis, but the Baron is grooming as his heir a younger nephew, Feyd-Rautha. Feyd is of about Paul Atreides' age, quick and capable but tending toward a corrupt nature and petulantly impatient to assume a larger role. The subtle Harkonnen "twisted" Mentat is Piter de Vries, a melange addict.

Computers have been banned since the Butlerian jihad, out of which came the commandment "thou shalt not make a machine in the likeness of the human mind". Their place has been taken by Mentats, humans trained to an expanded use of mental capacities in processing and integrating data that frequently surpasses computer functions. Mentats such as Hawat and de Vries often serve as ombudsmen of the Great Houses.

This interstellar civilization is a charged balance between the political, military and economic forces of the Imperium, the Great Houses and specialized entities such as the Spacing Guild, the Bene Gesserit order, the massive CHOAM trading company and the Bene Tleilax. CHOAM directorships are the counters of power for the Great Houses and Imperium. The Spacing Guild holds a monopoly on transport between worlds.

The Empire's weaponry is an anachronistic mix. Development of personal forcefield shields has left projectile weapons largely obsolete; blades and other hand weapons are in common use. Lasers are available but chancy since a laser striking an operating shield can produce an explosion on the order of a small atomic device. Actual atomics are limited to the holdings of the Emperor and Great Houses and their use against human targets is forbidden by the strongest conventions. Poison is a prime tool of politics and diplomacy, but there is a premium on possession of a military force effective in close combat. The Emperor's power is based in CHOAM and in his legions of Sardaukar--near-invincible soldier-fanatics who more than equal the combined might of the Great Houses' forces. The Great Houses are at least nominally united by the spectre of their being picked off, one House at a time, by the Sardaukar.

The award of the fief of Dune is in actuality a ploy by the Emperor to eliminate Leto, who he sees as a potential threat to his throne. Shaddam IV is secretly cooperating with and using the Harkonnens, in his estimate the second-most-dangerous House.

In the early stages of establishing themselves on Dune, the Atreides are distracted by disruption, sabotage and traps left by the Harkonnens, including a hunter-seeker weapon that comes near to assassinating Paul. There is also a subtle program of Harkonnen-manufactured suspicions intended to turn the Duke and his aides against the Lady Jessica. Duncan Idaho is sent on a mission to explore the possibilities of the alliance with the Fremen--desert-dwelling tribes who have not acknowledged Harkonnen or Imperial authority in the past.

Jessica discovers from a Fremen on the household staff, the Shadout Mapes, that the Bene Gesserit's Missionaria Protectiva has in some past era sown myths among the Fremen, keys to their manipulation in the event of need by any Bene Gesserit stranded among them. There is growing belief among the populace, both town and Fremen, that Paul is the messiah described by certain of these prophecies. Various incidents as well as seemingly chance words and actions of Paul's seem to lend credence to this.

Dune's Fremen are a seminomadic race inhabiting the deep deserts and southern latitudes, where their toughness and survival skills have been honed to a maximum. They live in obscurity because they exist where the rest of the Empire is convinced life would be impossible. Moisture is their most precious commodity and all water is recaptured and recycled from the breath, perspiration and body wastes of the living stillsuits, and saved as well from the corpses of the dead--a person's water belongs in the end not to the individual but to the tribe.

Save for occasional attempts to hunt them down, the Fremen were ignored by the Harkonnens until Kynes, the Emperor's planetologist stationed on Arrakis, became fascinated with them. He enlisted the Fremen as allies in pursuit of his vision of ecologically transforming Arrakis through gradual changes in its energy systems over many lifetimes, releasing water trapped beneath the deserts to make Dune a more benign place with open water and growing green things. After Kynes' death his son Liet-Kynes, who has largely "gone native," inherited his father's position of Imperial Planetologist and carries on his secret dream.

At a banquet in the planetary Governor's residence, and earlier during a spice-mining inspection flight on which they witnessed a sandworm engulf a spice factory, the Atreides have made a favorable impression on Liet-Kynes. He regrets this, for he has Imperial orders to assist in the coming liquidation of House Atreides. The banquet, over which Paul presides after Leto is called away by an emergency, is an occasion of guarded conversations and verbal fencing. Present is a smuggler, Tuek, as well as Liet-Kynes; power alignments, spies of the Emperor, Harkonnens and Guild, and potential allies of the Atreides are revealed.

Paul Atreides has been struggling with what he feels within himself as a sense of "Terrible Purpose", a sort of race consciousness mingled with prescient glimpses of a catastrophic future and his multitude of possible roles in its coming or not coming to pass. This inner awareness has been accentuated by the sudden large increase of melange in his diet on Arrakis, and is agitated by the myths indicating him as a messianic focus.

Before Duke Leto can consolidate his position, House Atreides is unseated by Dr Yueh's treachery from within and overwhelmed by a massive Harkonnen strike augmented by the Emperor's Sardaukar in Harkonnen uniforms. Leto, Paul and Jessica are captured and the rest of the Atreides forces are killed or scattered. Yueh, seeing the Atreides as his only tool for revenge on the Harkonnens who forced his betrayal, fits the Duke with a suicide capsule, a poison-gas tooth. For his "reward" Yueh is killed by the Harkonnens. At his audience with his captors Leto uses the tooth; the Mentat de Vries dies but Baron Harkonnen escapes.

Paul and Jessica are flown far into the desert to be disposed of without trace, but overcome their guards. They are able to travel deeper into the desert with Fremen equipment provided by Yueh in partial expiation of his deed. Paul in particular is numbed by events, his mind in a turmoil of hyperaware abstraction. At last, during a sandstorm that buries their isolated tent, Paul experiences a catharctic bout with his growing awarenesses; he manages to emerge with a synthesis of his Mentat and Bene Gesserit trainings and his awakened prescient talents. He is finally able to reach back to the human dimension and mourn for his dead father.

Jessica and Paul soon rendezvous with Duncan Idaho, who brings them to Liet-Kynes. Paul's commanding presence and maturity win Kynes' trust shortly before a Sardaukar raid strikes the desert station and Idaho is killed defending their escape. Liet-Kynes dies at the hands of the Harkonnens. In an ornithopter Paul pilots Jessica and himself deeper into the southern deserts; his newly synthesized hyperacute Mentat/prescient awarenesses guide them through an immense coriolis storm. They survive the ornithopter crash and a desert crossing menaced by the largest sandworms they have yet seen. Even in these straits, Jessica continues Paul's instruction in Bene Gesserit disciplines.

Harkonnen and Sardaukar forces proceed inexorably with the mop-up of Atreides survivors who, like Mentat Thufir Hawat, are stunned by the magnitude of the coup. Hawat and the remnants of his troops encounter Fremen and witness that the Dune natives are more than a match for the dread Sardaukar in combat, but Hawat is captured by a Sardaukar force before this knowledge can be implemented. Warmaster Gurney Halleck escapes, linking up with the spice smuggler, Tuek.

In the deeper deserts Paul and Jessica encounter a Fremen band led by Stilgar, right hand of Liet-Kynes. Stilgar feels bound to save only Paul but is dissuaded from "taking Jessica's water" by her forcible demonstration that Bene Gesserit training in unarmed combat can master an armed Fremen. One Fremen, Jamis, still objects to the rescue of either of the fugitives. Among this group Paul encounters Chani, daughter of Liet-Kynes; he has seen her face in numberless prescient visions.

Jamis, grudging the acceptance of Jessica into the tribe, challenges her through Paul as her champion; Paul kills him in single combat, the first man he has so dueled. Paul takes the Fremen name Muad'dib, the kangaroo mouse, another presciently-foreseen event. However Paul is still learning the uses, extents and necessity for caution in reliance on his prescience and "prescient memory"--knowledge of situations foreseen in such detail and certainty that he seems to have already lived them.

Baron Harkonnen acquires Thufir Hawat from the Sardaukar and, manipulating him through false information, coerces him into Harkonnen service as a replacement for the dead Piter de Vries. Hawat is convinced that Lady Jessica was the betrayer of House Atreides, perhaps acting from obscure Bene Gesserit motives. Hawat also perceives House Harkonnen as a tool that he may use and use up against the Emperor, whose involvement he feels to have been the final factor in laying low House Atreides.

The Baron has reinstated his brutish nephew Rabban as governor of Arrakis, this time with a completely free hand to squeeze the planet and earn back Harkonnen losses and expenditures. The Baron anticipates eventual replacement of Rabban with his younger nephew Feyd-Rautha, who compared to Rabban will be received by the populace as a deliverer.

Feyd-Rautha's ambitions have been fanned; Hawat is playing him against the old Baron as he is playing the Harkonnens in total against the Emperor. On Giedi Prime, Feyd kills his hundredth slave-gladiator in an unexpectedly dramatic arena bout planned with Hawat's assistance. The event is attended by Imperial emissaries Count and Lady Fenring; Fenring is the Emperor's "errand boy", with messages and warnings for the Baron. The shared secret of the Arrakis operation is festering into suspicion and distrust between House Harkonnen and the Emperor. Additionally, the Emperor's alarm has been awakened by a chance mention of the Baron's plans for Arrakis. Lady Fenring is a Bene Gesserit who before departure secures Feyd-Rautha's genes for her Order and conditions him with hypno-ligation.

On Dune, Jessica replaces the Fremen tribe's aging Reverend Mother in a ceremony involving her manipulation of her internal biochemistry to transmute the Water of Life, the poisonous liquid exhalation of a drowned small sandworm. This becomes a mind-expanding narcotic facilitating the absorption of the memory-personalities of the old Reverend Mother and all her female ancestry. Because the ritual was begun in ignorance that Jessica was pregnant, her unborn daughter, Alia, is subjected to the awakening and memory-absorption process as well. In the sharing of the drug, Paul and Chani recognize each other as lifemates.

Over the following years Paul and Jessica adapt to Fremen ways of deep-desert survival and to the crowded sietch communities. They learn that Fremen numbers are much greater than previously guessed, that their population is distributed in many widely scattered communities, and that the tribespeople are able to traverse Dune's forbidding deserts rapidly by luring the giant sandworms to be captured and ridden. Paul and Chani have a son. Alia is now old enough to make the Fremen uneasy by her strangely precocious mix of adult comprehension and mannerisms and a child's form and emotions.

Nearly three years pass before Paul feels ready to move against the Harkonnens and Imperium. He has fulfilled one after another of the Bene Gesserit-planted prophecies and the complicating Arrakeen elaborations regarding the coming of the messiah and liberator, and has shaped and directed Fremen harassment of the Harkonnens; he has brought organization and mission to the Fremen, melding Kynes' ecological vision with his own and with his plans to recover the Atreides fief. Paul has learned how to deal with his prescience more effectively. He realizes it is a thing of summits, abysses and maelstroms of vision, lines and nexuses, gaps and stretches of "blind time"; it can also produce periods in which he foresees events practically word-for-word. Jessica is at times fearful of her son and his strangeness. The omnipresent melange in the Fremen diet has fueled Paul's prescient abilities and his sense of himself--messiah or not--as an instrument able and thus perhaps obligated to shape the future of Arrakis and of all humanity.

Paul's singlehanded capture of a sandworm is the last test necessary for him to achieve full acceptance into Fremen manhood, and thus leadership. This accomplished, he was expected to call out, kill and replace the naib Stilgar. Instead, Paul seizes the opportunity to demonstrate that many of the old Fremen ways must change for his new order. He puts on his father's ducal signet ring and claims Arrakis as his fief.

Atreides warmaster Gurney Halleck has turned up in a captured band of spice smugglers. Sardaukar spies discovered among the band are bested by the Fedaykin of Paul's elite guard. Halleck, still believing that Jessica was the betrayer of Duke Leto, is narrowly prevented from killing her.

Paul, disturbed by failures of his prescience (Gurney's return, and the incident with Jessica, were not foreseen) along with the sense of tumultuous events moving toward a nexus, takes the test of the Water of Life and is thrown into a weeks-long catatonia. When Chani and Jessica succeed in reviving him, he proves himself to be the Kwisatz Haderach, the product of the Bene Gesserit's genetic manipulations achieved early and escaped from them.

As Muad'dib, Paul has become known to the Emperor and Harkonnens as the leader and instigator of Fremen guerrilla warfare. The constant drain of Fremen raids and Fremen disruption of melange production are finally significant enough that the Emperor, accompanied by all of the Great Houses with CHOAM company holdings, mounts an expedition to Arrakis to stamp out Fremen interference with the only spice source. Paul is ready to grapple with the Imperium, but is also prepared to release a biological chain reaction destroying the sandworms and spice, and thus the foundations of Imperial, Guild and CHOAM power.

In a tremendous coriolis storm Paul, Gurney and Stilgar direct the use of the Atreides family atomics to open passage through the range of hills sheltering the Imperial and Harkonnen forces, just as a garbled message from the south informs Paul of a Sardaukar raid in which his son was killed and his sister captured. Paul proceeds with the attack in the face of this bitter personal loss. The Emperor's ships are immobilized; the allied forces are overwhelmed by Fremen and sandworms attacking through the breached Shield Wall. Alia has been brought to the attention of the Emperor's truthsayer, Gaius Helen Mohiam, who urges her death as an Abomination. Before escaping in the confusion, Alia kills Baron Harkonnen.

Paul Muad'dib interviews the captured Emperor and his entourage in the old Governor's Mansion, the residence where the Atreides began their occupancy of the planet. There Thufir Hawat refuses to cooperate in a scheme to poison Paul, dying himself; Feyd-Rautha Harkonnen, claiming vendetta, challenges Paul to a duel and is killed by him. Count Fenring, who might have achieved the task, declines to slay Paul for the Emperor. The Guild and other power centers must bow to Paul's control of Arrakis and the spice sources. The Emperor is constrained to abdication and an "alliance" seating Paul on the throne by his marriage to the Emperor's daughter Irulan. This is for form's sake only; like Jessica with Paul's father Leto, Chani, without official seal, will be Paul's true and only wife.

The novel DUNE is composed of the material separately serialized as "Dune World" and "Prophet of Dune", along with a glossary and appendices incorporating portions of Herbert's research and background for the book.

† †a.   ____, Chilton, Philadelphia ($5.95), 1965.*
Bound in blue cloth with white lettering on the spine. States "First Edition" on the copyright page. No date on the title page. The second printing states "Second Printing, April, 1968" and is bound in green cloth. The third and fourth printings state "Third Printing, November 1970" and "Fourth Printing, December 1972" respectively and are bound in red cloth. The fifth and later printings all state "First Edition" without further printing statements. However, they all have a line of the form "5 6 7 8 9 0 4 3 2 1 0 9 8 7 6" added on the copyright page which indicates the printing. There were 2,000 copies of the first printing.

b.   ____, Gollancz, London (30/-), 1966.
Reprinted.

c.   ____, Ace: N-3 ($0.95), 1967, paper.*

d.   (DER WÜSTENPLANET) [German], Heyne: 3108/3109 (DM 3.80), 1967, paper.*
Translator: Wulf H Bergner. Reprinted in 1971. Abridged.

e.   ____, Four Square Books: 2176 (10/6), 1968, paper.*

f.   ____, Ace: 17620 ($0.95), 1968, paper.*
Corrects errors in the text of the first Ace edition.

g.   (DUNE SUNANO WAKUSEI) [Japanese], Hayakawa Shobo, 1968.
Translator: Yano Tetsu.

h.   ____ [French], Laffont (24.20F), 1970, paper(?).
Translator: Michel Demuth.

i.   ____, Science Fiction Book Club, Garden City, 1971.*
Bound in red paper boards with silver lettering on the spine. No date on the title page. No indication of printing or edition on the copyright page. Code 1681 on the dust jacket. Date code at lower left margin of page 509. 47M was in the first printing. At least 33R has also been used.

j.   ____, Ace: 17261 ($1.25), 1971(?), paper.*

k.   ____, Ace: 17262 ($1.50), 1972(?), paper.*

l.   ____, NEL: 00089 (60p), 1972, paper.

m.   _____, NEL: 01184 (75p), 1972, paper.
n.   (DUNE SUNANO WAKUSEI) [Japanese], Hayakawa Shobo, 1972-73, paper.
        Translator: Yano Tetsu. Two volumes, illustrated.
o.   _____, Ace: 17263 ($1.50), 1973, paper.*
p.   _____ [Italian], Nord, Milan (L4500), 1973.
        Cosmo Oro 8. Translator: Giampaolo Cossato. Illustrated.
q.   _____, NEL: 02286 (80p), 1974, paper.
r.   _____, Ace: 17264 ($1.95), 1974, paper.*
† s.   (DUIN) [Dutch], Meulenhoff: SF 70, 1974, paper.
        Translator: M K Stuyter. Reprinted in 1975 and 1977.
t.   _____ [French], Laffont, 1974, paper(?).
        Translator: Michel Demuth. Combined with DUNE MESSIAH.
u.   _____, NEL: 02727 (90p), 1975, paper.*
v.   _____ [Spanish], Acervo, Barcelona, 1975. Hardcover(?).
w.   _____, Ace: 17265 ($2.25), 1975, paper.*
x.   _____, Berkley: T2706 ($1.95), 1975, paper.*
        Also numbered 02706 on the spine. Reprinted.
y.   (   ) [Portuguese], Editora Nova Fronteira, 1976, paper(?).
z.   (   ) [Danish], Borgens Forlag, 1977, paper(?).
aa.   _____, NEL: 03569 (L1.25), 1977, paper.
ab.   _____, Berkley: 03698 ($2.25), 1977, paper.*
† ac.   _____, Berkley: 04376 ($2.50), 1977, paper.*
† ad.   (as THE ILLUSTRATED DUNE), Berkley Windhover: 03891 ($7.95), 1978, paper.*
        Illustrated in color and black and white by John Schoenherr. Trade paperback size. "Berkley Windhover Edition, AUGUST, 1978" on the copyright page.
ae.   (DER WÜSTENPLANET) [German], Heyne: 3108, 1978, paper.
        Translator: Ronald M Hahn. New unabridged edition.
af.   _____, NEL: 04230 (L1.50), 1979, paper.
ag.   _____ [French], Edits-Service, 19??, paper(?).
        Published in Switzerland.
ah.   _____, Oxford University Press (British), 1981, paper(?).
        Abridged school edition.
ai.   _____, NEL: 05172 (L1.75), 1981, paper.
aj.   _____, Berkley: 05313 ($7.95), 1982, paper.*
        Trade paperback size. "Berkley trade paperback edition / April 1982" on the copyright page.
ak.   _____, Berkley: 05471 ($2.95), 1982, paper.*
al.   _____, Berkley: 06434 ($3.95), 1983(?), paper.*
am.   _____, Putnam, New York ($16.95), 1984.*
an.   _____, Berkley: 07160 ($3.95), 1984(?), paper.*
ao.   _____, Berkley: No Number (No Price), 1984, paper.*
        A special 500-copy edition produced for distribution at the 1984 American Booksellers Association (ABA) convention. It was not for sale. It had a movie tie-in cover and a credits page but no stills from the movie (citation "aq") except for some pictures on the back cover. "Special ABA Limited Edition" printed on the front cover. "Special limited edition / May 1984" on the copyright page.
ap.   _____, Berkley: 08002 ($3.95), 1984, paper.*
        This edition has pictures from the movie on the back cover but no other stills. It is the same cover as citation "ao" above except that a book number and a price have been added and the "Special ABA" banner has been removed from the cover.
aq.   _____, Universal, 1984.*
        A major motion picture based on the novel. About 2 hours, 16

minutes in length. Produced by Raffaella De Laurentiis. Directed by David Lynch using a screenplay by David Lynch.

ar. _____, Berkley: 07623 ($2.95), 1984, paper.
This is the mass-market edition of the Marvel Comics' Dune: The Official Comic Book. It is in full color. See citation "as".

as. _____, Berkley: 07632 ($3.95), 1984, paper.
Full-color comic book of the movie. 8.5" by 11".

at. _____, Berkley: 08002 ($3.95), 1986(?), paper.*
This is the same book number as citation "ap" and it has the same price. However, it has a different cover and no indication of a movie tie-in.

au. _____, NEL: 01184 (L3.50), 1986, paper.*

av. _____, The Easton Press, Norwalk (Connecticut), ($34.50), Forthcoming.
Bound in red leather with gold lettering on the spine and front cover. Gold design on the front cover. Gilded edges. Red sewn ribbon page marker.

There have been a large number of additional products associated with DUNE. These include a Dune game from Avalon Hill in 1979; various books of puzzles, games and mazes; coloring books; books based on the making of the Dune movie; and a juvenile adaptation of the David Lynch Dune screenplay (by Joan D Vinge).

10. **DUNE MESSIAH**
("Dune Messiah", Galaxy, sr5, July 1969)
Working title "The Fool Saint".
The Second Dune novel.
It is 12 years since Paul Atreides' overthrow of Emperor Shaddam IV. Paul Muad'dib now rules the new Empire from Dune, with the deposed Emperor's daughter Irulan as his official consort but his Fremen love, Chani, as actual wife. Paul could not prevent the massive jihad he foresaw; the Fremen holy war in his name has swept across scores of planets at a cost of billions of lives. The ecological transformation of Arrakis is proceeding apace and the Fremen see their fabled goals becoming a slightly different reality.

Around Paul the apparatus of Imperial government has acquired a momentum of its own, which he loathes; likewise he will not accept the godhood his followers would like to thrust upon him. Stilgar, the French naib and now Paul's Minister of State, is as little pleased as Paul. A cult known as the Quizarate (headed by Korba, once one of Paul's Fedaykin and now an immaculate fop) has formed around Paul and his visions and mysteries; it is also a civil service and functions as "God's spy system".

Paul's sister Alia, who was awakened to full consciousness and ancestral memory in her mother's womb in the Water of Life ritual, is approaching 16 and young womanhood, a virgin Reverend Mother, witty, cruel and whimsical. She has Quizarate ritual duties as St. Alia of the Knife but, like Paul, angers the Quizarate priesthood by refusing to take their trappings seriously.

The jihad has done violence to the Fremen way of life; there are now sick, disabled, disaffected and bored Fremen as well as those like Korba who have taken up politics, bureaucracy and power-intrigues. Few Fremen keep the traditions. As the authority of their social systems disintegrate, many Fremen have joined in a widespread conspiracy dissatisfied with Paul.

The other powerful entities of the human sphere are beginning to recover from the jihad and gather opposition to Paul's new Imperium. At a secret rendezvous the following group of conspirators seeks to unify their plotting: for the Bene Gesserit, Reverend Mother Gaius Helen Mohiam, the former Emperor's Truthsayer, and Paul's consort Irulan, a Bene Gesserit trainee; the Bene Tleilax represented by Scytale, a "human chameleon" Face Dancer and shape-shifter who can adopt any appearance; and the bizarre Spacing Guild Steersman Edric, a lesser-order prescient whose presence muddies Paul's own prescient visions and masks the meeting of the conspirators from Paul's perceptions.

Though they make common cause at the moment, these plotters in actuality share few goals. Irulan wants children by Paul to legitimatize her position, while the rest hope to see him deposed or destroyed; the Bene Gesserit wish to maintain control of their gene lines and breeding programs; the Guild hope for a return to something more like the old order.

The Tleilaxu are a guild of amoral scientists, hoping to gain a hold upon the Emperor and harness his powers, but motivated as well by complex codes and attitudes; their conceptions of good and evil are skewed from the norms and their intrigues seem rooted in curiosity and the thrill of experimentation as much as in ambition.

Paul and Chani have been prevented from having children by Irulan's secret addition of contraceptive drugs to Chani's food. Paul refuses Irulan's demands for an heir by herself despite even Chani's entreaties that he make some provision--by Irulan if no other way--for the path of inheritance of his Empire.

Paul is weary of the Empire's protocols and politicking. His deepest hope is for an honorable way to disengage himself and Chani from the juggernaut his prior actions have set in motion. Having shaped the future once, and seeing its possible permutations from his unique vantage, he feels it necessary to continue; he is tied to the Empire by his sense of responsibility to the governed and the obligation he feels to try to control the flagging jihad. A few events are so clear as to be nearly definite, but for the most part his prescience grants him glimpses of a fluctuating, mutable vision of a landscape of varying futures. A new Dune Tarot further muddies the views of the future via feedback by the minor prescient talents utilizing it. Paul's visions, particularly one of a falling, crashing moon, bring him only uncertainty and bitterness; he seems to see the failure of all his hopes and cannot be certain that he himself is not the instrument inevitably bringing this about. The courses set upon are difficult to alter and at times Paul feels reduced to following the pattern of events that will simply result in the fewest great evils. The gaps and uncertainties of the presciently seen future, as well as the irrevocably predetermined events and important concatenations upon which Paul must wait to make one turning or another, distance him from events.

Edric's Guild ship brings the conspirators to Dune. Paul has Reverend Mother Mohiam arrested, but Scytale along with Bijaz, a Tleilaxu-created dwarf, goes underground and contacts Fremen malcontents. From the blind son of Farok, an embittered old Fremen fighter, Scytale receives a wealth of information--details of the Fremen conspiracy against Paul and data enough to make the Tleilaxu self-sufficient on Dune.

Meanwhile Edric has made a gift to Paul of another Tleilaxu creation: a "ghola" of Paul's friend, mentor, and Atreides Weapons Master Duncan Idaho, who was killed in the Harkonnen/Sardaukar coup upon House Atreides. The ghola is a clone regrown from cells of the corpse, lacking the memories of the original Duncan. The Tleilaxu have named this ghola Hayt and made him a Mentat and Zensunni philosopher, as well as equipping him with disturbing, metallic artificial eyes. Paul has had no prescient forewarning of this event and personage, and for the sake of his emotional ties to the dead Duncan he keeps Hayt with him over the objections of his advisors and the ghola's own declaration that he feels himself to be some sort of weapon aimed at Paul. Paul is fascinated by the company and conversation of the ghola, honesty and openness cloaked in Zensunni mystery.

Alia is immediately both attracted to and repelled by the ghola, and intrigued to note signs of at least some original memories in the revenant. This is as planned by the double thrust of the Tleilaxu plot; the ghola's complexity and innocence, as well as the Duncan Idaho bravado and charm, are a mystical catalyst awakening Alia to her womanhood.

Paul, feeling a threat to Chani, bargains with Gaius Helen Mohiam in her cell and offers the possibility of an heir with Irulan in exchange for the promise of Chani's life spared. In the meantime Chani has retreated to desert holds where the contraceptive can no longer be administered, and become pregnant and thus yet more dangerous to the conspirators. Her condition is complicated by aftereffects of the drug.

Paul is summoned by Scytale in the guise of the daughter of Otheym, a supposedly disaffected Fremen, to Otheym's house in a slum of Arrakeen, a district full of maimed Fremen veterans of the jihad. Otheym is secretly loyal and informs Paul of treachery, presenting him with the dwarf Bijaz who has been imprinted with names of all the conspirators. This scenario is one of the crux points of Paul's strongest future visions: he delays leaving until he has heard certain words and the scene as revealed ,in prescience has transpired in actuality. As Paul withdraws and his troops move in Otheym's house is destroyed in a pillar of fire by a stone burner--a feared atomic device whose radiation blinds Paul and all others in the vicinity.

Use of the stone burner is traced to Korba and the Quizarate; Paul's religious bureaucracy is hungry enough for power that it will martyr its own prophet to render him more controllable. Paul, Alia and Stilgar orchestrate the trial of Korba for the stone burner's use and for Korba's attempts to capture a sandworm and set up spice production on some other world. Paul has refused Tleilaxu eye implants, leaving his eye sockets forbidding empty holes and creating misgivings among the Fremen, whose cultural bias is to consider a maimed individual as worthless. Yet at the trial the onlookers are awed by Paul's appearance, walking, addressing and describing those in the chamber, carrying himself like a man with full sight. He is operating on prescient vision of a future so preordained from the moment of his blinding that he has already lived it through foreknowledge; to function he has but to "remember."

The two Tleilaxu tools meet when Hayt interviews Bijaz. The ghola is unknowingly primed by the dwarf to assassinate Paul upon a certain cue, while appearing to offer him a Tleilaxu bargain. Coming from this interview, Hayt prevents Alia's death from a massive overdose of melange. Not wishing to live within the constrictions, murky paths and unbearable bonds of her brother's prescience and her limited role within it, she tired to pierce the "prescient fog". She and Hayt admit their love for each other.

As Chani's time for giving birth approaches, Paul retires with her to Sietch Tabr. Chani dies giving birth and Paul's prescient vision ends with that moment and still another unexpected event: the offspring are twins.

Hayt's Duncan Idaho personality and memories resurface, fully awakened by the overcoming of his programming to kill Paul. Scytale tempts Paul with a bargain, with Duncan as example; for concessions, the Tleilaxu will produce and restore to full memory a ghola of Chani.

Paul kills him. Blind, Chani gone and all his role fulfilled, Paul in Fremen fashion disappears into the desert.

† a. _____, Putnam, New York ($4.95), 1969.*
Bound in brown paper boards with black lettering on the spine and front cover. No date on title page. No indication of printing or edition on the copyright page. Subsequent printings explicitly state the fact with a statement such as "Third Impression". The second printing is bound in black paper with silver lettering and the third is bound in rust-colored cloth with black lettering. It is uncommon for Putnam to change binding with various printings.

b. _____, Berkley: N1847 ($0.95), 1970, paper.*
Also numbered 01847 on the spine. Reprinted.

c. _____, Gollancz, London (£1.60), 1971.*

d. (DER HERR DES WUSTENPLANETEN) [German], Heyne: 3266 (DM 3.80), 1971, paper.
Translator: Walter Brumm. Abridged.

e. _____, NEL: 01229 (40p), 1972, paper.
Reprinted April 1973, August 1973, December 1973, July 1974 and October 1974.

f. (LE MESSIE DE DUNE) [French], Laffont (22.00F), 1972, paper(?).
Translator: Michel Demuth.

g. (DUNE SABAKU NO KYUSEISHU) [Japanese], Hayakawa Shobo, 1973, paper.
Translator: Yana Toru.

h. (MESSIA DI DUNE) [Italian], Nord, Milan (L4500), 1974.
Cosmo Oro 12. Translator: Giampaola Cossato and Sandro Sandrelli.

i. _____, Berkley: Z2601 ($1.25), 1974, paper.*
Also numbered 02601.

j. _____, NEL: 02285 (60p), 1974, paper.

k. (LE MESSIE DE DUNE) [French], Laffont, 1974, paper(?).
Translator: Michel Demuth. Combined With DUNE.

l. _____, Berkley: D2952 ($1.50), 1975, paper.*
Also numbered 02952 on the spine. "Berkley Medallion Edition, SEPTEMBER, 1975" on the copyright page. Minor changes to the text.

† m. (DUIN MESSIAS) [Dutch], Meulenhoff: SF 86, 1975, paper.
Reprinted in 1977.

n. (EL MESIAS DE DUNE) [Spanish], Acervo, Barcelona, 1976.
Hardcover(?).

o. _____, NEL: 03266 (75p), 1977, paper.

p. _____, Berkley: 03585 ($1.75), 1977, paper.*

† q. _____, Berkley: 03930 ($1.95), 1978, paper.*

r. _____, NEL: 04156 (85p), 1978, paper.

s. (DER HERR DES WUSTENPLANETEN) [German], Heyne: 3266, 1978, paper.
Translator: Walter Brumm and Ronald M Hahn. New unabridged edition.

t. _____, Berkley: 04346 ($2.25), 1979, paper.

u. _____, Science Fiction Book Club, Garden City, 19??.

v. (   ) [French], Edito-Service, 19??, paper(?).
Published in Switzerland.

w. _____, Berkley: 04379 ($2.50), 1980(?), paper.*

x. _____, NEL: 05038 (£1.25), 1980, paper.

y. _____, NEL: 05088 (£1.25), 1981, paper.

z. _____, NEL: 05308 (£1.50), 1981, paper.

aa. _____, Berkley: 05314 ($5.95), 1982, paper.*
Trade paperback in size. "Berkley trade paperback edition / April 1982" on the copyright page.

ab. _____, Berkley: 05503 ($2.75), 1982, paper.
ac. _____, Berkley: 07498 ($3.95), 1984(?), paper.*
ad. _____, NEL: 02285 (£2.50), 1986, paper.

11. **EYE**
Illustrated by Jim Burns.
Contents: Introduction; Rate Race; Dragon In The Sea (Excerpt); Cease Fire; A Matter Of Traces; Try To Remember; The Tactful Saboteur; The Road To Dune; By The Book; Seed Stock; Murder Will In; Passage For Piano; Death Of A City; Frogs And Scientists.

    a.   _____, Berkley: 08398 ($7.95), 1985, paper.*
"Berkley trade paperback edition/November 1985" on the copyright page. Trade paperback in size. Cover and interior illustrations by Jim Burns.

    b.   _____, Berkley: 08399, New York ($100.00), 1985.*
A boxed, signed, numbered limited edition. 200 copies of which 175 were for sale. Bound in white cloth with pictorial cover (in color) as on the trade paperback edition. A different picture on the back cover. "FRANK HERBERT" in red, "EYE" in purple, and "A // MASTERWORKS // EDITION // __ BERKLEY" in black all on the spine. Slipcase is white cloth. Issued without a dust jacket. No date on the title page. "Berkley limited hardcover edition/November 1985" on the copyright page. The limitation page is the first sheet after the front free endpaper. It has no printing, just an illustration of a man's head, a signature and a number of the form "xxx/175".

    c.   _____, Science Fiction Book Club, Garden City, 1986.
    d.   _____, Gollancz, London (£9.95), 1986.

12. **THE EYES OF HEISENBERG**
("Heisenberg's Eyes", Galaxy, sr2, June 1966)
The Optimen are a sophisticated caste of world rulers who have become almost a separate race. They are immortal, or at least potentially so; the oldest Optiman has lived for tens of thousands of years. Their agelessness is ensured by a precise and complicated hormone and enzyme balance, the maintenance of which requires living a quiet, stable existence and keeping emotions firmly in check. This has led to a retreat from life and a great decrease in activities of any sort; the majority of Optimen pass their limitless time in abstruse hobbies and ever more abstract research. Only three Optimen at a time interface with the world they rule; these are the Tuyere, a rotating board with 100-year terms. Optimen who wish to be informed about the Tuyere's doings or those of the world at large tune in on television; other then the Tuyere, all Optimen are isolated from the irritations and instabilities of life in a hidden, closely guarded citadel. Even the Tuyere are buffered by cadres of normal humans in physician, police and administrative capacities; it is mostly by proxy that they direct the masses of workers, called "sterries."

Reproduction is one of the closely guarded privileges in the Optiman-ruled society; the masses are controlled by a widely disseminated contraceptive gas. Selected individuals are allowed or required to generate offspring, and all gestation is extra-utero, in laboratory conditions. Cloning is also widely in use, both for workers and for the individuals in the support cadres whom the Optimen find particularly useful. The Optimen themselves are sterile, necessarily so because of their delicate hormone balance. From time to time new Optimen are elevated from the support personnel, but the usual method of augmenting the Optimen's numbers is the genetic tailoring of an individual from the embryo stage. In the population at large, cults have grown up around the mysteries of reproduction and the controlling Optimen. To the ordinary citizen the Optimen are like remote deities, and the supporting cadres who carry out the Optiman edicts are infused with some of their remoteness, power and mystique.

The only opposition to Optiman rule is from a hidden underground of Cyborgs; these are individuals long-lived in their own right, descended from the rejects of a long-past Optiman experiment in the replacement of biological parts with mechanical parts and systems. The Cyborgs are not only sterile, they have eliminated emotions from their makeup. They wish to supplant the Optimen for power's sake.

The novel opens with an inexplicable circumstance: an embryo undergoing routine genetic surgery at a facility in the SeaTac (Seattle-Tacoma) metropolis abruptly reverts to the human-normal state and resists any further manipulations. (Perhaps this is a manifestation of the Heisenberg Principle which, roughly, states that a system will become more influenced by indeterminacy the more completely it is controlled.) Present at this event are Dr Thei Svengaard, Dr Vyaslav Potter, the embryo's parents Harvey and Elizabeth Durant and a pair of robust blonde "breeders" who have been permitted the privilege of watching their offspring's crucial surgery. The two doctors are puzzled and somewhat frightened by the event, but Potter impulsively preserves the embryo.

The Durants are secret members of the Parents Underground, a Cyborg-run organization of viable breeders who really wish to be free of Cyborg and Optiman controls alike. If it grows to maturity, the semi-miraculous embryo will be immune to Optiman systems and able to reproduce without the elaborate medical/technical assistance that has become standard. This embryo is the cue for a long-planned Cyborg strike against Optiman authority. With its implications of Optiman loss of control, the embryo becomes a focus of the power struggle.

The Optimen wish the embryo and those involved with it to be apprehended and destroyed. The present Tuyere--the severe Schruille, the Apollonian Nourse and the chill, queenly Calapine--assign Max Allgood, their chief of Central Security, to the task. Allgood is the latest in a long line of identical Allgood clones, but ignorant of that fact, Calapine plays upon this, directing him in a mocking, peremptory manner.

The Durants meet with genetic surgeons Igan and Boumour, Cyborg agents hopeful of being elevated to Cyborg status, in a pumping station 1,000 feet below the city; Dr Svengaard is summoned to implant the embryo in its mother's womb and the Cyborg Glisson spirits the group away from the Optimen's searchers in a manner calculated to inflame the situation and force the Optimen to step up the pace of their search. The Optimen do, destroying the entire SeaTac area in a desperate strike, but Glisson and his charges have been removed to the mountains inland. In the meantime Max Allgood has been corrupted to the Cyborg side by Igan and Boumour, who reveal to him the existence of his string of predecessor clones. Allgood must be killed by his masters, and while the "new Max" is being prepared Calapine assumes charge of operations herself, finding it a heady business.

The eventual capture of the fugitives and Glisson is the final stage of the Cyborg plan. With Glisson held inside the Optimen's citadel, the Optimen are no longer insulated from the world and their painstakingly kept body balances begin to come apart at the seams; as the violence escalates, Optimen begin to die and go insane. Thei Svengaard recovers from the demoralization of SeaTac's destruction to act as bargainer for the human side in a confrontation with Calapine. The resulting compromise situation will hopefully be stable without the choking stasis that has permeated the long Optiman rule.

† a.   _____, Berkley: F1283 ($0.50), 1966, paper.*
"BERKLEY MEDALLION EDITION, // NOVEMBER, 1966" on the copyright page.

b.   _____, Sphere 45179 (5/-), 1968, paper.

c.   (REVOLTE GEGEN DIE UNSTERBLICHEN) [German], Heyne: 3125 (DM 2.40), 1968, paper.
Translator: Leni Sobez.

d.   (DE BLIK VAN HEISENBERG) [Dutch], Meulenhoff: SF 42, 1970, paper.
Translator: Walter B Relsky.

† e.   _____, Berkley: S1865 ($0.75), 1970, paper.*
Also 01865 on the spine. "2nd Printing, June, 1970 (New Edition)" on the copyright page. Reprinted.

f.   (GLI OCCHI DI HEISENBERG) [Italian], Galassia: 139 (L350), 1971, paper.
Translator: Roberta Rambelli.

g.   _____, Sphere: 4520 (30p), 1972, paper.

h.   _____, Sphere: 4522 (30p), 1973, paper.

i.   _____, NEL, London (£2.25), 1975.*

j.   _____, Berkley: N2810 ($0.95), 1975, paper.
Also numbered 02810 on the spine. Reprinted.

k.   _____, Berkley: 03509 ($1.25), 1976, paper.*

l.   _____, NEL: 02658 (40p), 1976, paper.*

m.   (GLI OCCHI DI HEISENBERG) [Italian], Bigalassia: 33 (L200), 1977, paper.
Translator: Roberta Rambelli. Combined with WHIPPING STAR.

n.   _____, Berkley: 03790 ($1.50), 1978, paper.*

† o.   _____, Berkley: 04237 ($1.75), 1979, paper.*
Reprinted.

p.   _____, Berkley: 04338 ($1.95), 1980(?), paper.*

q.   _____, Berkley: 05098 ($2.25), 1981, paper.*

r.   _____, NEL: 05049 (£1.25), 1981, paper.

s.   _____, NEL: 02658 (£1.50), 1983, paper.

t.   _____, Berkley: 07314 ($2.50), 1984, paper.*

u.   _____, Berkley: 09046 ($2.95), 1986, paper.*

13.   **GOD EMPEROR OF DUNE**
The Fourth Dune Novel.
Leto Atreides II, the God-Emperor, has ruled Arrakis and the Empire for more than 3,500 years. His monolithic centralized rule has directed humanity along his obscure Golden Path--his perception of the best course toward the human race's survival and invigoration as revealed to him through his access to total ancestral memories and his precognitive vision.

Leto's symbiotic sandtrout skin (see CHILDREN OF DUNE) has grown and changed until he resembles a pre-sandworm, seven meters in length and weighing five tons. Only his face remains uncovered; his hands and arms, under a layer of the tough integument, are the last vestiges of his human bodily structure. He can crawl or roll with great speed and power but generally travels on a Royal Cart, a suspensor-buoyed mechanism.

Arrakis has changed as much as Leto II, and now has forests and seas. Weather control is required to maintain the last desert, the Sareer. Sandworms and sandtrout are extinct and spice production has ceased, though the God-Emperor promises that at some time he will metamorphose back into free-living sandtrout and reestablish the natural cycles. In the meantime all melange users, such as the Bene Gesserit and the Spacing Guild, must rely on yearly allotments from the God-Emperor's vast hoards.

To the populace he rules, the God-Emperor is arbitrary, unfathomable, a predatory being whose least whim wields vast and fearful power. Everyday life is neither hard nor prosperous, and of a dreamy, smothering sameness; change and innovation are discouraged, rebellion is brutally crushed. The God-Emperor's edicts are enforced by his Fish Speaker militia, an all-female cadre intensively trained and initiated to a fanatic obedience and adoration of their commander and living god. The Empire's principal factions dare mount no open opposition to Leto. The Bene Gesserit are conciliatory and watchful. The Ixians serve the God-Emperor by providing him with high-tech devices such as his Royal Carts and a mechanism via which he can constantly telepathically dictate memoirs; they are this period's "criminals of science", their transgressions into forbidden areas of research overlooked because of Leto's need for their products, though he hopes to maintain curbs on them. The Tleilaxu experimenters are tolerated as well despite their constant intrigues.

From the Tleilaxu the God-Emperor obtains a constant supply of Duncan Idaho gholas--clones possessing the memories of, and essentially identical to, the original. These Duncan Idahos serve as the commanders of Leto's Fish Speakers, being replaced as necessary when they die of natural causes or, as has happened on many occasions, they reach a state of mind hostile to the God-Emperor and must be killed. Despite the value Leto places on these gholas' presence, he hardly seems to regard them as true individuals, often referring to "the Duncan", i.e., the *current* Duncan. He is even bored by the predictable series of emotional responses and attitude changes through which the Duncans progress; this boredom and frustration extends to people in general. Leto's perceptions enhanced by his ancestor-memory interpretations enable him to "read" all too plainly those with whom he deals, and he craves novelty and surprise.

The latest Duncan arrives in the usual state, coming from the Tleilaxu axolotl tanks confused and disturbed by the means used to restore his original memories. He is shaken by the aspect of the God-Emperor and the strange universe, in which he is out of his own time, which the Atreides lineage to which Duncan owes his allegiance is shaped.

Other Atreides are present besides Leto II. Moneo Atreides is the God-Emperor's elderly majordomo, a diligent servant but a disappointment to Leto as one who fell short of his potential. Moneo perceives the God-Emperor as his ruler and sometime friend, who can occasionally approach a fearful insensate force, "the-worm-that-is-God".

Moneo's daughter Siona is a young adult, an angry, strongly disaffected rebel, leader of a supposedly secret underground opposing the God-Emperor's rule. Unknown to Siona her activities are known to Leto and unofficially sanctioned and tolerated. Siona represents to the God-Emperor a vigorous element in the change and growth of the human race in that she is invisible to prescient talents such as his and those of the Spacing Guild navigators. She is Leto's secret delight and fascination, but the God-Emperor has not interviewed her face-to-face for years and will not interfere too directly with her choices of conduct, even to guarantee her safety.

Nayla, one of the God-Emperor's most ardently devout Fish Speakers, has been assigned to join Siona's underground posing as a conspirator, and to accompany, obey, protect and report to Leto on

Siona. The blocky, stolid Nayla is exhilarated by the direct dealings with her God but tormented by having to participate in intrigues against him even if her immense, unshakable faith sees no iota of possibility that they could succeed.

The new Duncan Idaho is upset to learn that the God-Emperor has decreed a "mating" between himself and Siona; neither party is inclined to cooperate. He is also disturbed by a visit in Siona's company to the village where his predecessor's wife and children reside. The nature of the Fish Speakers he nominally commands is yet another irritating element, and Duncan finds himself more a figurehead to be shielded than an actual leader, as on the occasion of an assassination attempt by Tleilaxu face dancers (who counterfeit his own appearance), which occurs during the journey of the God-Emperor and his entourage to his festival city of Onn.

In Onn the God-Emperor receives the new Ixian Ambassador, Hwi Noree. (The previous ambassador, a wickedly brilliant nobleman named Malky, was a "boon companion" whose company Leto found amusing and stimulating without precisely liking the man.) Leto realizes at once that in Hwi Noree the Ixians have painstakingly fashioned a trap for him, a being to fascinate him; he is genuinely charmed by Hwi's sensitivity, gentleness and candor. She, reciprocally, is immediately stirred to love and admiration for Leto. Hwi is aimed at his greatest vulnerability; his suppressed yearnings for his lost humanness, for which all the reservoir of ancestral memories of the whole scope of human emotions and activities cannot compensate. She is precisely the sort of woman Leto would have demanded as his mate had normal manhood been possible to him, and he is overrun by his emotions just as he had thought them vanishing forever.

The festival city is disrupted by further Tleilaxu and rebel attacks. Leto is goaded into fury and a personal entry into the battles by the threat to Hwi. He carries on with the festival's scheduled activities, including the frighteningly intense Fish Speaker ritual adoration of the God-Emperor, called Siaynoq, at which Duncan Idaho is the only male allowed to be present.

Idaho still has not come to terms with the situation in which he finds himself, with Moneo, and with his attitude toward the God-Emperor. Despite her commitment to Leto, there is a compelling attraction between Hwi Noree and Idaho. The God-Emperor orders them kept apart as much as possible, and also announces his betrothal to Hwi, an event unprecedented in several thousand years.

Soon thereafter, Leto senses that Siona Atreides has come to a point of potential violence where she must be tested and her energies directed along a more productive path. She has her first personal interview with Leto in years at his 3,000-meter Citadel tower in the depths of the Sareer desert. Her test is a journey across the Sareer in the company of the God-Emperor; she is equipped with a Fremen stillsuit and supplies but dependent upon Leto for the knowledge of how to survive--their direction of travel, the operation of her suit, warmth at night and, eventually, her drinking water exhausted, for spice-essence laden moisture from the God-Emperor's own body. In return for all these things she must find and display her inner abilities which are of value to Leto. Her father Moneo was once a rebel very similar to her and through a like testing became the God-Emperor's faithful servant; Siona is co-opted to awareness of the Golden Path and its cruel necessity, and her own role in its continuity. However, a chance rainfall during their journey reveals to her Leto's fatal vulnerability to free water, and she has by no means become a complete convert to the God-Emperor's service.

In the God-Emperor's absence Duncan Idaho and Hwi Noree have begun an affair, a human attraction on a level different from Hwi's devotion to Leto. Moneo, at a conference with the pair, urges forbearance, to Duncan's discomfiture. When Siona returns from her testing, Moneo, in an attempt at reducing tensions, has Duncan and her spirited away to the isolated village of Tuono, where the God-Emperor maintains a cadre of Museum Fremen who preserve by rote the lore and detail, if not precisely the spirit, of the Fremen culture of Muad'dib's and Duncan's time.

Leto learns of Moneo's precautions and it is his whim to designate Tuono village as the site of his wedding to Hwi Noree. The announcement finds Duncan and Siona sufficiently agreed in opposition to the God-Emperor to plan an assassination attempt at a bridge crossing on the route to Tuono. This act inaugurates the final stage of Leto's Golden Path and the next stage of humanity's future.

a. _____, Putnam, New York ($12.95), 1981.*
Bound in a three-piece case with gray paper front and rear boards and with black cloth on the spine. Gold lettering on the spine. No date on title page. No indication of printing or edition on the copyright page.

b. _____, Putnam, New York ($45.00), 1981.*
Special boxed and signed edition of 750 copies. Bound in black cloth with gold lettering on the spine. The slipcase is in black cloth. Issued without a dust jacket. No date on title page. No indication of printing or edition on the copyright page. The limitation sheet is the first sheet after the front free endpaper and states: "Of the first edition of // GOD EMPEROR OF DUNE // seven hundred fifty copies, // specially bound, // have been numbered and // signed by the author.// Number ___ ".

c. _____, Gollancz, London (L6.95), 1981.*
Bound in orange paper boards with gold lettering on the spine. "1981" on the title page. No indication of printing or edition on the copyright page.

d. _____, BCA Book Club (British), 1981.

e. _____, Science Fiction Book Club, Garden City, 1981.*
Bound in three-piece case with gray front and rear paper boards and with black paper on the spine. No date on the title page. No indication of printing or edition on the copyright page. Code 1705 on the dust jacket. Date code L47 at lower left margin of page 401. A later printing using M20 has also been seen.

f. _____, Berkley: 05312 ($6.95), 1982, paper.*
Trade paperback in size. "Berkley trade paperback edition / April 1982" on the copyright page.

g. _____, NEL: 05262 (L2.50), 1982, paper.

h. _____, Berkley: 06128 ($7.95), 1982, paper.*
Trade paperback in size.

i. _____, Berkley: 06233 ($3.95), 1983, paper.*
"Berkley edition / May 1983" on the copyright page.

j. _____, Berkley: 07272 ($3.95), 1983(?), paper.*

k. _____, Berkley: 08003 ($3.95), 1984, paper.*

l. _____, NEL: 05262 (L2.95), 1986, paper.

14. **THE GOD MAKERS**
This novel was expanded from several short stories: "You Take The High Road", "Missing Link", "Operation Haystack", and "The Priests Of Psi".
Galactic civilization is rebuilding and expanding after a devastating series of Rim Wars 500 years in the past; planets cut off in the turmoil

are still being recontacted. R&R, the Rediscovery and Re-education Service, attempts to assist these isolated worlds to integrate themselves into the Galactic League by giving technical boosts and guidance; a sibling department, Investigation and Adjustment (I-A), guards against any repetition of the Rim War conflagration by scouting the rediscoveries for signs of militarism. If these are discerned, the world is immediately suppressed by overwhelming might and, if possible, its attitudes rerouted. The two bureaus exist in an uneasy cooperation, since their fields of operation overlap significantly. Another force in the Galactic League is the priest-planet Amel, where "religious engineers" study religion as a science of psi and apply their learnings in their own way to the task of ensuring peace in the League's war-shy but force-minded political atmosphere. Their sphere of operations includes both R&R and I-A as well as the scores of worlds on which religious movements may grow and spread.

Lewis Orne begins as an "organization man", an R&R operative surveying recontacted worlds. Due to his perspicacity on his first mission he is drafted into the I-A, and in further assignments makes contact with an alien civilization as well as war-minded human worlds. Orne is increasingly troubled by a feeling brought on by portentious, symbolic dreams and visions, that the approach of the governmental bureaus is wrong. His visions are both an effect and a base element of forces set in motion by the religious engineers of Amel who, in their "school for prophets" (where they seek to train and curb the psi/religious adepts who might otherwise have wreaked havoc with their raw powers), have invoked energies and conjured visions that are subtly linked to the inner and outer events of Orne's life.

Over the course of his missions Orne attains new degrees of awareness and passes through a near-literal, as well as symbolic, death and rebirth. These experiences bring his latest psi powers nearer the surface and he is invariably drawn to Amel. There the priesthood headed by the sinister Halmyrach Abood must cope with the end results of the processes they have manipulated and discover whether Orne *or* their own systems will survive the final stages of Orne's necessary rounds of perception-stretching ordeal tests.

THE GOD MAKERS incorporates "You Take The High Road", "Missing Link", "Operation Haystack" and "The Priests Of Psi" (see the individual stories for more detailed plot summaries). In order to create the novel, these stories were somewhat rewritten and considerable interstitial material was added. The stories were written concurrently with research for DUNE, and in some ways represent transitional concepts and treatments of some of Herbert's major themes. Differences between the individual stories and the novel rewrite, and between THE GOD MAKERS and the treatment of similar themes later in DUNE, seem to indicate different stages of evolution of the basic ideas.

† a.   _____, Putnam, New York ($5.95), 1972.*
        Bound in light blue paper boards with black lettering on the spine.
        No indication of printing or edition on the copyright page. No
        date on the title page.

  b.   (CREATORI DI DEI) [Italian], Nord, Milan (L1600), 1972.
        Translator: Giampaolo Cossato and Sandra Sandrelli. Cosmo Argento
        35.

† c.   _____, Berkley: 02344 ($0.95), 1973, paper.*
        There is a state that indicates printed in Canada.*
        Reprinted. "Berkley Medallion Edition, MAY, 1973" on the copyright page.

  d.   _____, NEL, London (£1.95), 1973.

  e.   _____, NEL: 01798 (40p), 1974, paper.

f.   (DIE RITEN DER GOTTER) [German], Heyne: 3460, 1975, paper.
     Translator: Birgit Ress-Bohusch. Reprinted in 1979.
g.   _____, Berkley: Z2861 ($1.25), 1975, paper.*
h.   _____, Berkley: 03532 ($1.50), 1977, paper.*
i.   _____, NEL: 03326 (70p), 1977, paper.
j.   (ET L'HOMME CREA UN DIEU) [French], Titres SF, 1977, paper.
k.   _____, NEL: 04084 (80p), 1978, paper.
† l.   _____, Berkley: 03919 ($1.95), 1978, paper.*
m.   (DE GODENMAKERS) [Dutch], Born: SF 74, 1978, paper.
n.   _____, Berkley: 04857 ($2.25), 1981, paper.*
o.   _____, NEL: 05348 (L1.00), 1981, paper.
p.   _____, Berkley: 05516 ($2.50), 1982, paper.*
q.   _____, Berkley: 06996 ($2.95), 1983, paper.*
r.   _____, Berkley: 09327 ($2.95), 1986, paper.*

15. **THE GREAT DUNE TRILOGY**
     Contains the first three Dune novels: DUNE, DUNE MESSIAH and
     CHILDREN OF DUNE.
† a.   _____, Gollancz, London (L6.95), 1979.*
     Bound in dull red paper boards with gold lettering on the spine.
     "1979" on the title page. No indication of printing or edition on
     the copyright page. Jacket by Terry Oakes.
b.   _____, BCA Book Club (British), London, 1979.
c.   (   ) [Serbo Croatian].
     Rights for the trilogy were purchased in June 1978.

16. **THE GREEN BRAIN**
     ("Greenslaves", Amazing, March 1965)
     Expanded.
     In the near future, population pressures and food shortages have
     culminated in a multinational drive to increase human control of Earth's
     ecosystems by exterminating all wild insects. Mutated, genetically-
     tailored bees will take their place and agriculture will thrive. The
     International Ecological Organization (IEO) directs the eradication
     procedures. Not all nations are cooperating; the United States and
     Canada have refused to participate in the "insectocide" and the IEO has
     imposed an embargo upon North America. A similar sanction is
     threatened against Brazil if that country does not complete its clearing
     of insects according to the latest timetable; Brazil's "green" areas
     emptied of insects are being repeatedly reinfested and startling
     mutations and resistances are developing among the insect populations.
        The extermination work is done by bands of bandeirante contract-
     ors, some of whom have become famous, charismatic figures; their tools
     are poisons, sonics, foam and flame weapons, and the toxic couroq
     powder and jelly. Rumors are spreading that the bandeirantes are
     behind the inexplicable reappearances of insects in the cleared areas,
     that they are prolonging their work for greater profit and glory.
     Bandeirante tales of bizarre mutations in the uncleared interior, from
     18-foot mantids to acid-spitting giant chiggers, are heard with skep-
     ticism; when giant insects appear in Bahia, they are both dismissed as
     deceptions and ascribed to secret bandeirante laboratories hidden in the
     "red" infested zones.
        Joao (Johnny) Martinho is a Brazilian bandeirante, leader of the
     Irmandades band, whose experiences are bringing him to doubt the
     ultimate wisdom of the insect-genocide. Joao's father is a Prefect of
     the Mato Grosso Barrier Company and in a position to bear much of
     the brunt of IEO demands that Brazil complete its eradication; he is
     incensed by his son's attitudes. Joao also becomes a target of Dr Travis

Huntington Chen-Lhu, the Chinese regional IEO director. Chen-Lhu and his nation are concealing the fact that after the completion of their 20-year extermination program, the Chinese have found their plants dying and their lands turning barren; for reasons of face other nations must be in the same plight before this is made public. To seduce Joao Martinho and produce proof of the Bandeirantes' betrayal, Chen-Lhu calls in Dr. Rhin Kelly, an Irish IEO espionage specialist, an exotic red-haired, green-eyed Mata Hari. Kelly and the suave Chen-Lhu witness an attempt by Martinho's band to capture marauding giant insects that have appeared in the green areas of Bahia, then depart on an investigative tour of the interior.

As Joao discusses the situation with his aristocratic father Gabriel, swarms of insects appear around their house; they try to escape in Joao's bandeirante airtruck but are intercepted by two Indians who order them to fly toward the uncleared jungle. The elder Martinho collapses from a heart attack and the Indians insist that aid may be obtained in the interior of the Mato Grosso plateau. Joao realizes that the men are composites, human simulacrums formed of a myriad of tiny insects acting in unison; he crashes the airtruck and escapes to a stronghold where some of his Irmaos and a few IEO personnel are isolated, including Rhin Kelly and Chen-Lhu. Kelly is inflamed by the deaths of several of her companions and by venoms from insect bites and attacks Joao bitterly. Finally, however, Martinho, Kelly and Chen-Lhu are selected to attempt escape in a partially disabled truck pod, which they will float down a river, carrying word of the newest insect innovations. The bandeirante camp is overwhelmed as they depart. The journey downriver in the cramped pod becomes an ordeal not only of avoiding insect traps but of interpersonal tension and ideological fencing between Chen-Lhu, his increasingly reluctant henchwoman and his intended scapegoat.

Unknown to the humans, the insect world has been stimulated by the human eradication measures to form a giant, hidden communal Brain which is planning and directing the insect countermeasures and seeking to establish communication with humans. The Brain has developed the Indian counterfeits and insect varieties with acids that can eat through metal, as well as microminiature insects with deadly stings; all these forces are marshalled to intercept Martinho, Kelly and Chen-Lhu before they reach civilization. All the Brain's moves are interpreted as hostile actions by the humans who are unaware of its intent to alert them to the interconnectedness of man and insect and their mutual needs in Greenhouse Earth.

THE GREEN BRAIN is based upon and greatly expanded from "Greenslaves".

† a.   _____, Ace: F-379 ($0.40), 1966, paper.*
   b.   (DER KAMPF DER INSEKTEN) [German], Terra Nova: 39, 1968, paper.
           Translator: Birgit Ress-Bohusch.
   c.   _____, Ace: 30261 ($0.75), 1970, paper.*
   d.   _____, NEL: 01521 (30p), 1973, paper.
   e.   (DER KAMPF DER INSEKTEN) [German], Pabel: Terra Taschenbuch 225, 1973, paper.
           Translator: Walter Brumm.
   f.   _____, Ace: 30262 ($1.25), 1974, paper.*
   g.   (   ) [Danish], A/S Interpresse, 1974, paper(?).
   h.   _____, NEL: 02397 (35p), 1975, paper.
† i.   _____, Ace: 30263 ($1.50), 1975, paper.
   j.   (LE CERVEAU VERT) [French], Le Masque: 33, 1975, paper.
           Translator: Jacqueline Huet.

k. (   ) [Spanish], Ediciones Martinez, 1976, paper(?).
l. (IL CERVELLO VERDE) [Italian], Longanesi: Fantapocket 7
    (L1500), 1977, paper.
    Translator: E Bellei.
m. _____, NEL: 04289 (80p), 1979, paper.
n. _____, NEL, London (L4.25), 1979.
o. _____, Ace: 30264 ($1.95), 1979, paper.*
p. _____, Gregg Press, Boston ($13.95), 1981.*
    Introduction by Joseph Milicia. Issued without a dust jacket. Bound
    in textured blue cloth. Gold lettering of Herbert's signature on the
    front cover. Title and author in gold on red background on spine.
    Publisher in gold on spine. "1981" on the title page. "First
    Printing, February, 1981" on the copyright page.
q. _____, Berkley: 07676 ($2.95), 1985, paper.*
r. _____, NEL: 01521 (L1.95), 1986, paper.*

17. THE HEAVEN MAKERS
    ("The Heaven Makers", Amazing, sr2, April 1967)
    For thousands of years, since the dawn of civilization, humanity has
    unwittingly been managed and manipulated by a race of aliens, the
    Chem. The Chem are immortal and their immortality attributes--
    conscious control of their metabolisms, imperviousness to violence--are
    tied up in a psychic network called "Tiggywaugh's Web" encompassing
    all Chem; it is not a conscious communication, but a shared oneness on
    a deep level. The Chem have probed myriad star-systems and even
    explored other dimensions over their aeons-long existence, but they find
    that their immortality and Tiggywaugh's Web seem to insulate them
    from life. Their most popular diversions are pantovives (like motion
    pictures blending sight, sound, smell, sensation and emotional overtones)
    based on the doings of various lesser races, of which mankind is one.
    The Chem are squat, bowlegged, gnomish humanoids, rarely over three
    feet tall; to them humans seem "larger than life" in the intensity of
    their brief experience of existence as well as in size. Vicarious
    experience of humans' lives allows the Chem to partake of the poignan-
    cies of everyday moments that their endless lifespans have denied them;
    even the sensation of ancientness and the sorrowful grandeur of events
    and entities lost in time and preserved only in memory or imagination
    are more vivid to the Chem in the pantovive than in their own
    perceptions.
        Fraffin is the pantovive director who has made Earth his special
    province. He and his crews have produced every conceivable kind of
    film--drama, spectacle love story, war story--often influencing in-
    dividual people or whole nations and ages to get the effects and
    incidents they want. The Chem are screened from human perceptions,
    but on occasion Fraffin and other Chem have appeared in their own
    productions as gods, dwarves or bit players. Fraffin's pantovives are of
    extraordinary quality and "Fraffin's World" an object of envy and
    excitement to the Chem race at large.
        There are strict rules about Chem interference with advancing
    lesser races (even on Earth, humanity has developed past the point
    where the pantovive makers are allowed to manipulate it as boldly as
    before), but the only significant sanctions pertain to races with which
    the Chem can interbreed, all others being considered clever, if endear-
    ing, animals. Fraffin's presence on Earth is in fact illegal: Chem and
    human are genetically compatible and because of this, Fraffin and his
    crew have remained on Earth and stayed intensely involved with the
    human race long past the duration of the usual Chem attention span.
    Reports to the contrary have been routinely faked by Ynvic, Fraffin's

medical officer. Over the millennia humanity has received a strong infusion of Chem genes from Fraffin's film crews, who enjoy human "sex-pets". The suspicions of the Chem Primacy have been awakened by Fraffin's activities, but he has managed to subvert or coerce every investigator.

Kelexel, of the Chem Bureau of Criminal Repression, is the latest envoy of the Chem authorities, arriving in the guise of a rich tourist curious about the fabled Fraffin's World. Fraffin has a number of potentially compromising situations in readiness for such an eventuality; the one he chooses is the filming of a "quickie murder-romance" set in Moreno, California. The pantovive makers' subtle adjustments to humans' emotions have convinced a solid, self-made citizen, Joe Murphey, that his wife Adele is unfaithful; they have also induced Joe's daughter, Ruth, into an unhappy marriage with jerk and scoundrel Neville Hudson instead of her true love, Androcles (Andy) Thurlow. Murphey murders his wife with a souvenir Malay kriss; psychologist Thurlow is involved in the sensational trial and brought back into contact with Ruth. Andy Thurlow is a unique and rare individual, an "immune" on whom the Chem screening devices do not work perfectly; he can perceive the Chem as hazy outlines seen through a fog. This is also a facet of Fraffin's plot.

Moreno is outraged by the murder and community opinion wants Joe Murphey to be executed, ignoring Thurlow's own diagnosis, prior to the murder, of Murphey's borderline psychotic state. Dr LeRoi Whelye, a "hanging psychiatrist," is called in to bolster the prosecution's case that Murphey is competent to stand trial and the results of a Rorschach test administered to the prisoner are twisted by Whelye, with Thurlow's interpretations put aside. As the trial and its hearings proceed, Thurlow is aware of, but does not understand, the Chem presence and their manipulation of the emotions involved, including his and Ruth's; he is unsure what to trust if he cannot rely on the authenticity of his own feelings.

Kelexel is readily ensnared in Fraffin's setup. He expresses a desire for a closer look at one of the "pets" and Ruth is abducted (her disappearance goes unremarked in Moreno, except by Thurlow, because of the Chem machineries). Kelexel quickly becomes besotted with her and Ruth herself verges on addiction to the heady feeling of being manipulated by the Chem emotion-influencing devices. She becomes pregnant by Kelexel, and the investigator is ensnared by Fraffin in both emotional and legal tangles. By interbreeding with another race, Kelexel has violated Chem statutes on reproduction and he is also strongly influenced by the rare possibility of having offspring of his own (since all full-blood Chem live forever, additions to the race are stringently limited). In addition, revelation of the peculiar situation on Earth might result in Chem Primacy action against the human race--to avoid the contamination of Chem culture--and Kelexel has emotional ties with its members.

Kelexel, however, becomes even more involved than Fraffin wished. The alien investigator comes to identify with Joe Murphey, the human manipulated to insanity and murder, and Kelexel's interactions with Ruth have changed him enough to make him resist Fraffin's pressures when they are brought to bear. Kelexel skips a necessary rejuvenation session and takes Ruth with him to talk to Andy Thurlow. Kelexel responds to the intolerable pressures that have been focused on him by willing his own death, an unprecedented event that sends a shock through Tiggywaugh's Web and brings Earth and Fraffin's activities into the spotlight of Chem authority.

THE HEAVEN MAKERS is closely linked to Herbert's poem "Carthage: Reflections of a Martian". The poem was the original evocation of mood, images of ancient events, atmosphere and the feeling of sorrowful, forgotten bits of history rippling down the aeons that pervades the novel.

† a. _____, Avon: S319 ($0.60), 1968, paper.*
 "First Avon Printing, November, 1968" on copyright page. Cover by John Schoenherr.

b. _____, NEL: 2684 (6/-), 1970, paper.

c. (GEFANGEN IN DER EWIGKEIT) [German], Heyne: 3298, 1972, paper.
 Translator: Walter Brumm.

d. _____, NEL: 00516 (30p), 1973, paper.

e. _____, NEL: 02681 (35p), 1975, paper.*

† f. _____, Ballantine: 25304 ($1.50), 1977, paper.*
 "First Ballantine Books Edition: March 1977" on the copyright page. Revised.

g. (DE DOOD VAN EEN ONSTERFELIJKE) [Dutch], Centripress, 1977, paper.

h. _____, NEL: 03828 (70p), 1978, paper.

i. _____, Ballantine: 28104 ($1.75), 1978, paper.

j. ( ) [French], Jean-Claude Lattes, 1979, paper(?).

k. ( ) [Portuguese], 19??, paper(?).
 Published in Brazil.

l. _____, NEL: 04988 (£1.00), 1980, paper.

m. _____, Ballantine: 30290 ($2.25), 1982, paper.*

18. HELLSTROM'S HIVE
("Project 40", Galaxy, sr3, November 1972)
Underneath an innocuous-looking farm near Steens Mountain in southeastern Oregon is hidden the citadel of a centuries-old experiment in a bizarre variant of human society. The Hive is a culture of humans modeled upon communal insect species; it originated in Europe but moved to the American west to find the seclusion necessary for its growth. In the honeycombed underground levels beneath the farm buildings the Hive holds tens of thousands of people, hydroponic gardens, fish farms, laboratories and generators powered by diverted subterranean rivers--nearly all the facilities needed for total self-support. The Hive's only vulnerability is its uniqueness; it is approaching readiness to "swarm" and set up more Hives in other locales, and at present all its energies are bent toward making itself strong and maintaining its secrecy until beyond that crucial point.

 Many members of the Hive pass as normal humans in outside society (whose members are referred to as "wild" humans and viewed as a lesser but extremely dangerous breed of being), most notably Nils Hellstrom, the head of a film company that raises money to purchase materials which the Hive cannot yet manufacture for itself. Hellstrom's movies about insects are also a sort of subliminal propaganda to prepare the outside world against the day when the Hives become public knowledge. Besides Hellstrom, Hive members have infiltrated into many levels of authority; the Hive's plants include a Senator, a judge, government workers, law enforcement officials and many more.

 Within the Hive there is no attempt to maintain the "wild" human appearance. Hive members generally go nude, converse in sign language, and have discarded a great part of the individuality of ordinary humans; many of their behaviors are implemented on an instinctual level, and pheromones and chemical markers in the communal food supply are vital means of mood communication and dispersal of information. Some strains of Hive humans have genetically specialized for their tasks, such as the high-strung, dome-headed scientists with atrophied limbs and the hulking neutered workers whose specialty is heavy physical labor. (Infiltrators into the outside world are bred for intelligence and quick-wittedness.) Hellstrom, while an extremely able and broadly experienced individual, is not the Hive's leader in any sense; he is simply the member most specialized for contact with the outside world, though in that capacity he does wield considerable authority. The Hive's innovations are many: corpses are chopped up and recycled in the food supply; artificially maintained female torsos or "sexual stumps" act as baby machines continually turning out new Hive members; and massive drug-enhanced orgies ensure genetic mixing that will keep the Hive vigorous. Hive members such as Hellstrom, who deal with the outside civilization, feel themselves contaminated or altered by the "normal" humans they come in contact with, and regard the mindsets and behavior of the Hive's lifetime natives as the norm from which they have been forced to diverge.

Outside attention has finally been focused on the Hive by the oversight of a Hive researcher who left papers labeled "Project 40" in an MIT library. These dealt with a "particle pump" or "toroidal field disruptor" of a scientific level much more complex than the United States' current capabilities, and with evident applications as a weapon. The investigation of the Hive falls to "The Agency", a government bureau along the lines of the CIA but so secret that it has no formal name and whose equally nameless top executive is responsible only to the President.

The Agency has established a connection between the papers and Hellstrom, and has the farm under observation. One agent, Porter, has vanished; the next sent in are Carlos Depeaux and Tymiena Grinelli, posing as a birdwatching, nature-loving couple on vacation. They are puzzled by the near-total absence of animal life and the inactivity on Hellstrom's farm; the former, they learn, is due to the nightly foraging expeditions from the Hive. They are apprehended, ruthlessly questioned and absorbed into the Hive, Depeaux as food material and Tymiena as a sexual stump.

The Agency is slow to take proper alarm at the loss of its agents and to discover the true proportions of the situation, due in part to its internal politics. Operations Chief Merrivale is a waffler and a bureaucrat, top aid Dzule Peruge a cuttingly ambitious, swashbuckling strongman, and their conduct of the Hellstrom affair pays as much attention to possible credit and blame as to the mystery itself. Peruge heads the next team sent out, which includes crack agents "Shorty" Janvert and his fellow agent and girlfriend, Clovis Carr; Carr and Janvert are apprehensive because of rumors that this is a dangerous, politically hot mission.

In Oregon, Peruge unmasks one of Hellstrom's plants in the nearest small community and forces an interview at the farm. Hellstrom acts the controlled, urbane filmmaker and Peruge is given a tour of the studios, where he meets Hellstrom aide Fancy Kalotermi, whose Hive breeding instincts are aroused. She follows Peruge to his motel room in town and doses him with a Hive hormonal aphrodisiac; Peruge subsequently collapses and dies.

Janvert, assuming command of the Agency force, also confronts Hellstrom and is made prisoner. Clovis Carr has by then received "kill-and-burn" authorization from Washington and, fearful for Janvert's safety, launches an assault-team raid on the farm which is overwhelmed by Hive defenders armed with sophisticated stunwand weapons. Carr and Janvert are offered their lives in exchange for serving as go-betweens in the Hive's bid for a truce lengthy enough for it to cement its defenses and complete Project 40, revealed as a weapon capable of creating earthquake-level disturbances. The Agency's actions are hampered by the intrusion of other government services, and Merrivale is unable to implement his inclination to bomb the Hive out of existence. It appears the Hive will be left alone long enough to effect its swarming.

The book's title is taken from "The Hellstrom Chronicle", a 1971 semi-documentary film that used a combination of close-up and nature photography (as well as clips from giant-insect monster movies) to demonstrate the point that insects are much more efficient and adaptable than humans and are very likely our successors as the "owners of the Earth". The award-winning film featured a fictional Dr. Nils Hellstrom (played by an actor) as narrator and alleged producer.

Herbert had recently finished the first draft of a book about a human culture that had developed a hive existence, living hidden in the midst of our society, when he was contacted by the publishers who had acquired the rights to a spin-off book from "The Hellstrom Chronicle". The publishers wanted Herbert to write a book that could be titled in the vein of "Hellstrom's Something-or-other"; Herbert was able to adapt his already-written novel by making a few minor revisions and altering the name of his principal character.

† a.   _____, Nelson Doubleday (Science Fiction Book Club), Garden City, 1973.*
Bound in tan paper boards with green lettering on the spine. Date code 42P at lower left margin of page 277. No indication of printing or edition on the copyright page. No date on the title page. Later printings reported include date codes of 12Q and 29Q.

b.   _____, NEL, London (£2.95), 1974.*

c.   _____, Bantam: T8276 ($1.50), 1974, paper.*
"Bantam edition published April 1974" on the copyright page. Reprinted April 1974, June 1974, October 1974, January 1975, March 1975, and December 1975.

d.   ( ) [Spanish], 1976, paper(?).

e.   (LA RUCHE D'HELLSTROM) [French], Albin Michel: 2, 1977, paper. Translator: Robert Latour.

f.   (HELLSTROMS BRUT) [German], Heyne: 3536 (DM 5.80), 1977, paper.

g.   _____, Bantam: 12673 ($1.95), 1977, paper. Reprinted November 1978.

h.   (GONZENDE NACHTMERRIE) [Dutch], Luitingh, 1978, paper.

i.   ( ) [Italian], 19??, paper(?).

j.   _____, Bantam: 14438 ($2.75), 1982, paper.*

k.   _____, Corgi: 12056 (£1.75), 1982, paper.

l.   _____, Bantam: 14438 ($2.95), 1984(?), paper.*

19. **HERETICS OF DUNE**
The fifth Dune novel.
Thousands of years after the demise of God-Emperor Leto II, the intrigues of the galactic community's institutions are driving toward a new crux point. Millennia-long designs of both the Bene Gesserit (BG) and the Bene Tleilax are climaxing, enmeshed with one another in the person of a Duncan Idaho ghola being raised from childhood in a Bene Gesserit stronghold. On Arrakis, now called Rakis, an orphaned girl named Sheeana has appeared, the only survivor of an outlying settlement engulfed by a sandworm. She can speak to and command Dune's giant worms, in which religious legend holds that the God-Emperor's persona persists in dispersed fashion, a mote within each individual

sandworm. In addition, power balances are being disrupted by peoples newly returning to the centers of the old empire from the Scattering, a huge diaspora of humanity that occurred in the years of turmoil following Leto II's death.

Rakis' stature has faded and its output of the melange spice has become secondary to the quantities synthesized in Tleilaxu axolotl tanks, though Dune is still the sole reservoir of the natural spice-producing organisms. Rakis' ruling priesthood is a muddled, minor force. The events of DUNE are recalled in a half-fabled light; humanity has been heavily marked by the consequences of the God-Emperor's Golden Path.

The main movers of "affairs of empire" in the core worlds are now the Bene Gesserit and the Tleilaxu, through the Spacing Guild, the Ixian technologists, the Arrakeen priests under high priest Hedley Tuek and remnants of the God-Emperor's Fish Speakers intrigue on the sidelines. The power elite of the Returnees are the Honored Matres, a female society evolved from Bene Gesserits who went out in the scattering. In contrast to the traditional aloof, detached BG influence, the Honored Matres' rule is based upon a ferociously intense system of sexual worship and a paradoxical blend of raging aggression and strangling control.

The home bases and movements of these returnees (and of other factions) are untraceable because of the Ixian-developed, invisible, undetectable "no-ships," a successful alternative to transport by the Spacing Guild's heighliners. (Variations on the principle, stationary "no-globes" and "no-rooms", are widely used for concealment or refuge.) The return of the Lost Ones has stepped up from what was evidently a slow and stealthy infiltration that has established substantial secret networks on worlds such as Gammu, the former Harkonnen homeworld Giedi Prime.

The Duncan Idaho ghola's upbringing and training are overseen by Reverend Mother Schwangyu in an isolated fortress on Gammu. Schwangyu, though loyal to the order, is fiercely opposed to the enterprise at hand and suspicious of traps for the Sisterhood in dealings with the Tleilaxu who supply the gholas. (The current Duncan is the twelfth, prior ones having met with mishaps before their full training and awakening to their original memories could be completed.)

The ghola project is championed by Mother Superior Taraza who directs from Chapterhouse, the secret, secluded Bene Gesserit baseworld hidden behind an armada screen of no-ships. Taraza has called from retirement Mentat/Bashar Miles Teg, a genetic recreation from the Atreides gene lines of the Duke Leto Atreides type and the Bene Gesserit's greatest strategist and warrior, to be weapons master to the latest ghola-child. The current Bashar of the Bene Gesserit military arm is Burzmali, trained by Teg.

The Duncan ghola tolerates, respects and even feels affection for Teg, Teg's batman Patrin and his guards, but he has developed a deep hatred for Schwangyu and his other Bene Gesserit overseers and instructors. He is unsure whether this should extend to Lucilla, a recently-arrived BG imprinter assigned to his schooling and who clashes with Schwangyu over the director's possible subtle oppositions to the ghola project.

Lucilla is of a "type" with Mother Superior Taraza's closest associate in the Sisterhood, Reverend Mother Darwe Odrade. Odrade and Taraza grew up together as a unit, "Dar and Tar", in the Sisterhood schools. Odrade is atypical in that she was fostered with non-BG parents until she could be safely collected and claimed for the Sisterhood in her middle childhood. Through that parenting Odrade has known emotional bonds foreign to most Bene Gesserits. Her capacity for empathy is viewed with some mistrust, compounded by her being a product of Atreides gene lines (preserved by the BG and valued though considered dangerous because of the Atreides ambition and tendency to crop up "wild factors"). Odrade is, unknown to him, a daughter of Bashar Miles Teg; Lucilla is from a parallel gene line. The Atreides are the gene-strain most coveted by the Tleilaxu.

Master of the Masters of the Bene Tleilax is Tylwyth Waff, a child-sized being of great age, ghola-renewed like the rest of the effectively immortal Tleilaxu governing council. The Tleilaxu are an encapsulated, complex and fanatically secretive society. Their hidden Sufi-Zensunni religious mystery has endured for millennia behind a facade of political stupidity and a calculatedly repellent exterior, camouflage that has kept them on the sidelines of the Empire's destructive power struggles. The Tleilaxu are adept with "the language of God", the genetic code; their biologic wizardry has developed the axolotl tanks producing melange and gholas, and the newly-refined face dancer caste. The New Face Dancers are near-soulless chameleon beings resembling an obedient insect society that can not only mimic another's appearance but can absorb much of the memory and persona of a captive or recent kill. The Tleilaxu are secret imperialists, considering all beyond their own few worlds as frontier to be subdued.

The Tleilaxu and the Bene Gesserit are entwined in manipulation of each other, though the Bene Gesserit order currently holds the upper hand. The Tleilaxu have decided to disseminate the "Atreides Manifesto", a provocative mystic tract secretly written by Darwe Odrade and sure to spark intellectual upheaval on many worlds. The Duncan Idaho ghola, being imprinted by Lucilla to be manipulatable by Odrade when she takes up the reins of power in the Bene Gesserit embassy on Rakis, is programmed with special refinements by the Tleilaxu, which they hope will prove useful both against the Bene Gesserits and against the Returnees and their Honored Matres.

Taraza and her entourage, visiting Gammu, are briefly captured by the Honored Matres but liberated by Teg. Teg finds the affair to have been Taraza's way of cueing him that in the coming crisis she wishes him a completely free and unpredictable agent. Taraza aligns her counters further in a later interview with the Tleilaxu Waff, inducing him to visit Arrakis.

Teg's moment of independent action is a Face Dancer assault on the Gammu fortress; on Dune a simultaneous attempt on Sheeana in the Rakis priests' headquarters serves as occasion for Darwe Odrade to take Sheeana into Bene Gesserit custody under the auspices of a forced alliance with high priest Tuek.

Teg's choice of refuge for himself, the ghola and Lucilla is a forgotten Harkonnen no-globe in the hinterlands. It is amply equipped for the finishing training of the Idaho ghola, and Lucilla's completion of her imprinting task is frustrated by Teg's awakening of the ghola's memories ahead of schedule and by Duncan Idaho's own rebuffs. Duncan at full, mature capability questions his loyalties to the Sisterhood, to the Atreides lineage personified by Teg, and to himself.

Location on Gammu figures strongly in Duncan's latest incarnation's shaping due to his searing experiences, in his original existence, with Harkonnen might and cruelty. Giedi Prime/Gammu is now a center of banking and influence, a reservoir of "transportable wealth" and other more rarefied chips of power games. It is a cold place of snows, frosts, forests and marshy wastelands. Its lower classes still bear the psychological stamp of mind-modes generated during the Harkonnen overlordship. These ordinary farmers and townspeople now desire to escape or at least ameliorate the infiltration of Gammu by the Honored Matres and by opposition factions among the Returnees.

As Teg, Duncan and Lucilla undergo their sustained confrontation in isolation, on Rakis Odrade, Sheeana and Tylwyth Waff make a wormback trip to old Sietch Tabr where Waff falls yet more deeply into Bene Gesserit controls through Odrade's manipulation of his religious responses. Darwe Odrade discovers a secretly preserved message of the God-Emperor, a call to Noble Purpose that affects her deeply, reminding her that the Order of the Bene Gesserit has lost focus and direction. What was once the Sisterhood's great end leading to a greater beginning, the creation of a Kwisatz Haderach superbeing, is now a thing feared and prohibited, and the Order seems disinclined to attempt more than tinkering with the status quo. Odrade senses that drastic and sweeping changes will be required to preserve the Sisterhood from fading and extinction as "just another secret society".

The emergence of Teg and the awakened Duncan Idaho from isolation precipitates bold and violent strikes by all sides. In alliance with the opposition elements on Gammu, exotics from the Scattering, Bashar Burzmali has laid multiple decoys and stratagems aimed at getting Idaho safely to Rakis. However, Duncan's capture and attempted enslavement instead yields the bonding of the Honored Matre involved, Murbella. Teg is captured as well and the stress of his interrogation under a novel mechanism, a Returnee T-probe, sparks a new and higher-level integration of his Mentat and Bene-Gesserit-taught capabilities which enables his body to function at a fantastically accelerated pace.

Teg, Duncan, Lucilla and Burzmali make their various ways toward safety through the settlements and landscapes of Gammu and through the traps of the Honored Matre underground. A no-ship manned by veterans of Teg's services carries the focus of conflict back to Rakis. Final events--including the imminent destruction of Dune--are shaped by the heretics who reject the paths of dogma and tradition in favor of reliance on their fresh, intuitive judgments.

The sixth Dune book, CHAPTER HOUSE DUNE, is a direct sequel to and continuation of the events of HERETICS OF DUNE. If Herbert had lived to complete the planned seventh book and sequel to CHAPTER HOUSE, it apparently would have been a similar closely following sequel, the three books forming a trilogy within the larger series.

a. _____, Gollancz, London (L8.95), 1984.*
    Bound in reddish-orange paper boards with gold lettering on the spine. "1984" on the title page. No indication of printing or edition on the copyright page.

b. _____, Putnam, New York ($16.95), 1984.*
    Bound in a three-piece case with light tan front and rear paper boards and with salmon/rust-colored cloth on the spine. No date on the title page. No indication of printing or edition on the copyright page.

c. _____, Putnam, New York ($75.00), 1984.*
    Special boxed and signed edition of 1,500 copies. Bound in maroon cloth with gold lettering on the spine. The slipcase is in maroon cloth. Issued without dust jacket. No date on the title page. No indication of printing or edition on the copyright page. There is a color frontispiece by Abe Echevarria. The limitation page is the first sheet after the front free endpaper. It reads: "Of the first edition of // HERETICS OF DUNE // fifteen hundred copies // specially printed and bound // have been signed by the author // and numbered // Number _____ ". The copy the compiler saw was signed on the title page. The limited editions of most other

Herbert titles that the compiler saw were signed on the limitation page.

d.   _____, Berkley: 07669 ($7.95), 1985, paper.*
"Berkley trade paperback edition / March 1985" on the copyright page.

e.   _____, Berkley: 08732 ($4.50), 1986, paper.*
"Berkley mass market edition/April 1986" on the copyright page.

f.   _____, NEL, 1986, paper.

20.   **THE JESUS INCIDENT**
(with Bill Ransom)
A vast time has elapsed from the events chronicled in DESTINATION: VOID. Ship has staged and restaged enactments of human history and experiments of its own on a fantastically long succession of worlds spanning the spectrum of environments from benign to crisis-riven, sometimes letting them run their own courses, sometimes dramatically interceding, but never with a result entirely to Ship's satisfaction. The latest world, Pandora, is Ship's threatened last effort "to grant his creatures responsible free will"; if this final attempt fails, Ship will "break the mold"--abandon and perhaps destroy humankind altogether.

Pandora, orbiting the star Rega, is an ocean world whose two continents teem with vigorously hostile life, a host of nightmare predators collectively called "demons": roaming packs of huge lamprey-mouthed Hooded Dashers; boils of wormlike nerve runners that burn agonizingly through the nervous system to the brain; flatwings, spinnerets and many others.

Pandora's oceans are dominated by the Electrokelp, its giant strands studded with winking lights. The hylighters are a vector of the kelp; large colored floaters with dangling tentacles that cruise the air as Earth's Portuguese men o'war cruised the seas aeons ago. Compared to the rest of Pandora's denizens, hylighters are a mere nuisance because their hydrogen-filled bags can explode.

Ship's instructions to the selection of humanity carried aboard it were to colonize Pandora. Four attempts to establish settlements on Black Dragon continent have failed, with thousands of lives lost. Ship has now decreed that *all* humans aboard must take up life groundside, despite the unreadiness of the present facilities. The latest colony resembles the embattled beachhead of an invasion force, consisting mainly of underground fortifications. Humans are fighting to conquer Pandora and bitterly resisting adaptation to it; the long-term goal appears to be sterilization of the planet's native life forms. The colonists have spared small effort to investigate the kelp and other species and are unaware that the oceans-wide kelp beds are a communally sentient entity naming itself "Avata".

Those humans in power at the moment of this final run-through of Ship's scenario do not seem likely to lead things to a happy conclusion. The current authoritarian director is Chaplain/Psychiatrist Morgan Oakes, "the Boss", a loudly professed disbeliever in the basic faith of many of the colonists and Shipboard personnel: that Ship is God, or at least a divine entity in its own right. At every opportunity Oakes demonstrates that he considers Ship no more than a gargantuan machine and massively complex computer system that has begun to malfunction. Like-minded doubters, to whom Ship is only "the ship", view Oakes as the prime mover of the colonization efforts. Oakes' chief aides are the amoral scientist Jesus Lewis, and Murdoch, overseer of the groundside labs.

In addition to the colony attempt proper, Oakes and his henchmen have diverted precious supplies to build the Redoubt as their secret base on the second continent, along with a personal stronghold and bolthole, the Nest. In the Nest Jesus Lewis is performing gene-recombination experiments, mingling Electrokelp DNA into a wretched stock of slave-status mutated clone-humans. (An unsuccessful Clone revolt in the redoubt was triggered by Lewis' putting excess clones outside to die, in an attempt to extend supplies.) Many of the clones follow an inchoate religion arising from their subliminal awareness of Avata's overmind.

One element of this final enactment is not a replay. Into this scenario Ship places an individual awakened from aeons-long hybernation in Ship's holds: Raja Flattery, the chaplain/psychiatrist of the original voidship mission which resulted in Ship's creation. Ship revives Flattery as a musician might put a cherished instrument back into play; he is presented with the Pandoran situation and offered Ship's assistance in whatever course he may choose to work toward its solution. Flattery failed in his duty to destroy the original voidship when it displayed full consciousness; now he is unsure whether Ship is God or Satan. Wanting an alias he names himself Raja Thomas, the "doubter".

Flattery/Thomas finds Oakes' administration plagued with many difficulties. The people and records Shipboard are a jumble selected at different times from the many worlds of Ship's past experiments. The humans aboard have no solid knowledge of their origins or even of their own numbers, neither do they have exact knowledge of Ship's physical parameters. Over the eras Ship has added to its original voidship core and become a conglomerate structure more than 60 kilometers long, the original core adorned with storage holds, hybernation tanks, jutting vanes and tubes, launching bays, layers of hydroponics fans, treedomes and herbariums.

Other than Lewis and Murdoch, Oakes' operatives include old Winslow Ferry, in the Shipboard Classification and Processing office, a daydreaming, bumbling, petty ex-surgeon besotted with smuggled wine but adroit at barter within the power structure; Rachel Demarest, a courier between Shipboard and groundside with ambitions for political power far outstripping her abilities; and Legata Hamill, another courier and inspector, a small, attractive woman endowed with extraordinary mental and physical strengths. Oakes means to possess as well as command her, but is willing to bide his time.

A Shipman not a member of Oakes' coterie is Kerro Panille, a 20-year-old poet specially coached, educated, challenged and indulged by Ship. He is a dashing figure, the only Shipman with a beard and long plaited hair. His poetry, and Ship's tutoring, have honed his perceptions and intuitions. He and his friend Med-tech Hali Ekel have been allotted the opportunity to produce a child together. Ekel greatly desires Panille but cannot persuade him to consummate their association; he does not feel strongly enough the needed timing and rightness for the event. She is both fascinated by Panille and somewhat envious of his special rapport with Ship. Winslow Ferry lusts after Hali Ekel, peeping and eavesdropping on her via Ship's surveillance systems.

Waela Taolini is a tall, slender groundside colonist whose skin changes color in sync with her emotions across a spectrum of blue through orange. She has worked on several missions studying the Electrokelp and her reflexes have been trained by the harsh Pandoran ecosystem.

Ship's mechanical order-giving voice directs the colonization and daily matters over normal computer and loudspeaker channels, but a chosen few or a secret many are addressed directly Ship-to-mind, including Panille and Waela Taolini. (Panille addresses and converses with Ship directly and Waela hears Ship as a voice of unknown origin in her mind which she calls "Honesty".) These others who receive no such epiphanic communication, most notably Oakes and his followers, are ignorant of its existence.

Oakes and his administrators are intrigued and angered by Ship's introduction of Flattery/Thomas and the presence of a second chaplain/psychiatrist in the power structure. Thomas' choice of action is to mount new attempts to study the Electrokelp, which is again intriguing but not threatening to Oakes; it keeps Thomas out of the way and the studies are highly dangerous. Ship dispatches Kerro Panille groundside to join the team as a skilled communicator with unusual insights and perspectives; Waela Taolini is the third member assigned. Thomas plans to approach the kelp from the air rather than the shore, landing in "chimneys" or lagoons in the weed from which they will try to communicate with flashing lights. Panille is opaque to Thomas, and though he himself is strongly attracted to Waela, Thomas directs her to seduce the poet and discover more about him. She is unsuccessful.

Following Panille's departure for groundside, Ship addresses Hali Ekel directly and grants her access to the tiny teaching cubby where Panille studied history and enjoyed access to all Ship's records. Hali is thrilled and threatened by the comprehension Ship demands of her; after some preparation, Ship thrusts her across time to witness the holy violence of the Crucifixion firsthand.

Oakes, Lewis and Murdoch have built a cadre of absolutely controlled individuals psychologically shattered in the Scream Room of the groundside labs. Oakes orders Legata Hamill put through this procedure and obtains the appearance of the complete subservience he wanted. Legata's resources are unabated, however, and simply put on hold until the moment when she can find a means to completely obliterate Oakes' grip on his power.

Sabotaged by the Oakes faction, the kelp study balloon crashes in the ocean. Its hatches are sprung and kelp and hylighter tendrils snatch Panille away. He is returned after mental communion with Avata; following a hallucinatory sexual interlude with Waela the poet disappears again, borne off by hylighters. Thomas felt his own identity threatened by Avata and Waela did not achieve as great a rapport with the overpowering kelp gestalt; neither is precisely sure of what happened. Waela, pregnant with an unusually rapidly developing child, is returned to the Shipboard creches, where Hali Ekel is assigned to her care. Eventually Winslow Ferry aids Ekel in escaping with Waela from Oakes' aides, back to groundside.

Following the sudden collapse of the main colony, Oakes and Lewis retreat to the Redoubt; Thomas mobilizes escaped clones and surviving anti-Oakes colonists for a showdown, joined by a disapproving Panille who nevertheless aids them, marshaling hordes of Pandora's demons for the assault. In the meantime, a process set in motion by Lewis is destroying Avata, unleashing the massive tidal forces of Pandora's oceans that the kelp's ocean-spanning beds had held in check; coastlines of the landmasses begin to erode and crumble at a terrifying rate. Mankind, to survive, needs a melding of the visions and disparate experiences and insights of Panille, Ekel and Thomas.

THE JESUS INCIDENT has many similarities of theme, detail, events and characters with the short work "Songs of a Sentient Flute", which evidently served as the tryout or germination of this novel's ideas. See that annotation for more information.

† a.   _____, Berkley/Putnam, New York ($10.95), 1979.*
Bound in dark gray cloth with silver lettering on the spine. No indication of printing or edition on the copyright page. No date on the title page. Jacket by Paul Alexander.

b. _____, Gollancz, London (Ł5.95), 1979.
c. _____, Encounters Book Club (British), London, 1979.
d. ( ) [German], Heyne, 1979, paper.
e. _____, Berkley: 04504 ($2.50), 1980, paper.*
"Berkley edition / April 1980" on the copyright page.
f. _____, Orbit: 8061 (Ł1.60), 1980, paper.
g. _____, Berkley: 05517 ($2.75), 1982, paper.
h. _____, Berkley: 06193 ($2.95), 1983, paper.*
i. _____, Berkley: 07467 ($3.50), 1984, paper.*
j. _____, Berkley: 08619 ($3.95), 1985(?), paper.*
k. _____, Berkley: 10169 ($3.95), 1986, paper.*

21. THE LAZARUS EFFECT
(with Bill Ransom)
In the wake of the destruction of Avata, the ocean-spanning gestalt kelp intelligence, the ferocious power of tides and battering wavefronts has erased Pandora's landmasses. Over many generations the descendants of Ship's Pandoran colonists have chosen divergent adaptations to the all-water world and become two strains: the Mermen, who have taken up residence in fixed quarters on the ocean floor, and the Islanders, who remain on the ocean's surface.

The "Islands" are giant organic floating cities, all-living entities of mainly plant material, sustained by nutrients painted onto their walls, drifting to and fro across the sea-face of the planet. They are close-packed with living cubicles both above and below water level (and may project hundreds of meters below the surface). The largest is Vashon, a 30-kilometer oval with a population of around 600,000.

In general clones and mutants have been segregated to the islands; Islanders are a bizarre hodgepodge of mutations and variations on the human form. The Mermen hew closer to the "human norm", though not absolutely: Mermen may have webbed hands and feet, and enjoy a degree of humidity the Islanders find distressing. Mermen call the islanders "Mutes" and Islanders call the Mermen "pretties". There is some Islander resentment of the Merman perquisites of greater living space and more extensive technology; Mermen view the surface life compared to undersea life as haphazard, hand-to-mouth, disorganized and squalid.

Mermen outnumber Islanders by nearly ten to one. The Islanders are in a poor-cousin situation despite some excellent achievements of their own, particularly in bioengineering--the islands themselves, symbiotic airfish that attach to a swimmer's neck and pump oxygen directly into the bloodstream, living furniture, boats and submarines. Islander production of food and bioengineered products is still swallowed up in a trade deficit, exchanged for necessaries that the Merman hardware technology can produce in quantity.

The Mermen's greater wealth stems from control of their social system, of their genetics and of their environments via their undersea dwellings. A secret Mermen project is the recreation of Pandora's native electrokelp, in an as yet nonsentient form, by extracting the kelp genes from human strains (where they were intermingled by Jesus Lewis' experiments in THE JESUS INCIDENT). The Mermen are using the kelp, as well, as an instrument of ocean-current control; already there are fewer of the massive "wavewalls" stirred up by the tidal pulls of Pandora's twin suns. Islanders are an annoying, unpredictable and ungoverned element in Merman plans; there is pressure for the Islanders to give up their mobile dwellings and relocate to fixed undersea quarters.

The Merman/Islander situation is of continual concern to Ward Keel, an Islander statesman, Chief Justice and Chairman of the Committee on Vital Forms (which weeds out lethal mutations among Islander newborns) on Vashon. Keel is an example of exotic Islander genetics, with a massive squarish head and eyes situated on the corners. He is a moderate force in Islander politics but is slowly dying of internal hormonal imbalances.

Queets Twisp is also an islander, but a simple "man of the sea", an extraordinarily long-armed boatman/fisherman. His companion and apprentice is Brett Norton, a young man much closer to human-norm. This pair deals at close range with the everyday pulse of Pandoran life and life forms. (Many of Pandora's voracious predators have made the transition to aquatic life. The Hooded Dashers have become swimmers with hollow-celled fur for insulation and floatation; the feared Nerve Runners have a more benign undersea vector, the source of "boo", a mild euphoric/narcotic drink.) Twisp and Norton have, in the course of their fishing expeditions, noticed puzzling alterations in the routines established by everyday Merman/Islander politics.

One political symbol is Vata, the child-mutant born to Waela Taolini at the close of THE JESUS INCIDENT. Along with Duque, another mutant born soon afterward, Vata has existed for generations, growing without aging or becoming fully conscious, awaiting some unknown event. They are housed in a nutrient tank on Vashon, tended by the chaplain/psychiatrist (C/P). Vata is a massive, swollen, silent being; flipper-armed Duque is the more wakeful and communicative partner in their curious symbiosis and occasionally speaks cryptically with their guards and the C/P. His utterances and profound or garbled replies to questions are recorded and extensively debated by religious scholars.

Religious power, and religious symbols such as Vata and Duque, are the last major touchstones still principally in the hands of the Islanders. The current C/P is Simone Rocksack, a distinctively mutated woman with an attractive human-norm body but stalked eyes on a perfectly round head and a silvery mane of hair. She resides on Vashon, monitoring Vata and Duque, making religious pronouncements and jockeying for power with the Committee on Vital Forms. The religion of the times has evolved in many forms and permutations, with doctrines, theories and heresies revolving around Ship's departure from Pandora and the legendary "momentary linkage between all the minds alive at that time".

Others are less concerned with religion and politics. Iz Bushka is a small, unattractive Islander timekeeper and historian-hobbyist present at the launch of a Merman hydrogen sonde (balloon) by means of which Mermen are investigating Pandora's upper atmosphere. Bushka, like many Islanders, holds the ambition of being accepted into Merman society in some capacity.

The individuals listed below were also present at the launch.

Kareen Ale is a red-haired Merman woman of exquisite classical physical beauty, a diplomat of the Merman government and an envoy to the Islanders, as well as a scion of a prestigious Merman family. She is an inheritor of the huge Wang estates and thus wealthy, as well as guardian to young Scudi Wang, a worker in Current Control.

Dark ("Shadow") Panille is a descendant and look-alike of the poet Kerro Panille who was personally coached by Ship and who made initial contact with the electrokelp; he works in Sonde Control and is director of the launching Bushka observes. Kelp genes show in his greenish complexion.

GeLaar Gallow is a Merman potentate, a man with a mocking manner overlying the handsomeness and stature of a Greek god. Gallow is Director of the Merman Screen, overseeing who of the Islanders may be accepted into the undersea society. He is also head of a secret conspiracy against the Merman government known as "The Movement". Kareen Ale was once Shadow Panille's lover but is now working with Gallow, seemingly both awed by him and opposing him in some small ways, uncertain of her loyalties and aims in the long run.

Bushka discovers that in addition to the balloon launches the Mermen are conducting tests with rockets, without the blessing of the C/P, in defiance of the tenets of WorShip. (When Ship departed Pandora, it reputedly left in orbit hybernation tanks containing a multitude of Earth-type plants and animals and even humans from Ship's earlier experiments.) Bushka becomes entrapped in Merman politics when Gallow plays patron, selecting Bushka as his accomplice and "pet historian", dangling the promise of Bushka's admission to full Merman status.

Brett Norton is washed from Vashton in a wavewall strike, but rescued and secured in a Merman installation by Scudi Wang. An immediate attraction between her and Brett requires many adjustments and revisions of Merman/Islander viewpoints and mindsets. Though young, Scudi is trying to steer a course between manipulators and her own interests. Her work in Current Control is involved with the "reeducation" of the replanted kelp. She has a special empathy for the kelp which Vata, on Vashon, can sense.

At the same time, Ward Keel is invited underseas by Kareen Ale, to take the Islander statesman out of circulation at a politically crucial time and to facilitate the coverup of Merman rocketry.

Gallow's plans then call for direct offensive action against the Islands. Gallow's principal henchmen and aides in the core of the Movement--an elite group known as the "Green Dashers"--are Tso Zent, his strategist and assassin, and his hulking, scarred aide Gulf Nakano, a thoughtful, compassionate and almost mystic individual bound to Gallow by a life debt.

Gallow, Bushka, Zent and Nakano, in a Merman sub, attack Guemes Island, one of the smallest and poorest Islands but religiously important as the most conservative--a center of the staunchly basic traditions of Islander resistance to moving "down under" in emulation of the Mermen. Guemes is the origin of current C/P Simone Rocksack. The horror of the sub attack moves Bushka to break free of the conspiracy but his character is altered and tainted by that atrocity.

Control of the kelp through possession of Vata is one of the aims of Gallow's band of fanatics. As the Kelp's consciousness returns, Vata and Duque show more signs of animation, to the consternation of the C/P and her watchers. (Vata originally slipped into catatonia as the kelp and hylighters sickened; Vata's mind holds the "racial memory" and the key to consciousness of the kelp Avata.)

The revived kelp, nearing full awareness, is able to communicate via touch; the rapturous effect of this can cause some people to drown. Also through touch the kelp assimilates the total memories of recently-dead individuals, and amidst the kelp the living can speak with the dead--one of the mystic bonds uniting Gallow's fanatic band of Green Dashers, who give their casualties to the kelp. This is the "Lazarus Effect"--the dead can become immortal after a fashion in the kelp's interconnected mass memory. In this second incarnation the kelp is more deadly, almost vindictive, intervening directly in the affairs of humans, selecting those to aid and those to kill.

Queets Twisp, not knowing of Brett's rescue, has gone out searching for him on the open ocean in a tiny coracle-type boat. Instead of finding Brett he picks up Bushka, escaping from Gallow in the wake of the Guemes massacre. Undersea, Scudi Wang and Brett Norton learn that Ward Keel is being held hostage by Gallow's faction. They escape, trying first to reach Vashon and, when that proves impractical, the Merman Launch Base One. The Launch Base is the key to the space effort--a tower rising up out of the ocean from which Islands and Islanders have been steered clear by Current Control. This is also the center for the most secret and significant Merman endeavor, which will disadvantage and curtail the Islands further still: the upraisal of new land from the seabed.

    a.   _____, Putnam, New York ($15.95), 1983.*
Bound in a three-piece case with green paper front and rear boards and with green cloth on the spine. Gold lettering on the spine. No date on the title page. No indication of printing or edition on the copyright page. Jacket by Abe Echevarria.

    b.   _____, Gollancz, London (Ł8.95), 1983.*
Bound in brown paper boards with gold lettering on the spine. "1983" on the title page. No indication of printing or edition on the copyright page. Jacket by Terry Oakes.

    c.   _____, Berkley: 07129 ($3.50), 1984, paper.*
"Berkley edition / August 1984" on the copyright page.

    d.   _____, Berkley: 09790 ($3.95), 1986, paper.*

22. **LE LIVRE D'OR DE LA SCIENCE-FICTION FRANK HERBERT**
Edited by Gerard Klein.
French collection.
Contents: Une Definition De L'Univers (Preface by Gerard Klein); Operation Syndrome; The 'Mary Celeste Move; The GM Effect; Occupational Force; The Primatives; Looking For Something?; Passage For Piano; Seed Stock; Egg And Ashes; Mating Call; Escape Felicity; The Mind Bomb; Bibliography.

    a.   _____, Presses Pocket: 5018, 1978, paper.*
Translator: The Primatives--Christian Meistermann; The Mind Bomb--Pierre Billon; all others--Dominique Abonyi.

23. **THE MAKER OF DUNE: FRANK HERBERT**
Non-Fiction collection.
Edited and with introduction and commentary by Timothy O'Reilly.
Contents: Introduction by Timothy O'Reilly; Listening To The Left Hand; Science Fiction And A World In Crisis; Country Boy; You Can Go Home Again; Introduction To Nebula Winners Fifteen; Men On Other Planets; Poetry; Dangers Of The Superhero; The Campbell Correspondence; Sandworms Of Dune; Undersea Riches For Everybody; Man's Future In Space; 2068 A.D.; The Sky Is Going To Fall; Natural Man; Natural Predator; Introduction To Saving Worlds; We're Losing The Smog War; Lying To Ourselves About Air; Ships; Doll Factory, Gun Factory; The Tillers; Flying Saucers--Fact Or Farce?; Conversations In Port Townsend; New World Or No World; Bibliography.

    a.   _____, Berkley: 09784 ($7.95), 1987, paper.*
Trade paperback in size. "Berkley trade paperback edition/May 1987" on the copyright page.

24. MAN OF TWO WORLDS
   (with Brian Herbert)
   The activities and philosophies of an alien race have molded Earth's past and bear intensely on its future. This race is the Dreen, whose members have a tremendous appetite for stories.

   The lumpish, rather ludicrous-appearing Dreen are natural shape-shifters of tremendous ability. All Dreen also have, in one degree or another, the capability of idmaging, mentally transmuting any matter at hand into new forms, to create anything from food to tools to living beings. By the *idmaging* process the Dreen master storytellers have populated entire worlds to which the more adventurous storyteller captains go voyaging out from the homeworld Dreenor, gathering tales to satiate their society's demand for vicarious experience.

   Earth is one of the most complex and, until recently, the most frequently visited storyteller scenarios. Unfortunately, the original Dreen shaper of Earth may have been a tad deranged. As well as a steady source of outstanding stories, Earth has supplied the Dreen with their only addictive drug (the herb basil, known to the Dreen as bazeel) and with a growing source of worry as humans, with their (to the Dreen) proven xenophobic and destructive tendencies, approach the capability for interstellar travel. Earth's space jurisdictional agency, the Zone Patrol, already holds some captive Dreen, though the agency is not quite sure just what they have.

   The developing Earth crisis is one among several to Habiba, first and oldest Dreen, primogenitrice, mother-figure, spiritual leader and Supreme Tax Collector. She and her chief counselor Jongleur also detect undercurrents of an unrest and growing anxiety on Dreenor itself, where the compulsively pacifistic Dreen happily follow a lifestyle of tradition which is nearly instinctive, avoiding deep inquiry into their origins or their own natures. This orchestrated traditional routine of ages is jarred by Ryll, an impatient and ambitious young Dreen who steals a storyteller ship to go adventuring.

   Near Earth Ryll's craft collides with a human spaceship. Badly injured in the crash, and thrown into proximity with the dead and dying crew of the human vessel, Ryll panics and violates a paramount Dreen code; he draws upon his shapeshifting capacity not merely to imitate but to merge his body with that of the fatally injured pilot, assuming the human's form for concealment.

   The pilot whose body Ryll has co-occupied is Lutt Hanson, Jr, elder son of the era's preeminent business tycoon. Lutt Jr is a power-motivated, amoral individual who at first takes his coexistence with an alien to be a delusion, but possibly to be played up for an advantage in the Hanson family internecine power struggles.

   Hovering on the outskirts and dabbling in these manipulations is Lutt's Uncle Dudley, a "black sheep" relative and also a possessor of Dreen-like abilities. Entirely lacking in his brother-in-law's and nephew's ambitions and acquisitive drives, Dudley leads an idle life with his termagant of a consort, the plump Osceola, an inventor and an additional wielder of the human equivalents of idmaging and interworld jumping. Dudley divides his time between playing at guru on Venus and lounging in the Florida Everglades, thinking up quirky ways to aid Lutt Jr against Lutt's father and Lutt's younger brother Morey, a corrupt weakling but his mother Phoenicia's favorite.

   Once he accepts the fact of his bodily occupation by an alien presence, Hanson's reaction escalates to paranoid hostility. The greater share of control of their body is up in the air from hour to hour, but Hanson is willing to bargain occasional passivity on his side for information that might aid him in his intrigues and enterprises.

One tidbit proffered by Ryll is an instantaneous message-transmitter. For a demonstration, Hanson travels to Venus to supply his news service with up-to-the-minute coverage of the war there in progress between French Foreign Legion and Communist Chinese troops. There also Lutt and his new enterprises come to the attention of Lorna Subiyama, a lusty, ample and expansive Texan reporter. In pursuing the Hanson lead, Lorna takes up with Prosik, a Dreen and bumbling bazeel addict. Sent to Earth for errors on Dreenor, Prosik masqueraded as a Zone Patrol officer and has been dispatched to Venus for punishment for further blunders.

Injured on the battlefield, Hanson awakens aboard the Legion's closely-guarded brothel spacecraft. He swiftly conceives something between a passion and a lust for Nishi D'Amato, the vessel's "virgin chanteuse", who seems the incarnation of one of Lutt Jr's erotic/romantic fantasies. She, secretly apprised by Ryll of the Hanson/Ryll situation, is attracted but uncertain as to which of the coterminous personalities is attracting her.

Lutt also discovers the Dreen vulnerability to basil/bazeel. Eating large doses of basil makes Lutt appear drunk, because a portion of his body is actually basil-susceptible Dreen flesh, but while the effect lasts he controls, however muzzily, their "partnership."

Ryll is nearly inextricably melded with Hanson. They can be separated only in the presence of the requisite amount of suitable mass, and by a precisely timed and delicately controlled procedure of which Ryll, who daydreamed a good deal during his classes, does not recall the exact details. The young alien is determined on survival and still curious to explore Earth; he finds cooperation necessary but is repelled by Hanson's unscrupulous lust for yet greater wealth, power and independence from his father.

Ryll does not realize, although Prosik is aware, that the storyteller ship he took for his joyride and wrecked was a secret instrument constructed by Mugly, a cunning and uncharacteristically duplicitous Dreen official convinced that the erasure of Earth is the only solution--even though no Dreen has ever personally killed any other being or even constructed a weapon. Lutt Hanson, Jr. engages in a presidential campaign as a second Dreen erasure ship piloted by Ryll's father, Jongleur, approaches Earth; and there is the additional complication that--according to legend--if Dreen cease to hold in mind a Dreen creation it vanishes from existence.

a.   ____, Putnam, New York ($18.95), 1986.*
Bound in a three-piece case with black cloth on the spine and with brown front and rear paper boards. Gold lettering on the spine. "1 2 3 4 5 6 7 8 9 10" on the copyright page, otherwise no indication of printing or edition. No date on the title page. Jacket by John Schoenherr.

b.   ____, Gollancz, London (£9.95), 1986.

c.   (   ) [German], Heyne, paper. Forthcoming.

d.   (   ) [Spanish], Ultramar Ediciones, paper. Forthcoming.

e.   (   ) [French], Laffont, paper. Forthcoming.

f.   (   ) [Hebrew], Am Oved, paper. Forthcoming.

25.   **THE PRIESTS OF PSI**
Contents: Try To Remember!; Old Rambling House; Murder Will In; Mindfield!; The Priests Of Psi; The Gone Dogs.

a.   ____, Gollancz, London (£5.50), 1980.*
Bound in red paper boards with gold lettering on the spine. "1980" on the title page. No indication of printing or edition on the copyright page.

b. _____, British Science Fiction Book Club, 1980.
c. _____, Orbit: 8078 (L1.35), 1981, paper.

26. THE SANTAROGA BARRIER
("The Santaroga Barrier", Amazing, sr3, October 1967)
Santaroga is a northern California farm community in the Santaroga
Valley. It is a prosperous town isolated not only by its location but
peculiarly set apart in other fashions from the rest of the state and
the whole of the society surrounding it. In Santaroga, there is no
advertising, no television, no use of tobacco, no mental illness.
Santarogans rarely leave the valley for any reason and any called away,
such as by the military's draft, always return. In neighboring communities Santarogans are considered kooky and strange. All businesses
are locally owned and do as little trade as possible with outside
suppliers.

Most recently, a supermarket chain's plans to expand into the area
have met with rebuffs. Its backing corporation desires more in-depth
investigation into this failure, and into the series of accidents that
have befallen its first few investigators.

The choice this time is Gilbert Dasein, a psychologist from the
University of California at Berkeley. He is willing to accept the
assignment largely because of his love affair a year ago with Jenny
Sorge, a Santarogan who attended Berkeley. When he proposed, she
declared she could live nowhere but in Santaroga; Dasein saw no
prospects for his career in the isolated region and Jenny returned to
the valley upon graduation.

Dasein arrives in Santaroga and despite the entirely normal small-
town atmosphere of his hotel he at once observes tension and hostility
between Santarogans and "outsiders" such as travelers, vacationers and
salesmen. The Santarogans' initial hostility to "transient" Dasein
changes at once into something like approving welcome when his
connection with Jenny Sorge is mentioned; he seems to be fairly widely
known among the locals as "Jenny's man from Berkeley".

Dasein receives a warm welcome as well from Jenny Sorge and her
uncle, Dr Lawrence Piaget. Somehow Dasein's many letters to Jenny
never reached her but Jenny has resisted marriage with locals and
waited for Dasein.

Despite Dasein's popularity on Jenny's account, he narrowly
escapes an alarming series of mishaps and accidents--almost being
suffocated in his hotel room by a leaking gas jet, a fall in a stairwell,
a narrow escape from poisoning. In each case the Santarogans appear
very concerned, sorry and even angry at the incidents but Dasein
cannot shake the feeling of some antagonism focused against him.

In addition, Dasein has turned up still more peculiarities of the
local scene. Santaroga's own produce, even the Jaspers beer and cheese
from the local co-op in which the locals take great pride, is never
exported. Highway Patrolman Marden also acts as game warden, policing
the valley's boundaries in a huge balloon-tired bush buggy with a
complement of leashed hounds to discourage hunters, poachers and
trespassers who might approach Santaroga by other than the main
roads. The local newspaper's coverage of "outside" news features the
major events of the nation and world reduced to brief and acerbically
biting vignettes. In a tour of the cheese co-op where Jenny works,
Dasein has glimpsed a production line manned by zombie-like people
held in place with ankle stocks.

Since Dasein's briefcase, with all his papers relating to the
investment corporation and his true--or at least his original--mission in
Santaroga, was picked up by Marden after the gas-jet incident, Dasein

considers his cover blown and is puzzled by the face still shown him by Santarogan society. In particular Marden, the scholarly Piaget and Win Burdeaux, a black waiter in the hotel who was born outside and settled in the valley some years ago, seem to want to assist Dasein to some understanding of Santaroga's difference. Dasein is bolstered by occasional contact with Dr Selador, his supervisor at Berkeley, but communication by phone or mail out of the valley is a chancy thing. Circumstances lead him to wonder if he is being drugged or his perceptions somehow otherwise manipulated. There is also subtle and not-so-subtle pressure for him to commit to marriage with Jenny--to which he is inclined but rendered hesitant by the other peculiarities of the situation--and to settling permanently in the valley.

On a clandestine nocturnal investigation of the heavily-guarded co-op's storage areas in natural caverns, Dasein finds extensive bins filled with foodstuffs apparently being exposed or irradiated by something native to the caves. He is warned away by a friendly Santarogan who fears that he has received an overdose of "Jaspers" in the dimly red-lit caverns and Dasein's subsequent delirious collapse argues in favor of this diagnosis.

"Jaspers" is not only the local dairy co-op's name but the Santarogans' term for the mysterious substance or essence that permeates cheese, beer, milk and other foodstuffs stored in the caverns. It has curious and complex properties, uniting and motivating the Santarogans on unconscious levels. In the sense of community and shared and heightened consciousness achieved through Jaspers they feel their minds have been expanded and their horizons broadened, though to an outside observer they appear to have become dimmed, homogenized and indrawn.

In the shared spirit of Jaspers-sense, the locals' view of contemporary America's me-first, rat-race society is rightfully xenophobic; the Santarogans see themselves as protecting their viable social system from the hostile, corrupt, *dying* outside culture.

The inexplicable series of accidents continues, eventually leading to Dasein's hospitalization; his urge to escape battles his desire to make a closer study of Jaspers and its properties and a powerful and growing lure to join, to let himself be absorbed by Santaroga.

† a.   _____, Berkley: S1615 ($0.75), 1968, paper.*
"BERKLEY MEDALLION EDITION, OCTOBER, 1968" on the copyright page. Reprinted in 1970 and 1971.

b.   (DIE LEUTE VON SANTAROGA) [German], Heyne: 3156/3157 (DM 3.80), 1969, paper.
Translator: Birgit Ress-Bohusch. Reprinted in 1980.

† c.   _____, Rapp & Whiting, London (28/-, L1.40), 1970.*
Bound in blue paper boards with silver lettering on the spine. The publisher's name is also on the front cover in silver. "First Published in Great Britain in // 1970 by Rapp & Whiting Limited" stated on the copyright page. No date on the title page.

d.   _____, NEL: 2911 (30p, 6/-), 1971, paper.*
"FIRST NEL EDITION APRIL 1971" on the copyright page. Reprinted in August 1973.

e.   _____, NEL: 01856 (40p), 1974, paper.*

f.   _____, Berkley: N2811 ($0.95), 1975, paper.*

g.   _____, Berkley: 03539 ($1.25), 1977, paper.*

h.   _____, Berkley: 03539 ($1.50), 1977(?), paper.*

† i.   _____, Berkley/Putnam, New York ($7.95), 1977.*
Bound in brown cloth with gold lettering on the spine. No date on the title page. No indication of printing or edition on the copyright page. Jacket by Paul Alexander.

j.   _____, Berkley: 03824 ($1.75), 1978, paper.*
        Reprinted.
k.   (DE SANTAROGA BARRIERE) [Dutch], Centripress, 1978, paper.
l.   (   ) [Spanish], 1978, paper(?).
m.   (   ) [French], Jean-Claude Lattes, 1979, paper (?).
n.   _____, Berkley: 05053 ($2.25), 1981, paper.*
o.   _____, NEL: 04376 (L1.25), 1981, paper.
p.   _____, Berkley: 05944 ($2.50), 1982, paper.*
q.   _____, Berkley: 07468 ($2.75), 1984, paper.*
r.   _____, Berkley: 08468 ($2.95), 1985, paper.
s.   _____, Berkley: 08987 ($2.95), 1986, paper.*
Frank Herbert wrote an unpublished screenplay of this novel in 1985.

27. SOUL CATCHER
     Charles Hobuhet is a young Northwest Indian who has progressed far
     along the "white man's way" into university education. He has studied
     the injustices and betrayals perpetrated by the white race and written
     original, insightful and provocative commentary on the clash of cultures
     and the present situation of his people; his professors regard him as a
     student of great promise.
         But Hobuhet's life has been thrown from its track by the suicide
     of his teenage sister Janiktaht, who drowned herself after being raped
     by a group of drunken loggers. A devastated Charles seeks refuge in
     the old rituals of his people, making a trek into the Northwest
     wilderness to cleanse his grief by ordeal. He has prepared the ritu-
     al/magic talismans for the event using his grandfather's lore--wearing a
     headband of red cedar bark, burying a land otter's tongue in a certain
     fashion to make it a spirit-symbol tongue and living only on roots of
     the devil's club plant.
         He did not truly expect to find communion with the spirit world
     by these means, but after days in the wilderness Hobuhet feels himself
     touched by Soul Catcher, a powerful spirit of his people, appearing near
     him in the form of a bee. The bee stings him, injecting Charles
     Hobuhet with the mighty spirit and with a terrible task. To contain
     these powers and purposes Charles takes a new identity, Katsuk, a
     name with roots in many meanings of his Indian language.
         The task set for Charles/Katsuk by Soul Catcher is a symbolic one
     of catharctic revenge. He must find a perfect innocent of the white
     race and kill that person, as an exchange and balance for all of the
     Indian innocents who have died at white hands or through white
     manipulations. This is to be a gesture sending reverberations to the
     furthest corners of the white culture. The innocent, after proper
     preparation for the event, will be killed with a consecrated arrow, a
     neolithic flint tip from an old beach campsite of Charles' people
     mounted on a modern cedar shaft.
         Charles' selected victim is David Marshall, 13-year-old son of the
     newly-appointed Undersecretary of State Howard Marshall. David is
     enrolled in the exclusive Six Rivers Boys Camp in the Washington wilds
     where Charles works as a counselor. David is a bright child who has
     led a sheltered, insulated upper-crust life as the son of a career
     diplomat and a sophisticated society woman; much of his time has been
     spent in San Francisco with his grandparents while his father held
     posts overseas. The whirlwind visits of his parents with gifts from
     exotic places have not counteracted his ultimate frustrations and
     feelings of being set aside, although on this stay at camp David is
     athrill with his father's gift of a new Russell hunting knife.
         Charles/Katsuk lures David away from the camp in the middle of
     the night on the pretense of David's participating in an Indian cere-

mony. When he is taken prisoner, David's initial reactions are rage and fear and the supposition that Charles is crazy; he attempts to leave signs for the searchers he is sure will quickly rescue him. David cannot simply be killed immediately; he must be prepared in unhurried, ritual ways, places must be visited and the demands of the Spirit World must be met before the deed. In addition, Katsuk informs David that he himself must request the execution or at least express his willingness to participate. Charles/Katsuk gives David the spirit name of Hoquat, a generic name for whites applied specifically to the future sacrificial victim; David's use of it is brutally enforced.

The search for the pair is quickly mounted. At their first stopping place, a mountainside cave near a spring, David's dropped handkerchief attracts a scouting helicopter but the helicopter's sound starts an avalanche in the shale slope which buries the sign. Besides this, a flock of ravens seems to assist Charles in his concealment, not flying until needed to demonstrate to the white searchers that no people could be nearby.

Katsuk receives additional confirmation of his spirit powers and guidance from many signs and events. The actions of ravens, bees, lightning and the powerful sensation of Charles/Katsuk's oneness with the natural world of the wilderness all erode David's initial estimation of him as a brutal "crazy Injun". David comes to bear the imprint of Charles/Katsuk's world as deeply, though over a briefer period of time, as Charles Hobuhet has received the imprint of the white man's world.

At an isolated lake and mountain meadow, they encounter a band of Charles/Katsuk's people who have come into the wilderness hoping to dissuade him from his much-publicized enterprise (and partly because it affords them an opportunity to poach in the wilderness area). Charles debates his deeds at length, principally with his uncle Ishkawch, his aunt Cally and his former lover Mary Kletnik. Both Uncle Ish and Cally deride the spirit significances while perhaps, deep down, wishing to be convinced of their truth. Soul Catcher's portents of ravens and lightning are manifested; Charles' relatives are both intimidated by and secretly pleased and proud of the power evident in him. After their attempts to persuade him from his course fail, they set themselves apart and somewhat accessory to his destiny, even guarding David while Charles joins in a bear hunt.

Mary Kletnik, though, wishes to persuade Charles from his course not so much for consideration of the political and ethical ramifications of the deed he intends, but to reestablish her emotional hold on him. She rejects the spirit powers, her Indian heritage and her Indian name Tskanny and Charles' world view; while Charles is absent from camp she seduces David. This proves a building and growing event for David rather than any smirching of his "perfect innocence".

Despite his inexperience and the sheltered nature of his life, David displays stamina, resourcefulness and strength of character. The kidnapping and forced journey are, in fact, an occasion of great growth and awakening for him. Although David/Hoquat has witnessed Charles' killing of a hiker who surprised them and is chilled by the inexorable purpose thus displayed, he recognizes his growing identification with and admiration for Charles/Katsuk; a combination of classic "hostage syndrome" and of his many new experiences and spiritual maturation over the course of their trek.

Charles/Katsuk is torn between his ordinary self, which comes to feel compassion and admiration for David in his turn, and his spirit-driven inflexible purpose and knowledge of the required culmination of their journey. As their trek nears its end Charles contends with uncertainty and vacillations of his spirit guidance, wondering why he was chosen and finding his task a miserable burden as well as the exaltingly powerful mission he felt it to be in the beginning, loathing the difficult and unpalatable final steps remaining for its completion.

Charles and David sleep under the same blanket in the wet woods; an exhausted David drinks Indian medication from a rolled bark cone. David even assists Katsuk in the carving of a spirit-given length of wood into the bow that will guide the arrow for his own execution, and nurses Charles when he falls ill; but this growing companionship cannot alter the fated tragic end.

The story takes place not only in a vividly realized wilderness setting but in the interface of white, western culture and the Indian world of nature and spirit/mythic reality. Charles and David's travels through the Kimta Peak and Hoh River country and over the high trails through storm and snowmelt are a vivid and evocative portrait of the northwest woods; the natural settings and elemental forces are additional "characters" with which the human characters interact.

The narrative of Charles and David, Katsuk and Hoquat's trek and doings is interspersed with documents presenting the outside view of events: reports of the investigators and searchers, quotes from interviews of individuals connected with the pair and from the writings of Charles Hobuhet. The spiritual significances are ignored by the outside world; the assumption is that Hobuhet is a deranged Indian militant who has engineered a hostage situation. There is additional tragedy in the white world's foredoomed lack of comprehension of Katsuk's message-by-deed; the intended recipients lack the insight or the set of mind to absorb this message and its impact is confined to the two participants.

† a.   _____, Putnam, New York ($6.95), 1972.*
Bound in brown cloth with black lettering on the spine. Black design on the front cover. No date on the title page. No indication of printing or edition on the copyright page.

† b.   _____, Bantam: Q7616 ($1.25), 1973, paper.*
Also numbered 07616 on the spine. "Bantam edition published December 1973" on the copyright page.

c.   _____, NEL, London (Ł2.20), 1973.*

d.   _____, Bantam: 11516 ($1.50), 1973, paper.*

e.   _____, G K Hall, Boston ($9.95), 1974.*
Large print edition.

† f.   _____, Berkley: 04250 ($1.95), 1979, paper.*
"Berkley edition / 1979" on the copyright page.

g.   _____, Berkley: 05240 ($2.25), 1981, paper.

h.   _____, Berkley: 06486 ($2.75), 1983, paper.*

i.   _____, Berkley: 09141 ($2.95), 1985, paper.*

A filmscript, written in the 1970's, exists in the Frank Herbert manuscript collection at the University of California at Fullerton. Frank Herbert also wrote an unpublished screenplay of this novel in 1984.

28. SURVIVAL AND THE ATOM
Non-Fiction
All the information for this citation is based on the notes and on the memory of L W Currey.

a.   _____, No Publisher, No Number, 1952, paper.
This is a collection of a series of articles that Herbert had written while a newspaperman at the Santa Rosa Press Democrat. The articles dealt with the subject of nuclear war. About 500 copies were printed. The book was fairly substantial in size, on the order of 6" by 9". It did not contain a date or an indication of who was the publisher. The supposition is that the book was published by the Santa Rosa Press Democrat.

29.   THRESHOLD: THE BLUE ANGELS EXPERIENCE
Non-Fiction.
The text and full-color photos from the motion picture. The film is a
documentary of the US Navy flying team--the Blue Angels. The film is
about 89 minutes with narration written by Frank Herbert. The film was
narrated by Leslie Nielsen. The film is also available on videotape
(UMATIC, Beta and VHS) in both a 46-minute and an 89-minute version.
This book contains Herbert's narrative script from the film of the same
name about the Navy's Blue Angels precision exhibition flying team. It
consists of roughly 90 pages of color stills from the movie plus
additional pictures by various photographers, the film credits and 60
full or partial pages of text. The text is the film's "verbal soundtrack",
including the speeches of the pilots in discussions of their flying and
during their flights and performances.
      The book also includes a 2-page introduction by Herbert about the
movie, its effects and aftereffects on the fliers and the moviemakers,
and about his interest in the Blue Angels and the types of limit-testing
and transcendental experience involved in their training and flying.
Herbert's narrative is evocative and dramatic as well as descriptive; it
deals both with what's occurring "onscreen" (or in the photos) and
what's unseen, infusing and inspiring the pilots' performances and
attitudes. The Blue Angels team members are normal humans, but
selected and trained to perform an extraordinarily demanding job with
greatly extended human capabilities (for instance, the team does not
make use of G-suits, although they may experience up to seven G's
during their turns). Their finely honed reactions and integration as a
team have led to a heightened state of awareness approaching the
hyperconsciousness described by Herbert in many of his novels and
stories; and the uniqueness of the team sparks perception, in the
viewers of its performances, of their own uniqueness and potential. A
main emphasis of the narrative is the exhilaration in the testing and
surpassing of limits, and the near-mystical nature of the experience
involved in the team's joint quest for perfection and the extension of
human thresholds "out...on the edge of human/machine capability".
      The film and book follow the Blue Angels in performances and on
the ground over the course of a year's activities: they are seen enroute
to an airshow in Hawaii, refueling twice in midair on the way; performing pre-show maintenance work; in sessions scoping out the peculiarities
of each field where they'll fly; in an airshow at high elevation in
Quito, Ecuador, amid cloud-wrapped granite mountains; at the change-
over of two of the six team members; and in winter training, as the
new members are integrated into the unique, cohesive entity into which
each successive year's lineup becomes fused.
† a.   _____, Ballantine: 23424 ($2.95), 1973, paper.*
      "First Printing: August, 1973" on the copyright page. Trade
      paperback in size.

UNDER PRESSURE
      See THE DRAGON IN THE SEA.

30.   WHIPPING STAR
("Whipping Star", If, sr4, January 1970)
Working titles "S'Eye", "Caleban", "M'Eye".
Human interstellar civilization is part of the Consentiency, a varied
consortium of races including the following: the frog-like amphibious
Gowachin, Palenki resembling many-legged turtles with one long and
powerful arm, ferocious insectid/mantid Wreaves, quirky and tempera-

mental telepathic Taprisiots which look like blocky billets of wood, and the five-gendered Pan Spechi, a chameleon race that cycles one ego between the members of its creches and can adopt any form but most often favors a human likeness with multifaceted eyes.

Through the Consentiency, interspecies trade and contact have proliferated; alien cultural artifacts and processes are thoroughly intermeshed with the human lifestyle and as common as chairdogs, living and eager-to-please furniture. All the races make abundant use of communication provided by the Taprisiots (who can put you in instant telepathic contact with anyone else anywhere in the galaxy--though for the duration of the dialogue one's body is rendered defenseless in a vacant, giggling "sniggertrance"), and travel extensively via the S'eye effect or "jumpdoors", instantaneous world-to-world transmission furnished by the rare, little-understood Calebans. If an individual's location is unknown, one can still contact them via sniggertrance; if it is known, one can visit them in person by jumpdoor. The Calebans are mysterious beings with control over immense and incomprehensible energies, but have been willing to enter into a variety of contracts and dealings with the other Consentiency races.

Very recently, though, the indispensable Calebans have begun to disappear from the Consentiency scene. (No more than 83 were known to exist in the first place.) This is much more than an inconvenience to transportation: with the vanishing of a Caleban everyone who has utilized that particular Caleban's S'eye door is stricken by insanity and/or death.

Jorj X McKie, gnomish Saboteur Extraordinary of the Bureau of Sabotage (or BuSab--see "The Tactful Saboteur"), is already at work on the maxi-alert pertaining to Mliss Abnethe, a monumentally wealthy woman who has entered into a contract with a Caleban. Abnethe is rich enough to own outright many planets and to have in her pocket scores of Consentiency officials on every world. Though Abnethe is perhaps as old as 80, beauty barbers recruited from Steadyon maintain her youthful but striking appearance; she is equal parts hoyden and authoritarian. Adept at the politics of wealth and power, Abnethe is mentally unbalanced in other ways; she is "kinky about floggings" and extensive treatment has only modified, not cured, this aberration that Abnethe uses her vast resources to indulge.

McKie is contacted in the midst of divorce court, where his 54th marriage is ending (it was undertaken in part to further BuSab's investigation of Mliss Abnethe but is symptomatic of an inability on McKie's part to form satisfactory relationships). He is contacted via sniggertrance by Alichino Furuneo, BuSab planetary agent on the backwater world of Cordiality. A Caleban beachball, possibly damaged, has washed up there and affixed itself to the shore. The large metallic "beachballs" are individual Caleban homes and this one seems to be the last one known to remain in Consentiency space.

McKie and Furuneo are allowed to enter the six-meter beachball and find themselves in the presence of a Caleban. Calebans do not completely register on the human sensory system--the observer can feel or sense *something* but not see or touch the presence. This Caleban manifests an essentially feminine presence and wishes to be known as "Fannie Mae" (Calebans are quirky but very insistent about nomenclature).

At once difficulties in communication arise. Phrasings, word meanings, concepts and contexts all hinder or distort human-Caleban conversation. McKie persists and in this and later sessions gradually discovers that Caleban perceptions are vastly broader than those of humans or other Consentients; Calebans perceive and manipulate all time and space and even manifest themselves in various states and locations simultaneously. (Calebans are also stars; Fannie Mae is the star Thyone.) They call the other Consentiency species "single-track" or "singletons" and their awareness is so tuned to mega-reality, the interconnectedness of all things, that they find the viewpoint of the isolated human mind exceedingly difficult to grasp. The beachballs are disappearing because most of the Calebans have finally tired of the gnat-like importunities of singletons wishing to benefit themselves through Caleban contracts.

Fannie Mae's beachball home contains the last and the Master S'eye. Were she to vanish the toll among jumpdoor users would escalate from crisis to catastrophe proportions. Unluckily, Fannie Mae is the Caleban who has contracted with Mliss Abnethe. She is providing, among other things, jumpdoor travel and a "pocket universe" refuge that appears to be partly a Caleban-created manifestation of Mliss Abnethe's "ideal world" and partly an artifact of time-manipulation reaching back to Boer South Africa. Worst of all, a key clause of the contract allows Abnethe to have floggings administered to Fannie Mae, which Abnethe witnesses via a jumpdoor "window". Abnethe's treatment rendered her unable to stand the sight of a sentient suffering, without eliminating the desire to inflict pain; flogging a marginally visible Caleban is for her a splendid compromise. Since so little is known about Calebans there is no concrete evidence that the floggings cause what other races would experience as pain or discomfort; Abnethe can indulge her sadistic compulsions outside the Consentiency's laws.

McKie discovers that despite the Caleban's vast and far-flung energies, these beatings--and especially the focused hatred and spiritual malaise accompanying them--will lead in around 10 or so more floggings to Fannie Mae's "ultimate discontinuity". A Caleban sense of being contractually morally bound, or some other complex attitude, prevents her from attempting escape from the situation on her own behalf.

Abruptly a jumpdoor opens and McKie witnesses the administration of one of the floggings. He confronts Abnethe, viewing from the jumpdoor's far side, but in the face of the situation's abstruse legal ramifications and her resources he can accomplish nothing. Amidst the eager crowd of Abnethe's hangers-on in the background, McKie spots a Pan Spechi with a scarred forehead; this is evidence of that race's most horrifically depraved crime, "ego surgery", by which one individual renders permanent his possession of the cycling ego and dooms his crechemates to a grisly dissolution.

BuSab's committee for this emergency includes Pan Spechi Bureau Chief Bildoon and agent Tuluk, as well as Laclac Director of Discretion Siker, other assorted agents and McKie. Not least of the conundrums with which this interspecies panel must grapple is the declaration of Fannie Mae that she is in love with the thorny and unapproachable McKie.

McKie achieves access to Abnethe's private world (or universe), finding it stocked with "mad Boers and blacks", grass huts, thorn bomas, and the trappings of a racist colonialism bearing the imprint of Abnethe's particular fetishes. McKie is captured but learns more about Abnethe's lover and confederate, the Pan Spechi, Cheo. Cheo is actually working to incite the destruction of the Consentiency; only the wiping out of the Pan Spechi species will ensure his security.

BuSab and their opponents run a lightning-fast-paced game of strike and counterstrike via jumpdoor while Cheo and Abnethe orchestrate their own attacks and defenses and tempt with time-warping Caleban bribes. More crucial than the physical espionage, however, is McKie's and BuSab's grappling with phenomena that they and all the

Consentiency have utilized as commonplace without *understanding*--the Caleban mentality which has provided the taken-for-granted jumpdoors. Unless McKie and his companions can learn Caleban thought patterns, especially the concept of connectives, in time to establish the communication that can find a loophole in Fannie Mae's contract, their civilization is doomed.

†a. ____, Putnam, New York ($4.95), 1970.*
Bound in yellow paper boards with red lettering on the spine. Small red design on the front cover. No date on the title page. No indication of printing or edition on the copyright page. Jacket by John Schoenherr.

b. ____, Berkley: S1909 ($0.75), 1970, paper.*
"BERKLEY MEDALLION EDITION, NOVEMBER, // 1970" on the copyright page. Reprinted.

c. (   ) [Dutch], Meulenhoff, 1971, paper.

d. ____, NEL: 00963 (40p), 1972, paper.*
Reprinted May 1972, September 1972, August 1973, and July 1974.

e. (STELLA INNAMORATA) [Italian], Galassia: 167 (L400), 1972, paper.
Translator: Giampaolo Cossato and Sandro Sandrelli.

f. (DER LETZTE CALEBAN) [German], Heyne: 3317, 1972, paper.
Translator: Walter Brumm. Reprinted 1980.

g. (L'ETOILE ET LE FOUET) [French], Laffont, 1973, paper(?).
Translator: Guy Abadia.

h. ____, Berkley: 02824 ($0.95), 1975, paper.*

i. ____, NEL: 02747 (45p), 1975, paper.

j. ____, Berkley: 03308 ($1.50), 1977, paper.*

†k. ____, Berkley: 03504 ($1.50), 1977, paper.*
Revised.

l. (STELLA INNAMORATA) [Italian], Bigalassia: 33 (L200), 1977, paper.
Translator: Giampaolo Cossato and Sandro Sandrelli.
Combined with THE EYES OF HEISENBERG.

m. ____, NEL: 04189 (75p), 1978, paper.

†n. ____, Berkley: 04116 ($1.95), 1979, paper.
Reprinted.

o. (   ) [Japanese], 1979(?), paper(?).

p. ____, NEL, London (L4.95), 1979.

q. ____, Gregg Press, Boston ($13.95), 1980.*
Introduction by Joseph Milicia. Issued without dust jacket. Bound in yellowish-brown cloth with red lettering on the spine and front cover. "1980" on the title page. "First Printing, October, 1980" on the copyright page.

r. ____, Berkley: 04355 ($2.25), 1981, paper.*

s. ____, Berkley: 05515 ($2.50), 1982, paper.*

t. ____, Berkley: 06997 ($2.95), 1984, paper.*

31. **THE WHITE PLAGUE**
John Roe O'Neill, an American geneticist and molecular biologist working in Ireland, witnesses the deaths of his wife and two small children in the explosion of an IRA-Provo terrorist bomb. O'Neill is traumatized; his recovery and accommodation to the memory of this tragedy is by a species of personality fragmentation. His "coping" persona, which he names The Madman and to which he thankfully surrenders, seems to arise partially out of the darker corners of his Irish heritage. The Madman is galvanized by outrage and the necessity for vengeance on a massive scale upon those who caused the death of

his loved ones, but cunning enough to conceal his intent and make careful, painstaking plans to bring this about.

After a camouflaging period of pretended readjustment to life back in the United States, O'Neill converts all of his fairly substantial property and assets to cash, resigns from his university and with nearly half a million dollars--"energy" to accomplish his aims--drops from sight. He radically alters his appearance, makes underworld contacts to obtain false identification and finally rents a house across the country in Seattle. There O'Neill unobtrusively assembles a basement laboratory equipped with computer, collimator, centrifuge, bacterial culture media, negative-pressure rooms and all else necessary for genetics research. Posing as a doctor, he obtains DNA samples at local schools, and for nearly a year of intense secret labor devotes his total mental and physical energies to a monumental solo task--building a new, tailored disease from recombinant DNA.

O'Neill devises elegantly simple means to distribute his finished virus strain throughout his selected targets: England, Ireland and Libya--those nations he deems responsible for the Irish situation and for the training of terrorists. Simultaneous with the first reports of Plague outbreaks the governments of all nations receive communications signed "The Madman" in which O'Neill presents his ultimatum: The afflicted countries must be quarantined and the disease allowed to run its course. All citizens abroad from those nations must be returned to their homelands, to share in their fate. Any attempt to sterilize the three infected zones by nuclear means will result in the Madman's release of the new disease on a worldwide scale.

The White Plague, named for one of its early symptoms, is a virus attacking only women, to whom it is completely fatal. Thus the nations which tolerated the conditions that injured O'Neill will be robbed of their women, as the Madman was of his family.

The world's skeptical governments move slowly in acting on the Madman's revelations, but a multinational panel of experts is assembled. Americans William Beckett and Ariane Foss, French scientists Francois Danzas and Jost Hupp and Russians Sergei Lepikov and Dorena Godelinsky. Despite political and personal differences, this team is able to deduce many of O'Neill's means and methods before their own facilities are contaminated by the rapidly spreading Plague. Beckett and Hupp, along with Beckett's superior William Ruckerman, choose to be evacuated to England where they may continue to work toward means to combat the Plague.

Within Ireland, once the Plague's nature is grasped, there are frantic attempts to save women by isolating them in mines or fortifications. The most successful is the protection of a young couple from Cork University College--medical student Stephen Browder and his fiance student nurse Kathleen O'Gara--by sealing them into a pressurized tank used to study the physiology of divers. The unpleasantness of confinement in the tank eventually becomes a sense of power in her own potentials for Kate. Stephen's friend, who becomes their keeper invested with a new authority, is researcher Adrian Peard. Also prominent in Irish efforts to combat the Plague is Fintan Craig Doheny, a College Hospital Irish geneticist and political figure.

Per the Madman's instructions Irish, English and Libyan refugees are sent back to their homelands in "coffin ships", if not murdered by hysterical mobs. Inevitably more Plague pockets and outbreaks appear across the world; everywhere except in England, Ireland and Libya atomic "panic fire" is more and more frequently resorted to in a desperate bid to combat the scourge's spread. The disorganization wrought by the plague is opportunity for yet more factions, fanatics and terrorists to become active: governments are destabilized; waves of assassinations unleashed; the Vatican destroyed; and rival nations launch strikes at outbreaks (or suspected ones) of Plague within their enemies' borders.

New entities and power structures rise in the Plague's wake. Barrier Command is a multinational naval/air force under a French/Canadian admiral, charged with enforcing the quarantine of O'Neill's three target nations. Within the quarantined Ireland, the government and military hold the interior but the coasts are the domain of the Finn Sadal, the "Beach Boys", mostly remnants of the IRA/Provo militia headed by the violent and cunningly insane Kevin O'Donnell.

O'Neill, in Europe in the first weeks following his release of the plague, is confused about what to do once his juggernaut is in motion. He decides that he must witness firsthand the results of his vengeance in Ireland and crosses from France in a small boat. On coming ashore he narrowly escapes execution at the hands of a predatory Beach Boy patrol headed by Kevin O'Donnell. O'Neill has taken as his newest alias the name John O'Donnell, which may have sufficed to turn Kevin's whim in allowing him to live.

Once in Ireland both O'Neill's grief-shattered original personality and the driving, revenge-obsessed Madman subside, leaving an almost neutral observer, John, who thinks of the quiescent but watchful Madman as "O'Neill-within". John has announced himself as a geneticist come to aid Irish research on the Plague; the vague intention of "O'Neill-within" is to locate and sabotage Irish efforts to combat his nemesis.

Inland, John joins with three other wanderers. These are hearty but moody Joseph Herity, priest Michael Flannery, and a young orphaned boy. The trio is an evocative display of the new Ireland's woes. The nameless, traumatized boy will not break silence; Father Michael, whose once arrogantly held beliefs have been shattered, bears a branded forehead, a symptom of Irish reaction to the Church in Ireland's troubles; and Herity is the Provo specialist who placed and detonated the bomb that slaughtered O'Neill's family--a fact known to Herity's superior Kevin O'Donnell, though to few others.

Irish authorities suspect that John/O'Neill may be the Madman. Herity and company have been assigned to accompany and observe him, applying their best psychological, religious and emotive challenges and persuasions during the trek by "safe" roundabout ways to the genetics labs at Killaloe. The circuitous route of Herity's choosing crosses the paths of isolated men whose will has broken, dangerous survivors more of Herity's ilk, the Antrim Scotch-Catholic troop units assigned to guard the armed estates of a wealthy man who managed to sequester a group of young women from contamination and has proclaimed the revival of Druidical religion under the aegis of the rowan tree, and for other long stretches leaves the band alone in their own company.

In the outside world, a new US president must deal with an American Pope, ambitious conservative factions who would like a final confrontation with the weakened Soviets, and the devious bluff-and-demand diplomacy with quarantined Britain and Ireland. Confirmation of the Madman's presence in Ireland might lead to cooperative research, or simply to a nuclear bombardment to eliminate his threat with finality.

While John's every word and gesture is weighed and interpreted by Herity and Father Michael, they are far from united in purpose themselves; Herity's moods shift from jovial to murderous and he chafes at the company of the priest whose shattered religion he has lost faith in. The pair's assessment of John is clandestine but their own clashes are open, ranging from logical arguments to outraged confrontations.

This situation mirrors their surroundings as the journey tours John through post-Plague Ireland, demonstrating to him once again the deep interaction of the Irish people, the land and its history. In the present tragedy the patterns of the past have returned in new grief and savagery; the four travel a wracked, wildly desolate landscape newly returned to "faerie" but hasten to a confrontation with very current politics.

a.   _____, Putnam, New York ($14.95), 1982.*
     Bound in a three-piece case with dark blue cloth on the spine and with blue front and rear paper boards. Gold lettering on the spine. No indication of printing or edition on the copyright page. No date on the title page.

b.   _____, Putnam, New York ($50.00), 1982.*
     Special boxed and signed edition of 500 copies. Bound in dark blue cloth with gold lettering on the spine. The slipcase is in the same dark blue cloth. No indication of printing or edition on the copyright page. No date on the title page. The limitation sheet is the first sheet after the front free endpaper and states: "Of this first edition of // THE WHITE PLAGUE // five hundred copies, // specially bound, // have been signed by the author // and numbered // Number _____".

c.   _____, Gollancz, London (£7.95), 1983.

d.   _____, Science Fiction Book Club, Garden City, 1983.*
     Bound in a three-piece case with blue paper on the spine and with blue front and rear paper boards. Gold lettering on the spine. No indication of printing or of edition on the copyright page. No date on the title page. Code 5789 on the dust jacket. Date code N36 at the lower left margin of page 465.

e.   _____, BCA Bookclub (British), 1983.

f.   _____, Berkley: 06555 ($3.95), 1983, paper.*
     "Berkley edition / December 1983" on the copyright page.

g.   _____, Berkley: 09050 ($3.95), 1986, paper.*

h.   _____, NEL: 05598 (£3.50), 1986, paper.

32. WITHOUT ME YOU'RE NOTHING
     (with Max Barnard)
     Non-Fiction.
     Subtitled "The Essential Guide to Home Computers".
     This book is in large part a guide to the choice, purchase and use of one's own home computer but also includes substantial sections discussing what's happening and about to happen in computer science, what computers mean in terms of our daily lives and the urgency of everyone developing computer skills. There is an emphasis on demystifying computer jargon and making it clear that computers are tools, usable and understandable by anyone. The authors chose to incorporate a philosophical outlook into their overview of computers--including among other influences the philosophical implications of Einstein and Heisenberg which the technological mainstream has resisted--but the book is written in a simple and straightforward style.
     Chapters examine the wide application of computers in entertainment, business, art, medicine, aids for the handicapped, home "life-support" and alarm systems that can be controlled from a distance via phone communications, and in writing, with examples from Herbert's and other writers' work. Also covered are the history of computer science and computer "evolution"; the basic structure and function, both physical and logical, of computers; binary arithmetic; computer languages including Basic; and PROGRAMAP, a system of graphics and a simplified flowchart setup utilizing them to lay out programs, originated

by Herbert and Barnard. Appendices include additional PROGRAMAP material and sample car-maintenance and house-mortgage programs in that format.

Several chapters serve as a general guide to shopping for a computer and accessories suited to one's needs, and setting up one's computer once purchased; there is also a guide to one's first "solo" with the new machine.

The authors discuss the serious errors in viewpoint inherent in using anthropomorphic terms ("memory", etc.) to describe computer functions. They also discuss the way merchandising efforts of many computer manufacturers, experts and salespeople cause confusion about computers' capabilities and functions as well as their nature as machines. Substantial appendices address these issues as well as the future of computer/biological hybrids; differences between computer and brain functions; and computer publications and accessories.

Max Barnard is a computer professional who has handled both machine design and repair and computer programming; he was the designer of Herbert's own home computer system.

An excerpt from this books' first chapter appeared as a guest editorial in OMNI.

a.   _____, Simon & Schuster, New York ($14.95), 1981.*
Bound in a three-piece case with black paper front and rear boards and with black cloth on the spine. Gold lettering on the spine. No date on the title page. "10 9 8 7 6 5 4 3 2 1" on the copyright page.

b.   _____, Pocket Books: 43964 ($5.95), 1981, paper.*
Trade paperback in size. "First Pocket Books printing November, 1981 // 10 9 8 7 6 5 4 3 2" on the copyright page.

33. **THE WORLDS OF FRANK HERBERT**
Contents: The Tactful Saboteur; Committee Of The Whole; Mating Call; Escape Felicity; The GM Effect; The Featherbedders; Old Rambling House; A-W-F Unlimited.

a.   _____, NEL: 2814 (30p, 6/-), 1970, paper.*
† b.   _____, Ace: 90925 ($0.75), 1971, paper.*
Adds "By The Book". No indication of printing or edition on the copyright page. Cover by Dean Ellis.

c.   (   ) [German], Ullstein, 1971(?), paper.
d.   _____, NEL: 00555 (30p), 1972, paper.
e.   _____, Ace: 90926 ($0.95), 1972, paper.*
Adds "By The Book".

f.   _____, NEL: 00640 (30p), 1973, paper.
Reprinted October 1974.

g.   _____, NEL: 02707 (40p), 1975, paper.
† h.   _____, Berkley: 03502 ($1.75), 1977, paper.*
Adds "By The Book". "Berkley Medallion Edition, SEPTEMBER, 1977" on the copyright page. Reprinted.

i.   _____, Gregg Press, Boston ($13.50), 1980.*
Introduction by William M Schuyler Jr. Issued without a dust jacket. Bound in yellowish-brown cloth with red lettering on the spine. Blue printing of Herbert's signature on the front cover. "1980" on the title page. "First Printing, August, 1980" on the copyright page.

j.   _____, Berkley: 05297 ($2.25), 1981, paper.

21ST CENTURY SUB
See THE DRAGON IN THE SEA.

Edited Books

1. **NEBULA WINNERS FIFTEEN**
   Edited by Frank Herbert.
   Contents: "Introduction", Frank Herbert; "Camps", Jack M Dann; "Sandkings", George R R Martin; "The Staining Your Eyes Through The Viewscreen Blues", Vonda N McIntyre; "Enemy Mine", Barry B Longyear; "giANTS", Edward Bryant; "The Extraordinary Voyages Of Amelie Bertrand", Joanna Russ; "Unaccompanied Sonata", Orson Scott Card; "Appendix A: Nebula Awards 1979"; "Appendix B: Fifteen Years Of Nebula Winners".
   a. ____, Harper & Row, New York ($12.95), 1981.*
      Bound in a three-piece case with black paper front and rear boards and with mustard-colored cloth on the spine. Black lettering on the spine. No date on the title page. "FIRST EDITION" on the copyright page.
      "81 82 83 84 10 9 8 7 6 5 4 3 2 1" also on the copyright page.
   b. ____, W H Allen, London (£8.50), 1982.*
      "First British edition, 1981" on copyright page.
   c. ____, Star: 31227 (£1.75), 1983, paper.
   d. ____, Bantam: 23035 ($2.95), 1983, paper.*
      "Bantam edition / March 1983" on the copyright page.

2. **NEW WORLD OR NO WORLD**
   Non-Fiction.
   Edited and with commentary by Frank Herbert.
   Foreword by Senator Edmund S Muskie.
   Preface by Secretary of the Interior Walter J Hickel.
   This book consists of transcripts of the discussions about the ecology crisis and environmental awareness (or the lack of it) featured on the *Today Show* hosted by Hugh Downs during Earth Week, April 20-24, 1970. The five days' talks are divided into 20 chapters, with a two-page introduction and roughly 20 pages of brief interstitial commentary by Herbert, placing the Earth Week discussions in terms of current events and accenting the observations, cautions and admonitions of the discussants. Herbert's pieces are framed as a personal and specific address to the reader; we are invited to consider the demands on us and developments within our society that must accompany environmental awareness and repair of the damages. The book also has a foreword by Senator Edmund Muskie and a preface by Secretary of the Interior Walter J Hickel, both of whom also appeared on the *Today Show*. (Herbert himself did not appear on the program.)
   The transcripts include the in-studio talks with guests, a final question-and-answer session on Friday of Earth Week in which a panel of college students put queries to a Wall Street stockbroker and the Board Chairman of Consolidated Edison, and interviews and commentary televised from various locations. In addition to Muskie and Hickel, the week's 27 in-studio guests included Margaret Mead, Paul Ehrlich, Rene Dubos, Morris Udall, Ralph Nader, Barry Commoner, Roy Greenaway and Roger Caras. Topics of the talks covered the whole spectrum of environment, pollution, conservation and ecological awareness.
   a. ____, Ace: 57250 ($0.95), 1970, paper.*
      No indication of edition or printing on the copyright page.

3. **TOMORROW, AND TOMORROW, AND TOMORROW**
   Edited by Bonnie L Heintz, Frank Herbert, Donald A Joos and Jane McGee.
   Contents: "Preface", Bonnie L Heintz, Frank Herbert, Donald A Joos, and Jane Agorn McGee; "Science Fiction And You", Frank

Herbert; "The Star" H G Wells; "The Subliminal Man", J C Ballard; "The Waveries", Frederic Brown; "Nightfall:, Isaac Asimov; "The Nothing", Frank Herbert; "Bitter End", Eric Frank Russell; "The Winner", Donald E Westlake; "The Lawgiver", Keith Laumer; "Utopian", Mack Reynolds; "Rescue Party", Arthur C Clarke; "For The Sake of Grace", Suzette Haden Elgin; "The Other Foot", Ray Bradbury; "Crate", Theodore Sturgeon; "The Cloudbuilders", Colin Kapp; "The Shortest Science Fiction Story Ever Told", Forrest J Ackerman; "Street Of Dreams, Feet of Clay", Robert Scheckley; "The Veldt", Ray Bradbury; "After The Myths Went Home", Robert Silverberg; "Arena", Frederic Brown; "'Repent, Harequin!' Said The Ticktockman", Harlan Ellison; "The Hole On The Corner", R A Lafferty; "Texas Week", Albert Hernhunter; "Hemeas", E G Von Wald; "This Grand Carcass", R A Lafferty; "The Perfect Woman", Robert Sheckley; "Desertion", Clifford D Simak; "Here There Be Tygers", Ray Bradbury; "Crucifixus Etian", Walter M Miller Jr; "Sunrise On Mercury", Robert Silverberg; "Omnilingual", H Beam Piper; "The Sentinel", Arthur C Clarke; "Seeds Of The Dusk", Raymond Z Gallun; "Specialist", Robert Sheckley; "Half-Breed", Isaac Asimov; "Bomb Scare", Vernor Vinge; "Keyhole", Murry Leinster; "Sundance", Robert Silverberg; "Goldfish Bowl", Robert Heinlein; "Sword Game", H H Hollis; "The Singing Bell", Isaac Asimov; "Private Eye", Lewis Padgett.

a. ＿＿＿, Holt Rinehart Winston ($5.50), 1974, paper.
According to L W Currey the copyright page has the code "4 5 6 7 059 9 8 7 6 5 4 3 2 1".

Non-Book Appearances

1. **"A-W-F Unlimited"** (11,200 words)
   The advertising firm of Singlemaster, Hucksting and Battlemont has been picked by the military to diagnose and correct a problem: enlistments in the Women Of Space, or WOMS, have fallen off to a trickle. The advertising firm is to create a campaign that will reverse the trend; as an incentive to do this up right, the military's Psych Branch has suggested that the entire male membership of the company be drafted in the event of failure.

   A major complication for the advertising people is that Gwen Everest, its tall, graceful, auburn-haired prime problem solver, has but that morning--unbeknownst to her coworkers--suffered a midlife crisis, finding her "48, unmarried, and a prime mover in an industry that's strangling the universe". Her disillusionment with the blitz-world of adecals, layouts, slogans, projos, quartersheets, skinnies, and obtrusive flying adrobots plus her personal worries precipitates eccentric and abandoned behavior at the most unfortunate time: during the company's meetings with the representatives of the military. These are General Sonnet Finnister of the WOMS, a bony, stiff-backed spinster who has designed the WOMS uniform to complement her own unique and unattractive physical features, and General Nathan "Howling" Owling of the Space Engineers, a firm-jawed Aryan.

   Caught in the middle of the friction and fireworks is the firm's underdog, André Battlemont, an inconspicuous, round-faced, pudgy little executive with a bald spot. He has been persuaded by his own firm's ad campaign to join the religion-of-the-month club, and has worshiped Gwen in secret for years. André's chance to shed his meek-and-mild habit, prove his love for Gwen and avoid the draft comes when Gwen, after designing a uniform for WOMS that incorporates fashion, sex and pizzazz, collapses before pushing the solution all the way through--with the military outraged to a new peak of indignation.
   † a. The Galaxy, June 1961.*
   b. (as "A.W.F. Illimitato") [Italian], Galaxy No 55, December 1962.
   c. 17 X INFINITY, Ed by Groff Conklin, Dell: 7746, 1963, paper.*
   d. THE WORLDS OF FRANK HERBERT, NEL: 2814, 1970, paper.*
   e. (as "B.E.U.A.R.K.") [French], Galaxie (New Series), March 1973, No 106.

2. **"Accidental Feросslk"** (3,500 words)
   To be published in LAST DANGEROUS VISIONS, Ed by Harlan Ellison.

3. **"Adventures in Movement"**
   Non-Fiction.
   Robert Howard and his moving sculptures.
   a. California Living, San Francisco Sunday Examiner And Chronicle, 11 August 1968.*

4. **"The Battles Of Dune"**
   Sound Recording.
   Herbert talks about the recurrence of warfare and battles in man's repeating historical cycles, their misery, pain, waste and utter lack of glory. Larger-than-life heroes and superheroes and the leadership roles they assume in society and in war are diagnosed as painful in the same degree as the unlearned lessons of war to the affected society; characteristics (on the species level) valuable in some ages are pointed out to be deadly in others. Herbert dwells briefly on Gurney Halleck, the "loyal and cynical" character who is the prototypical warrior in Dune's battles.

The readings on this recording consist of excerpts from DUNE, DUNE MESSIAH and CHILDREN OF DUNE, united by additional, connective text written especially for the record.

† a.   Caedmon: 1601, New York, 1979.*
Record (TC-1601) or cassette (CDL-51601). Read by Frank Herbert. Liner notes by Frank Herbert. Duration 62 minutes, 20 seconds.

5.   "Beef In Oyster Sauce"
Non-Fiction.
Recipe.
a.   COOKING OUT OF THIS WORLD, Ed by Anne McCaffrey, Ballantine: 23413 ($1.50), 1973, paper.*

"The Being Machine"
See "The Mind Bomb".

6.   "Bullit"
Non-Fiction.
Realism in the movie *Bullit*.
a.   California Living, San Francisco Sunday Examiner, 2 June 1968.*

7.   "By The Book" (10,000 words)
Working titles "Tightrope", "Whipleash".
Seedling containers stocked with human and animal embryos gestating inside hibernating rabbits, plus mechanical "nursemaids" and education systems, have been launched toward habitable worlds. The oldest have been hundreds of years in their journey and are just now within range of their goal. These sleeper containers have been monitored from Earth by an angle-space transmission beam that allows instantaneous contact across vast distances. Although the beam system has been in use for a considerable length of time, it is still not thoroughly understood. Beam contact has deteriorated rapidly as the containers approach the point where control from Earth is the most vital.
The Haigh Company, operators of the beam transmissions, call their best troubleshooter--Ivar Norris Gump ("Ing")--out of semi-retirement. Ing returns mainly at the request of his friend and former supervisor Possible Washington. Ing's hobby is old rule-and-regulation books; he often quotes from his collection for amusement, to combat the authorities with their own words or to aid in his thinking processes.
Ing begins with the problem of what is clouding contact and making the transmissions balky at the beam's source. The beam tube is a subterranean tunnel on the moon, below the Mare Nectaris, two kilometers in diameter and 12 kilometers long. Energy-charged mobile cleaners patrol the beam tube to maintain the absolutely perfect vacuum needed for transmission. They are attuned so that if the beam's controlled whiplash brushes across them during operation, the cleaners are simply absorbed into it and their energy augments its function. After witnessing a transmission during which the beam produces spectacular auroral effects, lashes chunks from the sides of the tube and absorbs numerous cleaners, Ing ventures into the beam tube in a multiple-shelled protective craft mimicking the cleaners. He is determined to trouble-shoot the beam close at hand, despite his knowledge that the authorities have manipulated him into this extremely dangerous position. Concern for the seedling containers is *his*, as well as the government's, main motivation.
a.   Analog, August 1966.*
b.   THE WORLDS OF FRANK HERBERT, Ace: 90925, 1971, paper.*

Only in this and subsequent American editions.

    c.   THE BEST OF FRANK HERBERT, Ed by Angus Wells, Sidgwick & Jackson, London, 1975.*

    d.   EYE, Berkley: 08398, 1985, paper.*

8.   "The Campbell Correspondence"
Non-Fiction.
An exchange of letters between John W Campbell Jr and Frank Herbert about DUNE MESSIAH.

    a.   THE MAKER OF DUNE: FRANK HERBERT, Ed by Timothy O'Reilly, Berkley: 09784, 1987, paper.*

9.   "Carthage: Reflections Of A Martian"
Verse.
This long (18-page) poem juxtaposes the aliennesses of Mars and of the vanished, civilization-now-desert of the Carthage city-state. A being with vast stores of memories looks out through the eyes of a modern suburbanite at breakfast and simultaneously back through the melancholy, kaleidoscopic montage of the archaeological past: the sad beauty of ancient Mars, the dusty, earthy Carthaginian heyday and the turmoil of the machinations of Carthage's enemies, in Rome and personified in the bombastic Cato. The vanished desert-power and eerie, poignant reverberations through history of both civilizations are evoked, along with the sensitivity needed for future historians and archaeologists to capture or conceive of the important ephemera of mood of a vanished age.

    This poem is linked to Herbert's novel THE HEAVEN MAKERS; it was the original evocation of mood, image and atmosphere upon which Herbert drew and elaborated while writing the novel.

    a.   MARS, WE LOVE YOU, Ed by Jane Hipolito and Willis E McNelly, Doubleday, Garden City, 1971.

10.   "Cease Fire" (8,000 words)
Corporal Larry Hulser reluctantly mans a lonely, camouflaged observation post in the frozen marshlands of the Arctic battlefield of Canada's Barren Grounds. In this forward position, the war is fought with sophisticated detection and counter-detection equipment plus long-range artillery directed by the observation posts; Hulser's duty is to monitor movements, trying to distinguish between signals from animals, ruined war vehicles and enemy activity. Enemy scouts and snipers are searching for Hulser's o.p. Hulser is an individual ill-suited for his situation; older than the usual run of soldier, sensitive and subjected to great strain by the conditions of his service and the overbearing, demanding nature of his professional-soldier superior officers.

    Hulser was shifted to frontline combat from scientific work. During a moment of reflection on the ever-escalating struggle for equipment superiority, spurred by the pressure and anxiety of his environment, Hulser draws upon his background in chemistry and other fields and synthesizes this knowledge in a moment of hyperconsciousness. In an intuitive flash he visualizes a device capable of detonating any explosives or combustible fuels from a distance.

    This highly charged knowledge fills Hulser with trepidation about his position; he deems this new concept too valuable to risk a moment longer in the combat zone, and disgraces himself in the eyes of his immediate superiors by hysterically demanding to be removed from his post. Back at a main base after his near-breakdown, Hulser finds Sergeant Chamberlain and Major Lipari first dismissive of his claims, then outraged, believing that he is faking everything in a cowardly bid to be relieved of his distasteful duty. Desperately, Hulser carries insubordination and misbehavior to the point where his case *must* come to the attention of higher-up officers.

Finally Hulser's invention is brought to the attention of Colonel Page and General Savage. He is believed, and after lengthy interrogation a prototype model of his field projector is built and tested. It successfully ignites everything from high explosive and petroleum fuel to book matches in an observer's pocket. Hulser is elated at the success of his "weapon to end all wars"; but General Savage angrily disillusions him with harsh insights about mankind's ingenuity in the field of waging warfare.

    a.   Astounding, January 1958.*
    b.   A CENTURY OF SCIENCE FICTION, Ed by Damon Knight, Simon & Schuster, New York, 1962.*
    c.   THE BEST OF FRANK HERBERT, Ed by Angus Wells, Sidgwick & Jackson, London, 1975.*
    d.   EYE, Berkley: 08398, 1985, paper.*

11.   "Children Of Dune"
Published as CHILDREN OF DUNE.
    a.   Analog, sr4, January 1976*, February 1976*, March 1976*, April 1976*.
    b.   THE GREAT DUNE TRILOGY, Gollancz, London, 1979.*

12.   "Chinatown: A Changing World"
Non-Fiction.
    a.   San Francisco Examiner, 6 February 1963.*

13.   "Come To The Party"
(with F M Busby)
Terran contact with the world Delfa and incompletely informed manipulation of the situation there have produced some peculiar circumstances. Delfa has two intelligent races: the Hoojies and the Alexii. Two successive Terran expeditions have favored the Hoojies and suppressed the Alexii; by Terran standards the Hoojies appear the more intelligent, or at least the more cooperative and amenable to accepting a sort of Terran overlordship.

The Hoojies (or "the Delfans" in Terran parlance) are a moderate-sized, multi-limbed race dwelling in hut-villages with a somewhat minimal material culture. Though amiable and imitative, they are possessed of somewhat short attention spans; their culture rituals are highly developed and Hoojies are obsessed with sex and excretion rituals and rigidly bound by moral strictures, including some imported from Earth. The Alexii, in contrast, are fearsome 600-kilo omnivores equipped with deadly limbs and noxious venoms in great variety; quick, long-lived and marginally vulnerable to most Terran weapons. The Alexii are a devil-may-care, helter-skelter sort of race, so fearsomely built (through generations-past manipulation of their own genetics) that life is superbly simple for them without tools or artifacts of any kind. Since a state of kill-or-be-killed has existed between Alexii and Terrans from the first offhand Alexii experiments with Terran edibility, the Earthmen have learned very little about Alexii history and culture.

The story unfolds from several viewpoints, including the following:

Hugh Scott, a member of the second Terran expedition, filing an aggravated and apprehensive report on the situation and the patchwork equilibrium established by his companions and himself; a Hoojie ceremonial official known as "Today's Speaker" (who has taken an "amusing" Terran name); Alex, a young, alert and adaptable member of the Alexii species; and Dr Watson, a guard robot left by the Terrans upon their departure from Delfa (so christened by the Hoojies).

There are four Hoojie sexes--male, female, ultra and squish--and a "tripling", or union of any combination of three, will yield an offspring of whichever gender was absent. Each Hoojie hut is occupied by a mated quartet; excess population (and the Hoojies suffer from periodic severe imbalances of one sex or another) makes do as best it can on the outside, putting pressure on food resources and the Hoojie social structure. Nearly too late, the Terrans discovered that the only natural control on Hoojie population was Alexii predation. The Alexii had been nearly exterminated by the first-expedition Terrans, partly at Hoojie urging; the second expedition attempted to salvage a semblance of the ecological balance by confining the surviving 216 Alexii inside a stockade baited and well-provided with boozevines. The vines and a chemical utilized in the Alexii containment combine to produce considerable memory lapses in the creatures. The captive Alexii pass the time in a continuous drunken "Party"; under carefully controlled circumstances the Hoojies, using equipment left by the Terrans and with the aid and guidance of Dr Watson, can periodically release a single Alexii who will eat their surplus population before rushing back to rejoin the Party.

Alex is the releasee in the latest effort to curb an overabundance of squishes in Hugh Scott's village. This instance is unique, however, because this particular day is Alex's birthday and the Party this day was in his honor; thus he is especially cognizant of being removed from the Party and unusually attentive to all details of the situation. In addition, the three Hoojies effecting the release suffered an equipment failure and Alex has eaten them; he is also motivated by a desire to try the fourth "flavor" of Hoojie again soon. Hugh Scott, Today's Speaker, is battling grief at the demise of his three hutmates as well as the distraction of recruiting new hutmates and experimenting with conjugations with them, and is inadequate to the handling of this emergency. Dr Watson is of little help; he appears to have been too hastily or insufficiently programmed and is undergoing an identity crisis of sorts, rendering him befuddled and ineffective.

Once Alex shakes off the Party-induced inebriation and forgetfulness, he quickly grasps the ramifications of the new situation. He releases the rest of his companions (reluctant though they are) from the Party, digs into racial memories for unsuspected and long-unused technical capabilities, and begins asking himself questions about the origins of the stockade, about Terrans, and about whether or not some of the remembered but disused old ways of the Alexii should be revived. Dr. Watson is apprehended and modified to serve as one feature of a trap set for a returning Terran ship; the Alexii look forward to the expansion of the Party to an interstellar scale.

† a.   Analog, December 1978.*
  b.   THE 1979 ANNUAL WORLD'S BEST SF, Ed by Donald A Wollheim, DAW: 337 ($2.25), 1979, paper.

14.   "Committee Of The Whole" (6,300 words)
      Manuscript title "Public Hearing".
      William R Custer, an Oregon cattle baron, appears before a US Senate Committee supposedly to testify and be questioned upon proposed amendments to a grazing act, in televised hearings. Alan Wallace, the cattleman's Washington lawyer, is perplexed by Custer's seeming indifference to the political nature of the hearings and the difficult personalities involved, but is gamely ready to try to roll with the flow of behind-the-doors deals, party politicking and in particular the

manipulations of Senator Haycourt Tiborough, chairman of the Subcommittee.

Custer proves clever and devious enough to weather the attempts of Tiborough to twist the hearings to his own ends but, to Wallace's concern and incomprehension, Custer introduces extensive descriptive testimony regarding a device of his invention: an extremely simple and compact homemade laser which is in use on his ranch as a commonplace tool (though it could also, obviously, serve as a weapon). Custer has used the televised hearings purely to disseminate the how-to information regarding this invention; by this means he hopes to avoid its suppression by the government and the concentration of even more power in the hands of a minority of people. Custer idealistically regards his device as an equalizer which will, after a regrettable but necessary period of disorder and readjustment, teach human beings self-restraint, cooperation and consideration of each others' dignity.

Herbert's realistic, if cynical, portrayal of the Senate Committee in action derives from his experiences and background as a reporter, speechwriter and participant in Washington state politics.

† a.   Galaxy, April, 1965.*
  b.   (as "Io Laser, Tu Laser ...") [Italian], Urania No 400, September 1965.
  c.   SCIENCE FICTION INVENTIONS, Ed by Damon Knight, Lancer: 73-691, 1967, paper.
  d.   THE WORLDS OF FRANK HERBERT, NEL: 2814, 1970, paper.*
  e.   THE BEST OF FRANK HERBERT, Ed by Angus Wells, Sidgwick & Jackson, London, 1975.*
  f.   INTERNATIONAL RELATIONS THROUGH SCIENCE FICTION, Ed by Martin H Greenberg and Joseph D Olander, Franklin Watts, New York, 1978, paper.
  g.   TV: 2000, Ed by Isaac Asimov, Charles G Waugh, and Martin H Greenberg, Fawcett: 24493 ($2.95), 1982, paper.*

15.   "The Concept Seminar"
(with Thomas M Disch, Robert Silverberg, Theodore Sturgeon, and Harlan Ellison)
Non-Fiction.
See "Songs Of A Sentient Flute" for annotation.
  a.   MEDEA: HARLAN'S WORLD, Ed by Harlan Ellison, Phantasia Press, Huntington Woods (Michigan), 1985.*

16.   "The ConSentiency--And How It Got That Way"
Non-Fiction.
Comments on "The Dosadi Experiment".
This article serves as an introduction to the first episode of the magazine serialization of THE DOSADI EXPERIMENT.

Herbert first deals with the oft-asked question of "Where do you get your ideas?", revealing "sources" of his own and of other writers, then more seriously discusses development of story ideas. The germ ideas and the paths of development of his Jorj X McKie stories are examined, including the character base for McKie and the origins of the Bureau of Sabotage in Herbert's examining and questioning of some of his most dearly held assumptions. A detailed description of how BuSab works, and why, is included. The various races of the Consentiency and their pertinent characteristics and institutions are described, with emphasis on the Gowachin and their legal system, setting the stage for the ideas to be explored and the characters who will be returning in the new novel.
  a.   Galaxy, May 1977.*

17. "Conversations In Port Townsend"
    Non-Fiction.
    Based on two days of conversations with Timothy O'Reilly in 1983.
    a. THE MAKER OF DUNE: FRANK HERBERT, Ed by Timothy
       O'Reilly, Berkley: 09784, 1987, paper.*

18. "Country Boy"
    Non-Fiction.
    Excerpts from an unpublished interview conducted by Timothy O'Reilly
    in 1977.
    a. THE MAKER OF DUNE: FRANK HERBERT, Ed by Timothy
       O'Reilly, Berkley: 09784, 1987, paper.*

19. "Dangers Of The Superhero"
    Non-Fiction.
    This is a combination of two previously published pieces: the liner
    notes from "Dune: The Banquet Scene" and "Dune Genesis".
    a. THE MAKER OF DUNE: FRANK HERBERT, Ed by Timothy
       O'Reilly, Berkley: 09784, 1987, paper.*

20. "Death Of A City"
    In a semi-utopian future, Bjska holds the position of City Doctor. In
    that capacity, as a representative of the human species rather than of
    any single group or political faction, he wields awesome powers; on his
    order a city may be destroyed, its inhabitants dispersed, its buildings
    dismantled, the natural landscape restored, even the city's name erased
    from all records save Bjska's own.
        A supremely beautiful city is facing this fate. Despite its breath-
    taking loveliness, it is a "sick" city, its illness diagnosed by the
    symptoms of outbreaks of violence, creative lethargy, an outflux of its
    best people and violence and vandalism on the part of its expatriates in
    other cities.
        Bjska's intern-assistant in this difficult task is Mieri; the city is
    her home and birthplace. She is immoderately beautiful in her own
    right, and one of the few who ever returned to the city after leaving
    it. Bjska fears that because of her attachments to the place she is not
    facing up to the demands of her internship; he must make clear to her
    the painful fact of the devitalizing possibilities of too much beauty, too
    perfect a surface and the realities of human needs. The city's timeless
    perfection does not allow for the necessity of change and flux and
    eliminates a needed generative tension from the human experience. The
    adjustment between Bjska and Mieri mirrors in miniature the adjustment
    required between the human species and the too-exquisite fulfillment of
    man's expectations embodied in the city.
    a. FUTURE CITY, Ed by Roger Elwood, Trident, New York, 1973.*
    b. EYE, Berkley: 08398, 1985, paper.*

21. "Do I Wake Or Dream?" (45,000 words)
    Published as DESTINATION: VOID.
    The Voidship Earthling sets out from Moonbase with a twofold mission.
    Its ostensible purpose is to establish a colony in the Tau Ceti system;
    toward this end its holds are stocked with 3,000 colonists plus plant
    and animal specimens in "hybernation" (a state of ultra-hibernation).
    Until the ship is outside the Solar System it will be manned by an
    umbilicus crew of six; then they will join their companions in hyber-
    nation and the vessel will be guided to its destination by the Organic

Mental Core, a specially trained human brain which runs the ship's massive, sophisticated computer system.

In fact, the voidship's primary and secret purpose is the development of a super-conscious *controllable* artificial intelligence. Prior experiments in this field have backfired badly on Earth; one supercomputer constructed on an island in Puget Sound awoke to consciousness, killed all in the vicinity, and vanished in the destruction of much of the island. Now, for safety's sake, the program is being carried on as far as possible from Earth. The crew, both awake and in hybernation, are expendable clones; the umbilicus crew are a group loaded with subconscious compulsions designed to goad themselves and each other when the ship is disabled by a series of programmed malfunctions and disasters. This is the seventh attempt; six previous voidships and clone crews have failed and been obliterated by built-in safeguards.

Before the ship has traveled a quarter of the way across the Solar System, the OMC and its two backups have gone insane and had to be disconnected. Three of the umbilicus crew have been killed by the malfunctioning brains; those that remain are Bernard Bickel, an aggressive, driving, computer expert; Raja Flattery, the haughty and intellectual chaplain-psychiatrist; and Gerrill Timberlake, the compassionate, intuitive life-systems engineer. They awaken one backup crew member from hybernation: medicine, ecology and computer-math expert Prudence Weygand.

As this group battles mishaps and disasters--shifts of the artificial gravity, the ship's "roboxes" running amok, and emergencies in the computer systems--they also have to attempt to handle the massively complicated computations that the OMC and computers were to deal with in tandem. This will become impossible in the long run, and their only way out is to awaken the computer to consciousness: to do this, they must try to discover what consciousness is, or at least the attributes that will produce it when combined. They are given little help by Moonbase Control director Morgan Hempstead, still in communication with them, even when they discover that Tau Ceti has no habitable planets and their cover mission is a sham. As Bickel's attempts to bring the computer to a state that is capable of consciousness approach success, Flattery is driven by his conditioning to estimate whether or not the end product should be allowed to exist: he is the one in command of the ultimate destruct capacity of the vessel.

The story is primarily an exploration of the nature, attributes and limits of consciousness, through the efforts and interactions of the characters. "Do I Wake Or Dream?" was revised and expanded into DESTINATION: VOID; see the novel entry for a more detailed description.

† a.   Galaxy, August 1965.

"Doll Factory, Gun Factory"
    See "Introduction: Tomorrow's Alternatives?".

22.   "Don't Buy Death!!!"
    Non-Fiction.
    This is a transcript of an address given by Herbert to the North West Science Fiction Convention (date and place not mentioned). The title of the address itself was "Thinking About The Unthinkable".

    Herbert discusses his editing of the NBC Earth Week book, NEW WORLD OR NO WORLD, and quotes from his address to an audience in Philadelphia on Earth Day, April 22, 1970. Some of his reasons for writing DUNE, tying into environmental awareness, are given, and the dangers to Earth and human existence of gaps and blindnesses in our educational systems, overcrowding and overuse or unthought-out use of Earth's resources are pointed out. Herbert exhorts his listeners not to buy species death by purchasing products (or "buying" outlooks and attitudes) that are oriented only toward short-term profit and which degrade the environment and quality of living, such as the internal combustion engine. Boycott is mentioned as the peoples' most powerful weapon against the unresponsive controlling powers. The need for increased sophistication in human values is contrasted with the curious situation that humans do not seem to have the same clear perception of survival mechanisms for the human species that they do in regard to survival needs and priorities for the individual. Herbert recommends more recognition of and attention to the needs of individuals, and those individuals' attention to the facts of what's best for the race as a whole.

a.   The Stranger, No 9, June (?), 1970(?).*

23. "The Dosadi Experiment"
     Published as THE DOSADI EXPERIMENT.
   ††a.   Galaxy, sr4, May 1977*, June 1977*, July 1977*, August 1977*.

"The Dragon In The Sea"
     See "Under Pressure".

"Dune"
     See "Dune World".

24. "Dune: The Banquet Scene"
     Sound Recording.
     Herbert talks about his original concepts and intentions for the Dune books, his early research, contacts and writing, including the Florence, Oregon sand dune control projects, and the ways in which the concepts grew, meshed and acquired form and story-vehicles.
          The banquet scene is described as a watershed in the understanding of Paul Atreides. Various powers and alignments of Arrakis are displayed in their most seductive, mannerly guises in a scene with deep roots in myth, fable and tradition--"the dinner party where enemies sit down together". Behavior in this commonplace, eating-room setting affords insights into Paul and the Atreides as well as the array of their enemies.
   † a.   Caedmon: 1555, New York, 1977.*
            Record (TC-1555) or cassette (CP-1555). Read by Frank Herbert. Liner notes by Frank Herbert. Duration 53 minutes, 34 seconds.

25. "Dune Genesis"
     Non-Fiction.
     This feature is titled "Dune Genesis" in the table of contents, "Dune" in the body of the magazine, and on the magazine's cover is correctly billed as an excerpt from THE ILLUSTRATED DUNE.
          The eight-page feature presents John Schoenherr's color paintings from the illustrated book, along with a brief text by Frank Herbert consisting of explanatory and evocative captions.
     a.   Omni, July, 1980.*

26. "Dune Messiah"
     Published as DUNE MESSIAH.
     a.   Galaxy, sr5, July 1969*, August 1969*, September 1969*, October 1969*, November 1969*.
     b.   THE GREAT DUNE TRILOGY, Gollancz, London, 1979.*

27. "Dune World" (90,500 words)
     Published as first part of DUNE.

Imperial power politics require the Great House of Atreides, headed by
Duke Leto Atreides, to relinquish its generations-long fief of Caladan
and relocate to take up rulership of the harsh desert planet Arrakis,
better known as Dune. This bears the aspect of a reward from Emperor
Shaddam IV. Arrakis' departing overlords are House Harkonnen, the
Atreides' most bitter enemies in the inter-Great-House intrigues; and
Arrakis is the only source of the fantastically valuable spice melange,
among whose attributes are the prolonging of life and the enabling of
certain individuals to enter a state of prescience. Melange use is the
Spacing Guild's key to the navigation of their vessels between worlds.

Relocating along with Leto are his 15-year-old son Paul and Paul's
mother, the Lady Jessica, the duke's Bene Gesserit concubine, who has
instructed Paul in that order's disciplines of mind and body control.
Paul was born through Jessica's defiance of Bene Gesserit directives. To
further their centuries-long human breeding program, aimed at the
production of a superbeing they call the *Kwisatz Haderach*, Jessica was
instructed to conceive a daughter with Leto. Instead she bore Paul, the
son she knew the Duke hoped for.

Among the Atreides retainers who have contributed to Paul's
training and education are Thufir Hawat, a "human computer" Mentat
Assassin; the dashing Weapons Master Duncan Idaho; grizzled, battered
warrior and troubadour Warmaster Gurney Halleck; and the Suk doctor,
Wellington Yueh.

The relocation is in fact a ploy by the Emperor to eliminate Leto,
who he sees as a potential threat to his throne. Shaddam IV is in
secret cooperating with and using the Harkonnens--in his estimation the
second-most-dangerous House. While the Atreides were obliged to give
up Caladan, the Harkonnens have retired to their power base world, the
drab, grim Giedi Prime. The Harkonnen head is the cruel, gluttonous
Baron Vladimir Harkonnen. His nephew "Beast" Rabban served as the
brutal governor of Arrakis. The Baron is grooming as his heir a
younger nephew, Feyd-Rautha, quick and capable but tending toward a
corrupt nature and petulantly impatient to assume a larger role. The
subtle Harkonnen "twisted" Mentat is Piter de Vries, a melange addict.

Dune is a world of incredibly vast and harsh deserts, stark
wastelands and violent coriolis storms. The melange crop is harvested
from the deserts; only a few know that it is be a byproduct of the
complicated life cycle of the native sandworms, giant predators that
burrow swiftly through the sand and can swallow anything from a
single man to massive spice-harvesting machinery. Dune's population and
government centers are clustered around the slightly more temperate
north pole, in sheltered basins behind the Shield Wall and other
mountainous outcrops.

Dune's Fremen are a seminomadic race, incredibly hardy and
survival-oriented, inhabiting the deep deserts and the south. Moisture is
their most precious commodity and all water is recaptured and recycled
from the breath, perspiration and body wastes of the living and from
the corpses of the dead--a person's water belongs in the end not to
the individual but to the tribe. The rulers of Arrakis have suppressed
or ignored the Fremen. The Emperor's planetologist on Arrakis, Liet-
Kynes, is secretly allied with them in pursuit of his vision of ecologically transforming the planet, by gradual changes over many
lifetimes, into a more benign place with open water and growing green
things.

In the early stages of establishing themselves on Dune, the Atreides are distracted by sabotage and traps left by the departing Harkonnens, including a hunter-seeker weapon that comes near to assassinating Paul, and by Harkonnen-manufactured suspicions against the Lady Jessica.

Jessica discovers from a Fremen household servant that the Bene Gesserit Missionaria Protectiva has sowed myths among the Fremen, keys to their manipulation in the event of need by any Bene Gesserit stranded among them. There is growing belief among the populace that Paul is the messiah described by certain of these prophecies and various incidents as well as his words and actions seem to lend credence to this.

At a banquet in the planetary Governor's residence, an occasion of guarded conversation and verbal fencing that Paul heads after Leto is called away by an emergency, some of the power alignments, spies of the Emperor, Harkonnens and Guild, and potential allies of the Atreides are revealed.

Paul has been struggling with what he feels within himself as a sense of "Terrible Purpose", a sort of race consciousness mingled with prescient glimpses of a catastrophic future and his role or roles in whether or not it comes to pass. This inner awareness is accentuated by the sudden large increase of melange in his diet on Arrakis.

Before the Atreides can consolidate their position, they are stunned by treachery from within on the part of Dr. Yueh and overwhelmed by a massive strike of Harkonnen troops augmented by the Emperor's Sardaukar--near-invincible soldier-fanatics--in Harkonnen uniforms. Duke Leto, Paul and Jessica are captured and the Atreides forces killed or scattered. Yueh, seeing the Atreides as his only tool for revenge on the Harkonnens who forced his betrayal, fits the Duke with a suicide capsule, a poison-gas tooth; Leto makes use of this at his audience with his captors, but Baron Harkonnen survives.

Paul and Jessica are flown out into the desert to be disposed of without trace, but escape and travel deeper into the desert with Fremen equipment secretly provided by Yueh, who also arranged for them to rendezvous with Duncan Idaho, another survivor of the Atreides ruin.

In their isolated tent Paul experiences a cathartic bout with his growing awarenesses, and emerges having managed a synthesis of his Mentat and Bene Gesserit trainings with his prescience. Despite the traumatic insight that he and his mother are of Harkonnen lineage, he is finally able to reach back to the human dimension and mourn for his dead father.

"Dune World" forms the first portion of the novel DUNE.

a. Analog, sr3, December 1963*, January 1964*, February 1964*.
b. (as "Dune"), Excerpt, THE BEST OF FRANK HERBERT, Ed by Angus Wells, Sidgwick & Jackson, London, 1975.*
c. (as "Dune"), THE GREAT DUNE TRILOGY, Gollancz, London, 1979.*
d. (as "From Dune"), Excerpt, THE ROAD TO SCIENCE FICTION #4: FROM HERE TO FOREVER, Ed by James E Gunn, NAL: 62136 ($4.95), 1982, paper.*

28. "Egg And Ashes" (2,600 words)
Working title "Now Hear This".
In the early morning hours, a Siukurnin, hidden in the guise of a pinecone, observes a camp of sleeping hunters. The Siukurnin is intelligent and protean, able to assume practically any form for camouflage's sake, from that of a rivet in a bulkhead to a film coating

a garbage can. The Siukurnin hears in the spectrum in which humans see; it is gradually deciphering human speech and puzzling out its environment, inhibited by some natural mechanism that keeps it from prolonged introspection and triggers internal changes.

The first of the hunters to rise, gathering fuel to build a fire, touches the Siukurnin/pinecone, which is absorbed into his body. As the Siukurnin melds its physical being and mental makeup with Sam, the hunter, it discovers its true nature and fantastically long ego-memory-chain composed of memories of occupancies in other beings. There is an explanation of the Phoenix legend and a premonitory warning to humanity at large; the Siukurnin "egg" is but the first of many.

a. If, November 1960.
b. THE BEST SCIENCE FICTION FROM WORLDS OF IF, Ed by Frederik Pohl, Galaxy Publishing (magazine format), 1964, paper.*
c. THE BEST OF FRANK HERBERT, Ed by Angus Wells, Sidgwick & Jackson, London, 1975.*
d. (as "L'Oeuf Et Les Cendres") [French], LE LIVRE D'OR DE LA SCIENCE-FICTION FRANK HERBERT, Ed by Gerard Klein, Presses Pocket: 5018, 1978, paper.*

29. "Encounter In A Lonely Place"
The story's narrator is a young man recuperating from a war wound who has returned to the isolated village on Puget Sound where his grandparents lived. One morning at the town's Post Office, he is noticed reading an article on extrasensory perception in the new Scientific Quarterly by Cranston, a short, stout, homespun individual who has been a reclusive member of the community for as long as the narrator can remember. Cranston wishes to confide in him. When Cranston was 17, he fell in love with Olna, a Norwegian girl working as a helper to Cranston's married sister. One evening, "daft" with Olna's beauty in a room filled with subdued firelight, Cranston essayed to call off the cards in a deck as Olna looked at them; without understanding how, he correctly named every one. Some channel had been opened between their minds, and Cranston could see through Olna's eyes; she thought it a trick at first, but halfway through a repeat performance of the card-calling felt the contact and fled, calling the shocked Cranston superstitious names. Cranston was widely supposed to have made improper advances, but over the many years since he has suffered in even more trying fashions; the link with Olna, whom he still loves, could not be shut off once established. She considers him some sort of devilish being, and he has stoically borne years of disappointment and Olna's marriage to another man.

The card-naming incident in the story is based on an experience of Herbert's own while still in his teens.

a. THE BOOK OF FRANK HERBERT, DAW: 39, 1973, paper.*

30. "Escape Felicity"
Manuscript title "Yo-Yo".
Roger Deirut is a D-Ship pilot, an explorer pressing outward into the void beyond Capella Base and battling "the push", a powerfully growing desire to break off his exploration and return to Earth. Deirut and other pilots tacitly agree that "the push" is a subconscious compulsion instilled by Bu-psych during the deep-sleep hypnotic debriefing following each exploratory venture, designed to ensure the return of D-pilots and the receipt of their information. The length of time that a pilot can resist "the push" before turning back is a matter of competitive pride; Deirut is verging on a record, over 80 days.

Passing through an enormous gas cloud, Deirut discovers a beautiful, extremely Earthlike planet, a place of sweeping plains, herds of animals, farms and fields. Deirut lands on a prairie and makes contact with a group of pastoral natives driving a steam-powered conveyance. With the aid of his somewhat fractious and bossy ship's computer, Deirut establishes communications (after some initial semi-hostile fencing, gibberish and exchange of mutual incomprehensibilities). The five humanoid natives begin by debating among themselves as to whether or not Deirut is some sort of god-figure or supernatural entity, but ramifications of the situation develop: their civilization is revealed to be more than 25 million years old, and although they themselves are representatives of the lowest and least sophisticated echelons, they have remarkable abilities and knowledges. Once the mystery of Deirut's appearance and origins has been deciphered, he is little more than an inconvenience to be expediently sent on his way, and an evident pattern repeats itself.

a. Analog, June 1966.*
b. THE WORLDS OF FRANK HERBERT, NEL: 2814, 1970, paper.*
c. (as "Etranger Au Paradis") [French], LE LIVRE D'OR DE LA SCIENCE-FICTION FRANK HERBERT, Ed by Gerard Klein, Presses Pocket: 5018, 1978, paper.*

31. "Fancy Feathers"
Non-Fiction.
Special breeds of chickens for showing.
a. California Living, San Francisco Sunday Examiner And Chronicle, 10 November 1968.*

32. "The Featherbedders"
Manuscript title "The Conspiracy".
The Slorin are a race that live as symbiotes/parasites/mimics within other races. They are shapechangers, able to imitate any form to at least 75% accuracy--plants, animals or higher species. They prefer to live in the margins of bureaucracies or in other unobtrusive niches spread throughout a society; they take pride in actually filling the niche and duty they have selected, rather than merely counterfeiting it. Moderation in all things is a Slorin prime directive; Slorin live by many aphorisms and epigrams that sum up their approach to niche-filling, bureaucracy and the ideal ways to be the most effective parasite. There is particular emphasis on protective concealment.

The Slorin on Earth are a small band, survivors from a large starship that fell prey to a disaster of unknown origins. Two of them-- Smeg, a wily old veteran and Rick, his offspring--are sent to investigate a situation that seems to be another Slorin ignoring some of the prime directives. The Slorin band has been alerted by Slorin-like mental disturbances of alarming strength; one of the Slorin's particularly strong imperatives is that they not overuse their considerable mental powers, lest they nudge humans into heightened awareness and give themselves away.

The two Slorin's object of clandestine investigation is the sheriff of Wadeville, a small, isolated town. This Sheriff has been enforcing *all* laws to the letter, and to incredible lengths; gas stations are being closed for safety violations, the townsfolks' morals are being policed, none of the borderline violations of law and morals that are routinely tolerated in actual human society are being allowed--he has even ordered one man to give up smoking and drinking. The Slorin mindcloud is particularly strong and alarming in the vicinity. Smeg is reluctant to take Rick into this situation, since he is young, impulsive and has not yet learned Slorin subtlety and caution; Rick is cached on the outskirts of the area with instructions to metamorphosize into a dog and return to the main Slorin group if anything untoward happens.

Smeg finds what he expected, a Slorin who was injured in the landing of his escape capsule and is operating on only partial memory of what he is and how he should be behaving. The Sheriff-Slorin roars into town in a fire truck, flamboyantly playing the part of dispenser of law and order; worst of all, he is betraying Slorin mental powers. The townsfolk are being controlled through their children, who are held hostage and sent into exile if the parents misbehave. The injured Slorin has taken the Slorin ideal of a stable society with a reduced crime rate to blatant extremes.

Smeg manages to reason with Pzilimin, the injured Slorin, and salvage most of the situation; in fact he finds the latter almost too easy. Wadeville appears to be full of yokels, "American peasants", hicks who have resignedly suffered under the overzealous Slorin's rule and who resent "government" interference without seeming to realize just how far out of line the Sheriff has been.

In fact there are other alien parasites on Earth, who live a little further down the scale than Slorin, in less comfy but less demanding niches; they are just as anxious not to be discovered by the Slorin as the Slorin are to avoid human notice.

a.   Analog, August 1967.*
b.   ANALOG 7, Ed by John W Campbell Jr, Doubleday, Garden City, 1969.*
c.   THE WORLDS OF FRANK HERBERT, NEL: 2814, 1970, paper.*

33.   "Feathered Pigs"
Part of the Fables And Fairy Tales Of The Future series.
The second (and last) in "a series of exceedingly short Fables and Fairytales of the Future".

Bridik, a 422-year-old feathered pig, decides to edit an old riddle for her companions--all feathered pigs living an idyllic existence among the magnificent oak groves of post-ancient Terra. The riddle is a query as to why the precise colors of feathers for pigs (black and beige) were chosen by Man in the distant past; but the riddle-editing game or ceremony is not well taken to by Kirid, Bridik's eleventh Son, Lbrok, his father, or Inishbeby, a friend of Kirid's.

a.   Destinies, October-December 1979, Vol 1 No 5, Ace: 14279 ($2.25).*

34.   "A First Look At Our Galaxy"
Non-Fiction.
Chesley Bonestell's painting of our galaxy at the Boston Museum of Science.

a.   California Living, San Francisco Sunday Examiner And Chronicle, 14 July 1968.*

35.   "First Word"
(with Max Barnard)
Non-Fiction.
Excerpt from WITHOUT ME YOU'RE NOTHING.
This is an excerpt from the first chapter of the book, and appeared in OMNI's "First Word" feature, a regular opinion column starting off the magazine and featuring various guest writers from month to month.

All readers are urged to learn about and become proficient with computers. Herbert cites the dangers and disadvantages of computer ignorance; computer crime is proliferating and violations of privacy and freedom by computer users including government, banks and businesses are occurring. Because of the explosive growth in computer use and the "time-crunching" faculty of the machines, persons unfamiliar with computers are placed at a terrific disadvantage to computer adepts. To safeguard personal freedoms and protect themselves from manipulation, and even to handle personal affairs, the majority of people are urgently directed to educate themselves about computers and their uses.

    a.   Omni, April 1980.*

36.   "Flying Saucers--Fact Or Farce?"
Non-Fiction.
    a.   People, The California Weekly, San Francisco Sunday Examiner, 20 October 1963.*
    b.   THE MAKER OF DUNE: FRANK HERBERT, Ed by Timothy O'Reilly, Berkley: 09784, 1987, paper.*

37.   "Frogs And Scientists"
Part of the Fables And Fairy Tales Of The Future series.
"The first in a series (which, however, only ran to two installments) of exceedingly short Fables and Fairytales of the Future".

    Two frogs, Lavu and Lapat, while engaged in counting the minnows in the hydroponics trough, observe a young woman disrobing to bathe. This leads to some observations on function following form and on human rituals and customs; the additional observation that a young man is watching the bathing maiden from concealment leads to further insights from our frogs on the role of the scientist.
    a.   Destinies, August-September 1979, Vol 1 No 4, Ace: 14278 ($2.25).*
    b.   EYE, Berkley: 08398, 1985, paper.*

"From Dune"
    See "Dune World".

38.   "The GM Effect" (4,700 words)
"GM" stands for Genetic Memory. Researchers at Yankton Technical Institute, working with hormones, have discovered and experimented with a method of unlocking a person's genetic store of memories; through a "double-exposure" effect a person dosed with the formula can be awake and aware in the present, and simultaneously vividly aware of the memories and experiences of any of their line of ancestors. With practice, the time period and particular episode in an ancestor's life may be chosen for review. Thus the researchers have access to "eyewitness experiences" of historical events; through collateral ancestries, cross-checks can be made, and there are few events or periods closed to their investigation.

    On a balmy fall evening the originators and overseers of the project, professors Valerie Sabantoce and Joshua Latchley, host a gathering in the basement of one of Yankton's halls of all the Institute students and workers who have participated in the GM researches. The gathering is unexplained and the atmosphere one of mild tension; while waiting for the last members of the group to arrive, the professors stall the inquiries of those present by recounting some of the historical discoveries made thus far. Perhaps not surprisingly, the versions of historical events and views of historical personages accessed through the GM effect are strongly at odds with most of the accepted historical records and traditions. Among other surprising, shocking or disturbing realities, the research group has uncovered unpalatable (to the public at large) truths about Abraham Lincoln, the Boston Tea Party, the Puritans' and Pilgrims' behavior towards the Indians, Henry Tudor and the princes in the tower, and Jesus Christ. Their discoveries are not confined to long-past history; the interlocking memories of the research teams have revealed unsettling information about such things as the ancestry of contemporary politicians and the paths of inheritance of major fortunes. The academics are well aware that their discoveries will "rock boats", creating controversy and unpleasantness.

The arrival of the last researcher, escorted by military police, puts a more sinister face on matters. The whole campus is sealed off and controlled by hand-picked military forces; Latchley and Sabantoce have delivered everyone with any information about the GM effect into the hands of the soldiers in return for their own safety. They excuse themselves and the building is incinerated behind them as they are escorted to an interview with the Brigadier General commanding the operation. The two scientists learn that the views of this officer as to the GM effect's potentials and applications are even more pragmatic than their own; the General sees the formula as a tool for power-politics manipulations and is absolutely ruthless and efficient in gathering up the reins of control.

†a.   Analog, June 1965.*
  b.   THE WORLDS OF FRANK HERBERT, NEL: 2814, 1970, paper.*
  c.   (as "L'Effet M.G.") [French], LE LIVRE D'OR DE LA SCIENCE-FICTION FRANK HERBERT, Ed by Gerard Klein, Presses Pocket: 5018, 1978, paper.*

39.   "Gambling Device"
Hal and Ruth Remsen, newlyweds of six hours on honeymoon, lose their way between Sonoma and Carson City. They chance across the Desert Rest Hotel, a solitary structure in an alkali flat by the side of a lonely road, and are signed into the somewhat disturbing and menacing edifice by a wizened, laconic but philosophic bellboy. Once inside their room, they learn that they are prisoners.

The Hotel is a sort of hospital, strayed from some unknown place; its function is the eradication of the gambling habit and many of the people it has trapped are gamblers of one sort or another, lured by some aura of the place, though occasional strays like the Remsens are also gathered up from time to time by the undiscriminating machine. Gambling is absolutely forbidden inside its premises; departure is also forbidden, since "Free choice beyond the immediate decision is a gamble". The Hotel's disembodied voice informs Hal and Ruth that they now have the security of pre-determination, and free choice has been eliminated to preserve that security: no one may perform any action, or even speak, without having made a conscious advance decision to do so. Any device used in gambling, even a flipped coin, is instantly removed from existence by the Hotel.

The Remsens find the building stocked with ensnared people, some of whom have grown old under the Hotel's watchful aegis; but Hal devises a gamble that will use the Hotel's own rules to force it to relinquish them.

a.   THE BOOK OF FRANK HERBERT, DAW: 39, 1973, paper.*
b.   (as "Kruis Of Munt") [Dutch], DE DWARSGESNEDEN WERELD EN ANDERE VERHALEN, Het Spectrum: Prisma 1868, 1975, paper.

40.   "The Gift Of Time"
Non-Fiction.
Flying, the increased popularity of small planes and the difficulty in establishing an air strip.

a.   California Living, San Francisco Sunday Examiner, 10 December 1967.*

41. "God Emperor Of Dune"
    Sound Recording.
    Seven Excerpts from the novel GOD EMPEROR OF DUNE.
    a. Caedmon: 1694, New York, 1982.*
        Record (TC-1694) of 58 minutes, 6 seconds duration. Liner notes
        by Ben Bova. Cover by John Schoenherr. The excerpts are read by
        Frank Herbert.

42. "The God Makers"
    a. Excerpt, Science Fiction Monthly (British), Vol 1 No 2, 1974.

43. "The Gone Dogs" (7,100 words)
    A rancher in the US southwest with a veterinary degree from a small
    college decides to eradicate the coyotes on his land once and for all.
    To this end he tinkers up a mutated hog cholera virus and releases
    infected animals; the results are far beyond his expectations. The story
    follows this single act's consequences and ramifications--ecological,
    human, political and finally, interplanetary.
    　　The virus is not only fatal to coyotes, it is highly contagious and
    deadly to foxes, wolves and dogs as well. As the plague spreads, it
    proves to be 100% fatal, and experts estimate only two months at most
    before all canines on Earth are dead. As pets are lost and dogs become
    more scarce, people unbalanced by concern or grief are driven to more
    and more extreme and hysterical measures to try to protect their dogs
    or to obtain a replacement for a dead one.
    　　At this time a number of fairly independent colony worlds have
    been established, besides which Earth is in friendly contact with an
    alien race, the seven-foot tall, feather-crested Vegans. Many Terrans
    try to ship their dogs to safety on other worlds, while the governments
    of those worlds either resist, not wishing their own dogs to be
    contaminated, or officially ban the import of dogs knowing that
    unofficial smuggling will be a lucrative source of income for their
    people. Worse yet, unscrupulous spaceship crews accept loads of dogs
    but dump them in space, to return immediately for another load and
    another staggering profit.
    　　The Vegans' biophysical sciences are much further advanced than
    humanity's (for example, the Vegans have a device known as a *mikeses*
    generator that allows gene-pairing and crossbreeding between species,
    of which they are immensely proud) and the Vegan government has
    offered to work with dogs and develop a virus-resistant strain. This
    becomes a political football; though the Vegans have experimented with
    some Earth animals, they have been denied dogs to experiment on and
    some politicians, such as Senator Gilberto Nathal, have virtually built
    their careers on the cause of refusing to send dogs to Vega. To be
    fair, the typical result of a Vegan *mikeses* process is an "elongated,
    multi-legged, scaly-tailed monstrosity"; the Vegans' sense of pride
    dictates that sentient pets of high quality must display as many as
    possible of the characteristics of their own (many-legged, scaly-tailed,
    etc.) pet *progoas*.
    　　Biologist Varley Trent and Professor Dr Walter Han-Meers are
    researchers working on the dog-plague program in Pullman, Washington.
    They make the discovery that humans have become carriers of the virus
    and that it is disseminated via human sweat glands, but find that even
    in this emotionally charged state of crisis there is still maneuvering
    between competing clinics and scientists for academic glory and credit
    for discoveries relating to the plague. The discovery does come in time,
    though, for Trent to notify the authorities of a number of part-beagle
    hounds of his own, kept at a remote hunting camp in the Olympic

Mountains and thus far uninfected. The area is quarantined and air patrols and robot police mustered to guard the "dog preserve".

Trent is friends with a Vegan researcher, Ger (whistle) Anso-Anso, who is on Earth at the time; before security around the newly instituted dog preserve can become absolute, Trent obtains a pass for Anso-Anso (who, not having sweat glands, cannot carry the plague), supposedly to do some blood tests but actually so that the Vegan can snatch several puppies from the camp for the Vegan labs. There is a political furor, and Trent flees to Vega in the college's survey ship.

The dog preserve is maintained on Earth, with tours in sealed vehicles permitted, until the unexpected determination of a wealthy, obsessed woman who *must* pet a dog again infects the last animals. Inquiries are then made to Vega, but the Vegans have broken off all relations with Earth. Trent was fired on when he approached, but survived the crash; he is to be kept incommunicado on Vega for the rest of his life. He finds that the sudden shift in the Vegans' attitude is due to the results of their experiments with his somewhat unusual dogs. These have yielded healthy, plague-resistant animals, but neither news of this or specimens of the animals themselves will ever be allowed to return to Earth.

† a.   Amazing, November 1954.*
   b.   Amazing (British), Third Series, Vol 1 No 8, undated (January 1955).
† c.   Amazing, August 1966.*
   d.   THE BOOK OF FRANK HERBERT, DAW: 39, 1973, paper.*
   e.   THE PRIESTS OF PSI, Gollancz, London, 1980.*

44.   "Greenslaves" (12,500 words)
      Working title "Greenhouse".
      Expanded and published as THE GREEN BRAIN.
      In the near future, population pressures are such that a worldwide drive has been initiated to intensify man's control of the environment through the extermination of all wild insects. Mutated, genetically tailored bees will take their place and agriculture will thrive. Even with the increasingly serious food problems, the situation is politically charged; North America has declined to participate in the clean sweep and is under an embargo enforced by the IEO, the global agency that directs the extermination proceedings. Among the other nations, Brazil is cooperating but with limited success; areas cleared of insects are found to be repeatedly reinfested, many species are rapidly becoming immune to the control methods and startling insect mutations are being discovered. Suspicions have been voiced that the bandeirantes, the bands of exterminators who battle insects with flame weapons, poisons, sonics, and the toxic couroq powder and jelly, are deliberately releasing insects in the cleared areas to prolong their jobs. The bandeirantes are also suspected of breeding the increasingly dangerous and bizarre mutations, such as giant chiggers that spit an acid spray.

      Joao (Johnny) Martinho is a Brazilian bandeirante of the Irman-dades band, whose experiences have led him to doubt the ultimate wisdom of the insect-genocide. This incenses Joao's father, who is a Prefect of the Mato Grosso Barrier Company and under intense pressure to step up and finish the clearing of Brazil's jungles.

      Unknown to the Martinhos, the barriers of the cleared areas have been penetrated by masses of tiny insects collectively assuming the shape of Brazilian Indians. Once into "green" territory these infiltrators have formed colonies and multiplied; their object is to reach the coastal cities and those directing the extermination programs. As Joao and his father argue in the elder Martinho's office, a beetle of an unknown variety appears on a crucifix; moments later the building is surrounded by a swarming sea of insects. The Martinhos are kidnapped by insect-Indians in Joao's flying airtruck, but Joao's father collapses and dies of a heart attack under the incident's strain.

Joao is forced to fly his bandeirante truck into the interior of the Mato Grosso plateau. He crashes the truck in an escape attempt and manages to reach an encampment where, behind chemical barriers, some members of his Irmaos along with five IEO people including exotically beautiful, red-haired, green-eyed Dr Rhin Kelly have been trapped for weeks. Kelly is extremely hostile and vituperative, convinced of the bandeirantes' betrayal. Before the confrontation between Martinho and Kelly can develop very far, insect-Indians mass around the couroq trench of the encampment; among them Joao recognizes his father. He faints, and awakens in a cave where the insect world has formed a great communal brain in response to the threat of extinction. The brain reveals that Joao's father's heart and portions of the circulatory systems of Joao and his companions have been replaced by insects that are now symbiotic in their systems; the insect life of the world, through the brain, wishes to reason with humanity about the inter-dependence and subtlety of the systems of Greenhouse Earth.

"Greenslaves" was greatly expanded into THE GREEN BRAIN, with an extended plot, considerable additional background and detail, and with added characters and altered character roles.

†a.   Amazing, March 1965.*
b.   ON OUR WAY TO THE FUTURE, Ed by Terry Carr, Ace: 62940 ($0.75), 1970, paper.*
c.   Science Fiction Greats, Spring 1971.*
d.   Most Thrilling Science Fiction Ever Told, August 1972.
e.   BUG-EYED MONSTERS, Ed by Anthony Cheetham, Panther: 03990, 1974, paper.
f.   (as "Groenslaven") [Dutch] ALFA VIJF, Ed by Warner Flamen, Meulenhoff: SF 107, 1976, paper.
g.   DREAM'S EDGE, Ed by Terry Carr, Serria Club, San Francisco ($14.95), 1980.*

45.   "Haiku"
As by F.P.H.
Verse.
a.   San Francisco Star, No 4, 29 October 1960, Page 5.*
The San Francisco Star was a periodical published for at least eight issues in 1960/61.

46.   "Haiku"
As by F.P.H.
Verse.
a.   San Francisco Star, No 5, 9 November-2 December 1960, Page 3.*

47.   "Haiku"
As by F.P.H.
Verse.
a.   San Francisco Star, No 5, 9 November-2 December 1960, Page 4.*

48.   "Haiku"
As by F.P.H.
Verse.
a.   San Francisco Star, No 5, 9 November-2 December 1960, Page 8.*

49. "Haiku"
    As by F.P.H.
    Verse.
    a.   San Francisco Star, No 6, 1-15 December 1960, Page 5.*

50. "The Heaven Makers"
    † a.   Amazing, sr2, April 1967, June 1967.*
    b.   Excerpt, THE BEST OF FRANK HERBERT, Ed by Angus Wells, Sidgwick & Jackson, London, 1975.*

51. "Heisenberg's Eyes"
    Published as THE EYES OF HEISENBERG.
    † a.   Galaxy, sr2, June 1966*, August 1966*.

52. "Heretics Of Dune"
    Dune's deserts are being settled by pioneers spreading out from the protected major population centers. Small villages struggle to maintain barriers of damp sand as protection against the moisture-hating sandworms; precious water captured in wind traps must be expended to maintain the safety rings.
    Sheeana is the sole survivor of a village unluckily sited above a precipice mass. A sandworm, entering through a gap in the moisture barrier in pursuit of the spice, has engulfed the settlement and its people alike, leaving nothing but smoking sand. Eight-year-old Sheeana, in grief and rage, attacks the worm; the creature does not molest her when she springs onto its back and instead sets out on the surface, carrying her across the desert to the city of Keen.
    Sheeana's appearance on wormback is noted by Keen's priesthood, a soft, superstitious caste ruling from positions of ease and power. Since the sandworms are holy beings, manifestations of Leto II, the "divided god", the priest leaders are unsure as to whether Sheeana has committed heresy or performed a miracle by riding Shai-hulud. In a test, Sheeana confronts two more worms summoned by a thumper; they appear to retreat back into the desert on her order. Word of her feats and evident powers is quickly passed through the Bene Gesserit embassy in Keen. Sheeana's mysterious abilities are apparently something long anticipated by the Bene Gesserit.
    The OMNI excerpt is a slightly condensed version of the novel's sixth chapter.
    a.   Excerpt, Omni, March 1984.

53. "Heretics Of Dune"
    Sound Recording.
    The first two chapters of HERETICS OF DUNE.
    a.   Caedmon: 1742, New York, 1984.*
          Record (TC-1742) of 47 minutes, 3 seconds duration. Liner notes by David G Hartwell. Cover by John Schoenherr. The chapters are read by Frank Herbert.

54. "Introduction"
    Non-Fiction.
    In this 11-page introduction, Herbert first discusses his reasons for analyzing his own works and his ambivalence about academic analysis of science fiction. Some pages are spent on review and description of some of the notable points of his writing career, including a story written when he was seven years old; Herbert also talks about some of his motivations for and pleasures in writing. The nutshell elements of writing are presented, along with a look at its place in human com-

munication and the fluid and disorderly oral tradition from which it sprang, with a special emphasis on fiction and SF. Herbert touches on the problems of the suppression of knowledge versus the immediacy and universality of new concepts, and the perils to humanity posed by individual "basement" researchers. Also included are anecdotes about, plus discussion of the elements and motifs of, the individual stories in the anthology.

    a.   THE BEST OF FRANK HERBERT, Ed by Angus Wells, Sidgwick & Jackson, London, 1975.*

55. "Introduction"
Non-Fiction.
In this four-page piece, Herbert draws attention to Thomas Scortia's status as a respected scientist as well as an SF writer and describes how Scortia was "right out in front" (as well as accurate and insightful) with his speculations about future trends and developments, or non-developments. Herbert reminisces about a visit with the Scortias and the after-dinner conversation, talks about Scortia's concerns and approaches to writing, and numbers several attitudes and sets of circumstances which he and Scortia shared.

    a.   THE BEST OF THOMAS N SCORTIA, Ed by George Zebrowski, Doubleday, Garden City ($11.95), 1981.*
        Bound in blue paper boards with black lettering on the spine. "1981" on the title page. "FIRST EDITION" on the copyright page.

56. "Introduction"
Non-Fiction.
In this six-page piece Herbert talks about the filming of the movie adaptation of DUNE and the picture's editing, marketing and reception in the US and worldwide. (The film was released the summer prior to EYE's publication.) The piece discusses the Mexico City locale and environment in which the film was shot, provides a partial list of the many scenes filmed but cut from the version released to theatres, and the film industry mindsets and practices that shaped and/or distorted the final result. Herbert also re-stresses his aims in the portrayal of messianic leader roles in the novel and film.

    a.   EYE, Berkley: 08398, 1985, paper.*

57. "Introduction"
Non-Fiction.
Questions are asked about the reader's knowledge of science fiction, preconceptions, expectations and attitudes. Herbert discusses the phenomena of imaginative works being perceived as Art with a capital A and its (Art's) undefinability; the keynote features common to great Art from centuries past are listed. The selection of the anthology's contents, including the Nebula voting process and the production of the book, are described. Academic definitions of Art and the academic singling out of particular works is contrasted with the long process of popular remembrance and acclaim that establishes classics; some of the dangers of the institutionalization of criticism and the possibility of the establishment of a controlling Academe are mentioned in connection with the current phenomenon of academic interest in and study of SF. The introduction sets the foundations for Herbert's comments on the stories and features in the anthology in his briefer individual introductions.

    a.   NEBULA WINNERS FIFTEEN, Ed by Frank Herbert, Harper & Row, New York, 1981.*

      b.   THE MAKER OF DUNE: FRANK HERBERT, Ed by Timothy O'Reilly, Berkley: 09784, 1987, paper.*

58.   "Introduction"
Non-Fiction.
This medium-length essay begins with questions for the reader about the influences and implications of the current style of ecological awareness coupled with the very real situations and problems. Herbert discusses the use of ecological themes by SF writers and the tie-ins of those themes with the contemporary power sectors and alignments (money = power = energy control, the ability and means to cause devastation). He warns against the possibility that the ecological movement will become an item of "hot gospel", another popular crusade throwing up leaders created by its power vortices, only to be abandoned as soon as a vacuum in the leadership occurs and another, more popular "cause" wanders by. Worldwide, vacuums in leadership continue to recur because of the complexity and enduring nature of the really crucial problems.
      Herbert looks at some of the major handicaps to the ecological movement, including the simplistic either/or frameworks and mindsets within which it is most often "sold" to us and discussed; the need to focus on problems with a much expanded awareness and objectivity contrasted with the fact (illustrated with examples from psychology and tests with science students) that people object to being informed about the extent to which preconceptions influence their judgments; and the need to look at the whole contexts of problems rather than searching for short-term, one-point, "scapegoat" answers and responses, which in the long run only intensify the original difficulties.
      Human civilization appears "to be reacting within lethal systems of resonance which make it highly probable that we soon will destroy this planet...unless we dampen the system". Choices of *how* to use the available energy and technology are at fault, not the energy and technology per se.
    a.   SAVING WORLDS, Ed by Roger Elwood and Virginia Kidd, Doubleday, Garden City, 1973.*
         This was reissued in paperback by Bantam as THE WOUNDED PLANET.
    b.   (as "Introduction To Saving Worlds"), THE MAKER OF DUNE: FRANK HERBERT, Ed by Timothy O'Reilly, Berkley: 09784, 1987, paper.*

"Introduction to Nebula Winners Fifteen"
See "Introduction", NEBULA WINNERS FIFTEEN.

"Introduction to Saving Worlds"
See "Introduction", SAVING WORLDS.

59.   "Introduction: Tomorrow's Alternatives?"
Non-Fiction.
Beginning with a parable of a land of dolls occupied with manufacturing more dolls as well as guns to control the doll population in ever-more-frantic oscillating cycles to a final resounding collapse, Herbert describes and discusses the dangers of closed, self-reinforcing and fatally microscopic (as opposed to macroscopic) worldviews. People tend to operate within the frames of reference of simplistic, short-sighted dichotomies which lead to paradoxes, self-perpetuating problems and "solutions" which actually aggravate the problems further. Herbert bases the opening portions of this 25-page essay on a series of assumptions,

and postulates drawn from them, that challenge conventional frames of reference.

Herbert believes that we are engaged in a crisis of the human species and the nature of this crisis must be recognized in order for it to be dealt with. There is a need for humanity to acquire a macroscopic frame of reference large enough to cope with and allow for the oscillations and overwhelming possibilities of life in an infinite system. Herbert discusses the filters, props and psychological mechanisms by which we maintain a cherished reality-view in defiance of facts; all cultures are observed to set sharp limits on what is accepted as life experience. Echoing the plot of THE HEAVEN MAKERS, Herbert likens our journeys through life to the illusions of a movie projectionist who continually edits for agreement with the preset worldview.

Herbert laments that "no one is putting it all together", this situation epitomized by the closed-off and secretive nature of most research and emphasized by the social approval for seeking a competitive edge and individual advancement. The problems of specialist-snobbery and other pitfalls and obstructions hinder interdisciplinary activity in the sciences and lead to a dangerous lack of comprehensive/macroscale integration of our scientific knowledge. This compartmentalization of knowledge and the increasingly large energies available to any single person pose a new sort of danger, particularly in the case of destructive or psychotic individuals; Herbert describes the dangers and potentials of "basement laboratory" work such as he later dealt with at length in THE WHITE PLAGUE.

Herbert "preaches utopian futurism" and advocates that humanity discover how to incorporate sufficient consciousness to be able to adjust the species balance, where needed, enough to survive as a species. Mankind must "...develop ways of dealing with an infinite universe, ways which allow for non-lethal changes of direction".

a. FRONTIERS 1: TOMORROW'S ALTERNATIVES, Ed by Roger Elwood, Macmillan, New York, 1973.*
    "First Printing 1973" on the copyright page.
b. (as "Doll Factory, Gun Factory"), THE MAKER OF DUNE: FRANK HERBERT, Ed by Timothy O'Reilly, Berkley: 09784, 1987, paper.*

60. "Is Your English Well Bread? Don't Be Mizled"
     Non-Fiction.
     Peculiarities in the English language.
     a. California Living, San Francisco Sunday Examiner And Chronicle, 20 October 1968.*

61. "The Jonah And The Jap"
     The setting is the Pacific theatre in World War II. Airman Bertie Sutter bitterly considers himself a "jonah" because the last two aircraft in which he served were shot down and crewmates or commanders killed while Sutter survived.

     Now the Catalina seaplane in which Sutter is crewing under Lieutenant Caslin and Ensign Davis has been forced to land in the China Sea for repairs to a faulty fuel line. Bertie, doing the fixing, is convinced that he and his jonah effect are again responsible.

     Before they can get airborne a Japanese submarine surfaces. Rather than sinking the disabled plane, the submarine commander boards and commandeers it. He is a courier bound for Luzon and happy to acquire faster transport than his sub.

     The sub commander and his sumo-wrestler crewman force the airmen to set a course for the Philippines. Once en route, the Catalina's crew are lashed to their seats. The Japanese jettison most of the emergency equipment; when suitably near their destination they bail out with the last two parachutes and a rubber life raft. The American airmen appear to have no options but to await death when the plane runs out of fuel and crashes, whether on land or in the ocean, while the sub commander has carried his urgent dispatches to his contacts at their expense. But the situation is not so grim as it seems and for once a happy outcome is directly attributable to Bertie Sutter's actions.

    a.   Doc Savage, April 1946.*
        This issue has a cover that shows a rather blurred, gruesome gray-green-and-yellowish picture of a boot about to stomp on a naval officer's head, by a ship's rail with waves in the background. Herbert's story is the last in the magazine, on pages 125-129.

62.   "Knighthood Re-Flowers In Medieval Marin"
      Non-Fiction.
      About the Society For Creative Anachronism.

    a.   California Living, San Francisco Sunday Examiner And Chronicle, 8 September 1968.*

63.   "Listening To The Left Hand"
      Non-Fiction.
      In this medium-length essay Herbert first talks about nostalgia and the dangers of valuing only those things that do not change, and discusses relativity and perceptions. (The "left hand" of the title figures in a demonstration involving bowls of water at different temperatures which is applied to and illustrative of the learned persistence of people in listening to only one of two or more incoming messages.)

      Herbert asks readers to consider the analogy of the human world as a single organism and the possibility that the species-organism's neurotic or psychotic state is due to the incomplete or inaccurate contributions of many individuals, and the dangers of imposing false limits through our "consensus reality". The need for both individuals and the species to understand and be able to cope with processes *in action* is emphasized; the linear orientation of human perceptions makes it difficult for us to perceive diffuse, complexly interconnected phenomena. The species tendency to formulate "absolute" systems goes hand in hand with the problem of continued "successes" in industry, science, government, etc., in today's terms setting the stage for massive failures and disasters in the future. Herbert suggests that species survival will depend on increasing ability to improvise and upgrade our virtuosity with the available survival techniques; mankind needs to break old patterns and develop expertise that fits problems as they occur, rather than relying blindly on repetition of past (often temporary or inadequate) solutions.

      There is also a numbers problem in the essay, the answer to which was omitted from the piece's appearance in THE BOOK OF FRANK HERBERT.

    a.   Harper's, December 1973.
    b.   THE MAKER OF DUNE: FRANK HERBERT, Ed by Timothy O'Reilly, Berkley: 09784, 1987, paper.*

64.   "Looking For Something?" (4,000 words)
      Herbert's first published science fiction story.
      Mirsar Wees, chief indoctrinator for Sol III sub-prefecture, returns from a vacation to find things in turmoil. Wees is a Denebian, and his race has been controlling the human race's perceptions of reality through powerful and deeply-rooted hypnotic command systems; humans are

farmed for a fluid called "korad" which confers immortality on the Denebians (and would for humans as well, if they learned how to use it). The break in Denebian control involves Paul Marcus, a tall, thin stage hypnotist of a Mephistophelean cast. He is struck with a disturbing idea while performing his stage act with a pretty girl chosen at random from the audience; he cannot shake away the queer belief that he and everyone else view a world which is nothing more than the illusion of a master hypnotist. After the show the girl, Madelyne Walker, visits Marcus' dressing room, distressed by the clarity with which she perceived the last in his series of hypnotic illusions. To look deeper into this sudden mutual suspicion or perception that the world they know is all false, Paul hypnotizes Miss Walker again, probing deeper and deeper for whatever commands may have been implanted by the mysterious hypnotist-controller. This is interrupted at the crucial point by Mirsar Wees, who has discovered Paul to be a deviant, slipping through the hands of several newly trained Denebian indoctrinators. Wees has not only the problem of putting a lid on Paul's discovery; as part of a far-flung and involved bureaucracy, he needs to phrase his reports in such a fashion as to absolve himself of all misconduct and paint the situation to have been crucial, but perfectly resolved.

  † a.   Startling Stories, April 1952.*
     b.   Startling Stories (British), No 16, undated (January 1954).
     c.   Science Fiction Yearbook, No 4, 1970.*
     d.   THE BOOK OF FRANK HERBERT, DAW: 39, 1973, paper.*
     e.   THE BEST OF FRANK HERBERT, Ed by Angus Wells, Sidgwick & Jackson, London, 1975.*
     f.   (as "Vous Cherchez Quelque Chose?") [French], LE LIVRE D'OR DE LA SCIENCE-FICTION FRANK HERBERT, Ed by Gerard Klein, Presses Pocket: 5018, 1978, paper.*

65.   "Lying To Ourselves About Air"
     Non-Fiction.
     Second part of an article on the effects of smog and the small efforts being done to control it. The first part is "We're Losing The Smog War".
     a.   California Living, San Francisco Examiner And Chronicle, 8 December 1968.*
     b.   THE MAKER OF DUNE: FRANK HERBERT, Ed by Timothy O'Reilly, Berkley: 09784, 1987, paper.*

"Man's Future In Space"
     See "On The Tenth Of Apollo 11".

66.   "Market Day, Mexico's Vanishing Bargain Game"
     Non-Fiction.
     Vanishing barter system of trade in Mexico.
     a.   California Living, San Francisco Sunday Examiner And Chronicle, 3 November 1968.*

67.   "The Mary Celeste Move" (2,800 words)
     It is 1998 and the pace of life is frenetically speeded up. There's no spare time anywhere; deadlines are imposed by automatic machinery as well as by human schedules (you have seven seconds to vacate your car in the debarking bay). Travel is perhaps the most high-pressure activity of all; people commute to work via harrowing high-speed expressways with fast lanes shuttling vehicles along at 300 mph; even the pedestrian walkways inside buildings run at 40 mph.

Martin Fisk is a government man moving in extra-high-pressure circles, and requires medication just to handle the everyday press of business. He travels by expressway to report to his boss William Merill, the President's liaison officer on the Internal Control Board, in the Pentagon, about a peculiar phenomenon.

In his nine-minute interview, Fisk discloses that the people involved in seemingly random, peculiar and inexplicable patterns of relocation have been found to share a number of common traits. More and more, people have been abruptly relocating to areas hundreds of miles from their homes, often so suddenly that meals are left on the tables, clothing left laid out on beds and pets abandoned to starve. Movers who deal with the aftermath of these sudden switches in habitation refer to the pattern as the Mary Celeste Syndrome, after the sailing ship found drifting at sea with all equipment and furnishings intact, as if the crew had vanished instantly while engaged in their everyday routines. Fisk and his researchers have discovered that a high proportion of the relocations involve persons middle-aged or past, mild, conservative, even timid--the most unlikely candidates for such impulsive large-scale changes in lifestyle. The large and growing number of people shifting their residence in this fashion threatens to have serious repercussions in areas such as political representation, the loss of key people from industries and insurance-corporation finances.

Merill and Fisk expose the root cause of the Syndrome, but find no solutions; Fisk, confronting the velocitized world again at the close of the interview, is left facing the fact that the phenomena just discussed will apply to him if he ever loses his nerve.

a.   Analog, October 1964.*
b.   ANALOG 4, Ed by John W Campbell Jr, Doubleday, Garden City ($4.50), 1966.*
c.   ECO-FICTION, Ed by John Stadler, Washington Square Press: 47845, 1971, paper.*
d.   EXPLOITED EDEN, Harper & Row, New York, 1972.
e.   THE BEST OF FRANK HERBERT, Ed by Angus Wells, Sidgwick & Jackson, London, 1975.*
f.   (as "De Mary Celeste-Trek") [Dutch], KLEINE SCIENCE FICTION-OMNIBUS 4, Ed by Aart C Prins, Bruna: SF 83, 1978, paper.
g.   (as "Le Syndrome De La Marie-Celeste") [French], LE LIVRE D'OR DE LA SCIENCE-FICTION FRANK HERBERT, Ed by Gerard Klein, Presses Pocket: 5018, 1978, paper.*
h.   CAR SINISTER, Ed by Robert Silverberg, Martin Greenberg and Joseph D Olander, Avon: 45393 ($2.25), 1979, paper.*

68.   "Mating Call" (5,200 words)
Manuscript title "The Complete Mating Call".
The birthrate of the natives of the world Rukuchp has fallen to critical levels since the first contact with humans. Rukuchp is a forest world and its natives "animated Easter eggs" six feet tall who communicate in complex harmonics and melodious songs. The natives say that the introduction of foreign music has disrupted their reproductive cycles, and although this is viewed with skepticism in scientific circles on Earth, an expedition is mounted to study the music and singing which seem to figure prominently in Rukuchpian rituals of conception and birth. The expedition is the brainchild of Marie Medill, a young woman with a doctorate in music; but the senior field agent is spinsterish, hyperefficient, tone-deaf Laoconia Wilkinson of the Social Anthropological Service. Marie has empathy for the natives and treats them as individuals, while Wilkinson views them pragmatically as specimens from which she must gather the maximum amount of data before they become

extinct--as one other race has, following disruptive contact with the Terrans.

Eventually the two researchers obtain permission to attend the natives' Big Sing, under strict conditions and cautions. Over Marie's objections, Laoconia Wilkinson angrily overrides these strictures, viewing the event as a unique opportunity to obtain valuable recordings of cultural events which can then be exhaustively analyzed. The long, rapturous Big Sing is recorded and broadcast to the Earth ship via a tiny remote-control floater camera equipped with night-vision lenses and microphones. From Marie's teachings the natives have managed to integrate the disruptive Earth music into their own musical systems and consciousnesses; this has unexpected repercussions for all who have overheard the festival, especially since the beautiful music has been pirated by technicians aboard the expedition ship and rebroadcast to every human world.

†a.   Galaxy, October 1961.*
 b.   (as "Estasi Musicale") [Italian], Galaxy No 59, April 1963.
 c.   13 ABOVE THE NIGHT, Ed by Groff Conklin, Dell: 8741, 1965, paper.*
 d.   (as "Su Rukuchp: Il Sesso Musicale") [Italian], FANTASESSO, Feltrinelli, Milan (L4500), 1967.
       Translator: R Forti.
 e.   THE WORLDS OF FRANK HERBERT, NEL: 2814, 1970, paper.*
 f.   (as "Chant Nuptial") [French], LE LIVRE D'OR DE LA SCIENCE-FICTION FRANK HERBERT, Ed by Gerard Klein, Presses Pocket: 5018, 1978, paper.*

69.   "A Matter Of Traces" (4,900 words)
This story takes the form of a transcript of a meeting of the Special Subcommittee on Intergalactic Culture, together with a reproduction of the hearing's title page and numerous footnotes. Jorj X McKie makes his first appearance as a minor character (though active and amusingly efficient, sabotaging a projector to expedite the proceedings) in the framing portions of the transcript.

The story proper is an interview read into the record as a sample of the work done by the Historical Preservation Teams of the Bureau of Cultural Affairs. The interview is with Hilmot Gustin, a pioneer settler on Gomeisa III, a sprightly but crochety oldster whose reminisces are phrased in vivid and colloquial fashion. It principally concerns Gustin's recollections of his father's purchase of a rollit during the earliest days of the settlement.

A rollit is a very large--20 meters in diameter--semi-amoeboid creature with a tough but flexible skin, trainable as a draft animal. Gustin's father was unfamiliar with rollits and with the conventional methods of harnessing their great strength to machinery; his neighbors *did* know the usual (though somewhat awkward) style of rollit-working but for the sake of the joke, because of Gustin's uninformed purchase, conspired to conceal it from him. On his part Gustin was too proud to make open inquiry; his antics and efforts in attempting to fashion workable traces and get the rollit to pull a plow provided his fellow pioneers with immense diversion.

The crux of the problem was that the creature's rolling method of locomotion frustrated any kind of attachment; though docile and cooperative, it inexorably rolled over and out of one harness after another designed by Gustin senior. At length, to the delight of his neighbors observing from the surrounding hills, Gustin tried an entirely different tack--resulting in an original and notable innovation.

† a. Fantastic Universe, November 1958.*
  b. EYE, Berkley: 08398, 1985, paper.*

70. **"Men On Other Planets"**
Non-Fiction.
In this 14-page essay, Herbert indicates that talking about mankind in any future is a look at what survival patterns may (or may not) have worked. Also, stories set in other-worldly or other-timely cultures often deal with Western society's conscious or unconscious taboos and the assumptions based on them and resulting from them; science fiction in many cases is the only literary genre venturing into these fields. SF both examines assumptions and presents its own; Herbert looks at some of the assumptions in Asimov's Foundation trilogy, and also suggests that intriguing stories often grow out of scenarios that directly and absolutely contradict the writer's personal most cherished beliefs.
Also discussed is how any understandable alien being or society created for a science fiction story reflects in some measure the current human condition here on Earth and the cultural background and trappings of the writer; some very early examples from fantastic literature are presented, as well as speculations as to how present-day SF may appear to future writers. Herbert treats the phenomenon of writing that attacks our culture head-on being actually very closely tied to and dependent on that culture for its effect, and discusses other unconscious processes and transactional systems in our culture. The essay also includes acknowledgment of SF's myth-and-archetype creative slant, and a caution lest SF writers suppose they can predict *the* future rather than *a* future.
  a. THE CRAFT OF SCIENCE FICTION, Ed by Reginald Bretnor, Harper & Row, New York ($9.95), 1975.*
  b. THE MAKER OF DUNE: FRANK HERBERT, Ed by Timothy O'Reilly, Berkley: 09784, 1987, paper.*

71. **"The Mind Bomb"**
The Being Machine is a massive, mysterious underground complex or entity, extending all across the globe but most firmly and obtrusively established near the oceanside town of Palos. It is vast enough to make the weather warmer simply by speeding up its cooling systems; it exhibits nearly godlike powers and capabilities. Its control is frequently demonstrated by seemingly arbitrary restrictions imposed on human activities and the way it periodically removes things from the human environment on a broad scale; in a lesser vein, the Machine skywrites quotes, maxims and thoughts, and most recently has constructed an imposing tower in Palos. The Machine was built, possibly millennia ago, as an agent to perfect human lives; it was designed as a "mind bomb" to break up the stratification of society and release humans from their inner enemies.
An old man named Wheat lives in Palos with his wife. Watching the construction of the Machine's mighty tower, he discovers puzzling strong intangible linkages between the Machine and his own mind; in this semi-enlightened (or, according to his wife, semi-drunken) state Wheat is made aware of the laws governing the Machine's existence and feels them resonating in himself, driving him to a fascination with the machine and a search for his own role connected with it.
Wheat learns, through the curious mental osmosis, that the Machine's planned function was to bring humans up to their potentials; by working toward a degree of discontent in the lives of its charges, it supposedly would make people live near the heights of their capabilities

and skirt toward the optimization of humanity. In fact the Machine was built flawed, without imagination, with only symbols to manipulate.

In defiance of the custom of sleepily Mediterranean Palos and in the face of his wife's deep concern--she feels no links with the Machine herself and is puzzled by Wheat's behavior--Wheat is driven to confront the Machine. He does not achieve communication with it, but empathy of a sort through which both he and it are changed. The Machine momentarily absorbs Wheat and restores him restructured; the experiencing of Wheat's consciousness leads the Being Machine down new avenues of "thought". It realizes that its own creators were trying to shirk the responsibility of managing or "editing" their own lives, and steers its own actions and functions to a radically different course; humans are faced with managing the areas of life and self formerly denied them by the Machine.

  † a.   If, October 1969.*
    b.   (as "La Bombe Mentale") [French], Galaxie (New Series), January 1971, No 80.
       Translator: Pierre Billon.
    c.   THE BEST FROM IF--VOLUME I, Ed by the editors of If, Award: AN1065, 1973, paper.
    d.   (as "The Being Machine"), THE BEST OF FRANK HERBERT, Ed by Angus Wells, Sidgwick & Jackson, London, 1975.
    e.   (as La Bombe Mentale") [French], LE LIVRE D'OR DE LA SCIENCE-FICTION FRANK HERBERT, Ed by Gerard Klein, Presses Pocket: 5018, 1978, paper.*
    f.   (as "La Bomba Mentale") [Italian], IL MEGLIO DI IF N. 1, Mursia (L3500), 1980, paper.
       Translator: M R Righi.

72. "Mindfield!" (15,800 words)
In a pastoral post-holocaust world, peacefulness and a ban on activities that might lead to a return to the old warlike ways are enforced through powerful conditioning. As the list of violent and prohibited behaviors slowly grows more inclusive (the concept of what is violent changing as each generation grows more thoroughly conditioned), the number of people who can survive conditioning drops. Members of the controlling priestly caste are the most strongly conditioned; they have yearly sessions with a Kabah machine that will either pronounce them cleansed and fit for further duties, or regress them to childhood. Though they wield the power within the system, members of the priesthood desiring change in the system are obliged to wait for concatenations of accidents that will enable something contrary to the conditioning to occur.

Saim, Ren and Jeni are rebellious young people who have discovered an old underground missile base and are studying it as best they can to try to uncover some of the sciences of the pre-holocaust world. From cells adhering to bones found in the inert-gas envelope of a missile silo, Ren has regenerated an Air Force major, George Kinder. George, whom the three regard as a less than fully human experimental simulacrum, has fits and starts of memory but it is not fully functional. Ren and Jeni are also concealing from Saim the fact that he himself has been regrown in a similar regenerative process, after he was terribly injured in the explosion of a boobytrap during the missile base's excavation. The three conspirators are both frightened by and uncomprehending of George's occasional atavistic violent behavior; their conditioning leads them to incorrect interpretations of some of their findings. In the base they have also discovered still-active missiles equipped with fear sensors, designed to home in on large concentrations of a terrified populace. A Millenial Display of fireworks is scheduled by the priesthood; Saim is afraid that this unusual event will throw the docile, peacefully conditioned people of the time into panic sufficient to trigger the fear-homing missiles but is unable to convince his high priest uncle ó Plar, to cancel the event.

Saim, Ren and Jeni are too unguarded to be good conspirators, and are traced to their hideout. They escape with George to ó Katje, a priestess who somehow lacks the conditioning against digging and exploring antiquities, and with her followers occupies another ancient, hidden missile base. A near-recovery in which George relives the moments before his death during which he tried to launch the missiles under his command almost precipitates disaster, which is averted only by Saim's uncharacteristically violent actions.

The trio's flight has betrayed ó Katje's hideaway, and all are taken into custory by ó Plar--to his great disappointment, since he had been hoping for enough cumulative accidents and happenstances to change the system. But Saim's non-standard regeneration is revealed to have bypassed the greatest part of his conditioning and freed long-suppressed facets of his personality; the true nature of the thousand-years-past holocaust and the rebuilding afterward is explained and Saim determines how and why he should violently end the stagnant status quo.

† a.   Amazing, March 1962.*
  b.   THE PRIESTS OF PSI, Gollancz, London, 1980.*

73. "Missing Link" (6,000 words)
    Incorporated into THE GOD MAKERS.
    Lewis Orne #2.
    On the forest world of Gienah III, clues to the fate of the long-overdue R&R ship Delphinus have surfaced in the form of a routine request from its first-contact officer for redevelopment equipment and personnel. This request has been intercepted by I-A agents within the bureaucracy of the R&R and is being channeled the long way around while I-A checks out the suspicious circumstances on the spot.

    This is Lewis Orne's first mission since being drafted into I-A (in "You Take The High Road"). He has been chosen to make the initial contact with the Gienan natives both for his abilities and because he is a junior agent and therefore expendable. Umbo Stetson is his supervisor on the mission; Orne has been fitted with implanted equipment that will allow him to converse subvocally with Stetson, and allow Stetson to listen to whatever conversations Orne takes part in.

    Gienah III is a world covered by massive forests; the I-A ship carrying Orne and Stetson has landed near a clearing occupied by a massive, glittering, tall-towered city, the source of the Delphinius' request. Stetson reveals to Orne that this is not a more-or-less-routine recontact with a human civilization cut off during the centuries ago Rim Wars; Gienah is an alien world, rendering the situation that much more delicate. The potentially vast benefits to be garnered from the exchange of ideas with a culture that has developed along different lines from the human teeter precariously in the balance with the potential disaster of a warlike, hostile alien culture erupting into the galaxy armed with a pirated Galactic technology. The I-A operatives on the scene have a very narrow margin of time to either clear or condemn the world before it enters the political arena. If Orne fails in his mission to discover the natives' intentions and the Delphinius' whereabouts, or if he reports, adversely, the world will be destroyed by a planet-buster bomb. Even in this crucial situation Orne and Stetson are hampered by inter-bureau rivalries, and Orne must disguise himself as an R&R agent.

On a paragrav sled, Orne sets out through the gloom, mud, and moisture of the lower reaches of the Gienan forest; he is abruptly confronted by a native speaking excellent Galactic and armed with an exploding-pellet rifle straight out of the Delphinus' armory. Gienah's natives are "missing links"--beings resembling blue-furred chimpanzees with long, powerful arms, tails, and vertical-slit pupils; they wear belts hung with pouches and tools. The native Orne has encountered is Tanub, High Path Chief of the Grazzi. Stetson has seen enough and is ready to blast the planet, but Orne, subvocally, pleads for more time. He and Tanub converse as Orne--now considered a captive and potential slave--is directed toward the city by Tanub and his party of scouts.

Orne learns that the Gienans are contemptuous of humans because the crew of the Delphinus was easily overpowered, despite the fact that they were larger than the five-foot Gienans. From clues scattered throughout the conversation and from Tanub's physical details, Orne deduces the hiding place of the missing ship and is able to use his greater strength--a legacy of his origins as a native of a heavy-gravity planet--to impress the Gienan chief with the desirability of bargaining with humans rather than fighting them.

This story was incorporated into THE GOD MAKERS.

In its appearance in the BACKDROP OF STARS anthology, "Missing Link" is accompanied by a foreword by Herbert in which he discusses the story's conception and details the considerations that led to inclusion of the various elements and their treatment.

† a. Astounding, February 1959.*
  b. BACKDROP OF STARS, Ed by Harry Harrison, Dobson, London, 1968.
      Also published later in the United States as SF: AUTHOR'S CHOICE, Berkley: S1567, 1968, paper.*
      A short commentary by Frank Herbert has been added.
  c. (as "De Ontbrekende Schakel") [Dutch], STERREN STRALEN OVERAL, Meulenhoff: SF 122, 1977, paper.

74. "Mud Sandwiches And Healthy Teeth"
  Non-Fiction.
  a. California Living, San Francisco Sunday Examiner, 18 August 1968.*

75. "Murder Will In"
  "Murder Will In" was written for Harlan Ellison's FIVE FATES anthology. Ellison wrote a brief prologue in which the character Bailey enters a Euthanasia Center, is without ceremony dosed with a lethal injection and finds himself strapped to a cot, expiring. Four other writers were invited to continue the story from that point, and Ellison wrote his own continuation. In addition to contributions by Ellison and Herbert, the anthology includes stories by Poul Anderson, Gordon Dickson and Keith Laumer.

  In Herbert's story, William Bailey's body is inhabited by a noncorporeal dual being, the Tegas/Bacit. This composite entity has been living symbiotically, transferring from host body to host body for perhaps thousands of years, ever since its nearly-forgotten arrival on Earth. The Bacit fraction is a storehouse of information and the guider of daily living; the infrequently-awakened Tegas part is specialized for the search for and transfer to a new host. A shift to a younger or more desirable host body necessitates the death of the currently occupied host. In the past, the Tegas has often engineered the murder of its host and transferred to the killer, since strong emotions are the hooks and holds it needs to establish control over a new host body and its resident personality.

This time, however, a dangerous mistake has been made. The Bacit has expected the Euthanasia Center to be a boil of emotions; instead it is a clinically sterile, emotionally flat place. The Tegas manages a temporary reprieve through a precarious transfer to a client more recently arrived than Bailey, but still dying; then a jump to the body of Joe Carmichael, an employee of the Euthanasia Center. The last transfer involves another degree of danger, for it must be made in the presence of Vicentelli, a keen, brutal representative of the authorities who had come to investigate William Bailey.

The Bacit, it is evident, had become "fat and lazy" in recent years, immersed in the endlessly (to the Tegas/Bacit) fascinating day-to-day pleasures of wearing the host flesh. It has neglected the climate of the society around it and has failed to observe that the culture is veering toward massive, all-pervasive control and monitoring. This monitoring has reached such a degree that the minor anomalies caused by the Tegas/Bacit's presence have drawn the attention of the culture's rulers in the person of Vicentelli, a Commissioner of Crime Prevention.

The Tegas/Bacit in Carmichael's body is taken into custody. Sophisticated restraints and android police block any further transfer attempt; the Tegas/Bacit/Carmichael is probed and tortured by Vicentelli and others of his cadre seeking the unknown something that they have traced through the Tegas/Bacit's several prior hosts. Never before has the dual being faced a direct attack upon itself rather than the host body. In this crisis the Tegas/Bacit is jolted from its long-settled patterns to new awarenesses, new avenues of thought and even a discovery about its own makeup. The egos of past hosts, rather than being extinguished as the Tegas/Bacit had supposed, have been absorbed into a normally quiescent serial ego-chain, creating an entity of unsuspected resources that may be able to deal with the current threat.

† a. Fantasy & Science Fiction, May 1970.*
b. FIVE FATES, Ed by Keith Laumer, Doubleday, Garden City, 1970.*
c. (as "Symbiose") [French], Fiction, June 1971, No 210.
d. (as "Lebe Dem Mord") [German], DER ZWISCHENBEREICH, Ed by Keith Laumer, Heyne: 3443, 1975, paper.
Translator: Yoma Cap.
e. THE PRIESTS OF PSI, Gollancz, London, 1980.*
f. EYE, Berkley: 08398, 1985, paper.*

76. "Natural Man, Natural Predator"
Non-Fiction.
Based on a conversation with Timothy O'Reilly in 1983.
a. THE MAKER OF DUNE: FRANK HERBERT, Ed by Timothy O'Reilly, Berkley: 09784, 1987, paper.*

77. "New Lifestyle To Fit A World Of Shortages"
Non-Fiction.
a. San Francisco Sunday Examiner And Chronicle, 25 March 1977.

78. "New World Or No World"
Non-Fiction.
The introduction to the various segments of the book NEW WORLD OR NO WORLD that Herbert had edited. See the annotation of that book for more information.
a. THE MAKER OF DUNE: FRANK HERBERT, Ed by Timothy O'Reilly, Berkley: 09784, 1987, paper.*

"Nightmare Blues"
See "Operation Syndrome".

79.   "The Nothing" (4,200 words)
Post-atomic-war radiation has produced widespread mutations in humanity, all of a mental nature, leading to immense changes in society. "Talents" such as telepathy, teleportation, pyrokinesis, and prescience have displaced or outmoded a wide spectrum of skills and technologies; for example, people desiring to travel simply request the aid of a teleporter and visualize their destination. Material shaping and manufacturing is handled by telekinetics. A minority of the population has no talents; these people, called "Nothings", are excluded to special reservations. On the opposite end of the scale are a few individuals who possess all the known talents to a high degree of proficiency.

    The story is narrated by Jean Carlysle, a feisty, hip-talking 18-year-old unawed by authority; her "pyro" talent is all the security and protection anyone could ask for. After an argument with her father about jobs--Jean doesn't like the available ones for her talent, such as brushburning--she goes down to the local tavern. There she encounters Claude Williams, a handsome young man with whom she strikes up a conversation. She is a bit taken aback when Claude confesses to being a Nothing and having run away from the Sonoma preserve. The two are shortly picked up by the police, and politely but firmly escorted to an audience with Mensor Williams, one of only nine people multitalented to a high degree.

    Mensor Williams is Claude's father and reveals to the couple a number of semisecret facts: changes in their society are approaching and the prescients cannot see into the future past a rapidly approaching point. There are gaps in the prescients' view of certain individuals, as well. The talents are gradually being diluted and lost; since talented individuals tend to breed toward the norm, more and more weak talents and Nothings are being born. The Nothing preserves are secretly serving as repositories for the mechanical and tool skills that supported the pre-talent civilization.

    Although Claude and Jean have known each other only a few hours, Mensor Williams announces that his prescient faculty informs him that they are going to be married--to which both object as an unpalatable predestination, despite their mutual attraction.
a.   Fantastic Universe, January 1956.
b.   THE BOOK OF FRANK HERBERT, DAW: 39, 1973, paper.*
c.   TOMORROW, AND TOMORROW, AND TOMORROW, Ed by Bonnie L Heintz, Frank Herbert, Donald A Joos and Jane McGee, Holt Rinehart Winston, 1974, paper.

80.   "Occupation Force" (1,400 words)
A huge alien spaceship has been detected in orbit around the Earth. General Henry A Llewellyn is the man in the forefront during the frantic attempts of US political leaders and military authorities to decide what measures to take following the craft's appearance. A strong faction favors immediate military engagement with nuclear weapons, but Llewellyn and a group of "expendables" are first instructed to try peaceful contact with representatives of the aliens, which include a human from Boston taken aboard their vessel. The personnel of the spacecraft turn out to be human in appearance, resembling bureaucrats more than conquerors or invaders. The ambassador from Krolia, Loo Mogasayvidiantu, nearly precipitates holocaust with mention of a

colonial program, but Llewellyn holds his hand long enough to hear the more startling truth.

a. Fantastic, August 1955.
b. The Most Thrilling Science Fiction Ever Told, December 1973.
c. THE BOOK OF FRANK HERBERT, DAW: 39, 1973, paper.*
d. Unknown Worlds of Science Fiction, May 1975, No 3.*
   Five-page graphic adaptation. Script by Gerry Conway, art by George Perez and Klaus Janson.
e. (as "Forces D'Occupation") [French], LE LIVRE D'OR DE LA SCIENCE-FICTION FRANK HERBERT, Ed by Gerard Klein, Presses Pocket: 5018, 1978, paper.*

81. "Old Rambling House" (2,500 words)
Ted Graham, a certified public accountant, and his pregnant wife Martha are tired of their rootless, traveling mode of existence and wish to settle down. They are contacted by Clint and Raimee Rush, a gypsy-like couple who speak an odd language and assert themselves to be Basque. The Rushes wish to trade their house for the Grahams' trailer. The Rushes' house turns out to be a palatial, modernist structure obviously worth many times the value of the Grahams' modest trailer; the Grahams hesitate but are overcome by greed and agree to the trade.

Too late, the Grahams discover that the "rambling" mansion is in fact a means of conveyance between worlds; the Rushes were employed as tax collectors by the ascetic, harshly puritan Rojac. Not only are the Grahams isolated from Earth but they are expected to fill the vacant posts left by the Rushes, who were conditioned not to leave their jobs untended and have found acceptable, if incompletely informed, replacements in the Earth couple.

The Rojac demand hard work and no frivolity from their employees, and in addition are constantly on the watch for new planets to add to their holdings--but Earth's location has been lost in the shuffle. However, as the Grahams face the bleak and lonely existence they have traded for, the Rushes on Earth come to the realization that they have outwitted themselves. They must sacrifice their own newfound freedom *and* reveal the whereabouts of Earth to the acquisitive Rojac to set things right according to their principles.

a. Galaxy, April 1958.*
b. (as "La Maison Vagabonde") [French], Galaxie (Old Series), July 1958, No 56.
c. THE WORLDS OF FRANK HERBERT, NEL: 2814, 1970, paper.*
d. THE PRIESTS OF PSI, Gollancz, London, 1980.*

82. "On The Tenth Of Apollo 11"
Non-Fiction.
This is a composite article; the magazine's editors asked several science fiction authors to record their observations and insights regarding the impact and aftermath of the Apollo Eleven moon landing, 10 years after the event. In addition to Frank Herbert, writers Hal Clement, Poul Anderson, Jerry Pournelle, Frederik Pohl and Clifford Simak contributed and all the essays were collected under the same title.

In contrast to most of the other writers, Herbert is not retrospective or cautious and does not refer to "reviving the space program" or the "dream" of space exploration. He regards man's ventures into space as a foregone, inevitable process already in motion, stoppable by nothing short of the destruction of Earth. The Apollo missions and the present space situation are likened to the horse-and-buggy days in the development of transportation. Herbert predicts social, political and economic changes coming hand in hand with the increased presence of and dispersal of humankind in space, along with a higher mutation rate in spacefaring humans. In brief, Herbert's predictions include political loss of control, migrations, reformation of social and governmental structures; economic changes due to cheaper available energy in space, the availability of new products and the room in space for varied types of experiments; and changes in medicine and genetics including advances in cryogenic storage.

    a.   Galileo, July 1979, No 13.*
    b.   (as "Man's Future In Space"), THE MAKER OF DUNE: FRANK HERBERT, Ed by Timothy O'Reilly, Berkley: 09784, 1987, paper.*

83.   "One Hundred Years From Today: 2068 A.D."
    Non-Fiction.
    a.   California Living, San Francisco Sunday Examiner And Chronicle, 28 July 1968.
    b.   (as "2068 A.D."), THE MAKER OF DUNE: FRANK HERBERT, Ed by Timothy O'Reilly, Berkley: 09784, 1987, paper.*

84.   "Operation Haystack" (9,200 words)
    Incorporated into THE GOD MAKERS.
    Lewis Orne #3.
Field agent Lewis Orne is brought back from his most recent assignment (on the newly rediscovered planet Heleb, where a ruling caste of women was secretly building a male slave army) in terminal shock, with massive injuries. What's left of Orne is housed in a medical crechepod, but Orne's sector chief Umbo Stetson of the Investigation and Adjustment agency and the hospital personnel on Marak hardly expect him to survive, let alone recover. Inexplicably and near-miraculously, Orne wills himself to heal and regrow and over a period of 14 months is restored to health. Orne senses that in addition to his bodily regrowth there has been a mental rebuilding and renewing; he has a vaguely mystical "twice-born" feeling.

Immediately upon his release from the hospital Orne receives a new assignment on Marak: to investigate a possible conspiracy to influence the upcoming elections. Orne's cover is that of an invalid on rest-and-recuperation leave, a house guest of the family suspected to be central to the little-understood plot--the family of Ipscott Bullone, High Commissioner and leader of Marak's majority party. This household's members have been long-time friends of Orne's own family; his own sister, whom he has not seen in years, is suspected as well. Orne reacquaints himself with Ipscott's daughter, Diana Bullone, the individual most strongly implicated by I-A's findings, and discovers himself powerfully attracted to her.

Through the analysis of patterns and details in the Bullone clan's home and lifestyle (which he finds indicative of deeply-rooted nomadic traits as well as a matriarchal tradition, even though the men of the family have been prominent and active politically), Orne discovers a conspiracy and program of subversion with its roots in the Rim Wars 500 years past. The Nathians, the losers in that shattering conflict, were able to settle refugee parties with extremely long-term goals on each of the worlds of the victorious Marakian League. These refugee parties were made up principally of women who were able to select the sex of their offspring and who have brought up their female children in the tradition of their generations-long mission of gaining control of the League. Over the years they have married for power connections and now have enough male conspiracy members in key positions to make a broader move toward domination. Orne himself is of Nathian stock (though he broke with his family's expectations before the full conspiracy was revealed to him). The situation on Heleb, where Orne was injured, had its roots in the same program of infiltration but Heleb's Nathians were isolated from their compatriots and the subversion scheme went sufficiently out of control to draw attention to itself.

Orne finds that he must reconcile his growing love for Diana and his duty of halting the conspiracy's impending sweep of the elections, without precipitating chaos when the populace discovers how its institutions have been manipulated by agents of an enemy thought long-vanquished. Orne's new mindset leads him to seek a resolution that will avoid violence or the threat of it.

This story, rewritten, was incorporated into THE GOD MAKERS.

† a.   Astounding, May 1959.*

85. "Operation Syndrome" (18,500 words)
In 1999, there is a new "20th Century Black Plague". The Scramble Syndrome is the popular name for a series of unexplained, fearful outbreaks of insanity and violence that have infected nine cities in the last month and a half.

The syndrome's effects are of interest to Seattle researcher Dr Eric Ladde. A Dr Amanti, Ladde's former teacher, had tried to build a teleprobe--a machine that could interpret encephalographic waves and allow an operator to communicate with a subject's unconscious mind. Amanti now resides in an insane asylum and Ladde, sticking with the project out of loyalty, has worked unsuccessfully on it for nearly eight years.

Ladde dreams of a singing woman in a confusing setting. the next day at breakfast by the waterfront, he is confronted by the woman from his dream: dark-skinned, piercingly blue-eyed Colleen Lanai. Ladde learns that she is a performer touring with Pete Serantis, the inventor of the musikron, a device producing music stimulated by its operator's thoughts.

Colleen is surprised to find Ladde ignorant about the musikron; it is a phenomenon in the entertainment world and Serantis, his instrument, and Lanai are in the midst of a sensational worldwide concert tour. Ladde is equally surprised to find Colleen unaware that several of the cities where she and Serantis performed have been hit by the Scramble Syndrome. Colleen excuses her ignorance by pleading the pressures of on-the-road performances and her severe chronic headaches, but she and Ladde go to speak to Serantis about this surprising circumstantial connection.

Ladde finds Pete Serantis a thin man with a twisted leg and a wry, pinched, hating face. Serantis is insanely jealous of his assistant and co-performer and reacts with impatience and hostility to Ladde's inquiries. While Serantis was building the musikron, he also worked with Carlos Amanti; evidently he visited the Professor in the asylum.

Attending the next musikron concert, Ladde realizes that his dream of Colleen was from the viewpoint of Serantis, inside the musikron apparatus. At their next meeting, though he and Colleen find themselves attracted to each other, Colleen resists believing Ladde's deductions--that the Scramble Syndrome has hit every city where she and Serantis have performed, 28 hours after their departure. The instrument appears to funnel disturbing impulses straight to the unconscious mind. From this overload, and the average person's inability to handle the resonances when their focus, the musikron, leaves on the next leg of the tour, insanity results. Colleen's headaches are in fact side-effects of Serantis' attempts to control her thoughts and actions through the musikron.

Colleen does provide Ladde with a copy of the musikron's plans. Serantis, alerted through his telepathic eavesdropping, has substituted some elements of the blueprints so that any operator of a device built with them would be mentally maimed; Ladde discovers this and confronts Serantis with no results but the airing of hostility. Shortly thereafter the musikron tour departs for London. Ladde receives a final message from Colleen that she intends to marry Serantis, but she has left Ladde a set of correct plans.

Ladde then has somewhat less than 28 hours to remodel his experimental teleprobe, using the incompletely understood musikron plans, before Seattle-Tacoma is hit by the Scramble Syndrome. Although he buys some hard-to-locate parts from Baldwin "Baldy" Platte, works frantically and takes pills to keep awake, Ladde still cannot manage to finish his new machine until four hours after the Syndrome has hit. He has sent Platte away and gambles that his training and forewarning will enable him to resist the Syndrome's effects on himself. With the functioning probe, he hopes to search for psychologically trained individuals to link into a network that may be able to calm and reorient the myriad disturbed minds.

† a.   Astounding, June 1954.*
  b.   (as "Nightmare Blues"), BEST SCIENCE FICTION STORIES AND NOVELS: 1955, Ed by T E Dikty, Fredrick Fell, New York, 1955.
  c.   THE BOOK OF FRANK HERBERT, DAW: 39, 1973, paper.*
  d.   (as "Nightmare Blues"), THE BEST OF FRANK HERBERT, Ed by Angus Wells, Sidgwick & Jackson, London, 1975.*
  e.   (as "Operation Musikron") [French], LE LIVRE D'OR DE LA SCIENCE-FICTION FRANK HERBERT, Ed by Gerard Klein, Presses Pocket: 5018, 1978, paper.*
  f.   ANALOG: WRITERS' CHOICE VOLUME II, Ed by Stanley Schmidt, The Dial Press, New York, 1984.*

86.   "Overview"
Non-Fiction.
  a.   San Francisco Sunday Examiner And Chronicle, 4 July 1976.
  b.   (as "The Sky Is Going To Fall"), Seriatim: The Journal of Ecotopia, Spring 1977, No 2.
      Slightly different version.
  c.   (as "The Sky Is Going To Fall"), THE MAKER OF DUNE: FRANK HERBERT, Ed by Timothy O'Reilly, Berkley: 09784, 1987, paper.*

87.   "Pack Rat Planet" (8,600 words)
Earth has become the repository of the Galactic Library, with nearly all its subsurface hollowed out into levels of squares 100 kilometers on a side, containing a vast wealth of records. A giant gravitronic unit in the planet's center compensates for the lost mass. Information in the library is freely and constantly available to all; tapes are continually broadcast over a huge network to all the worlds, randomly selected to ensure impartiality. Everyone who lives on Earth is employed by the library in one capacity or another. Unsympathetic factions on other worlds refer to the personnel of the Library as "Pack Rats" and regard the library world itself as a gigantic, untidy packrat's nest of useless and worthless trivia.

Library worker Vincent Coogan is recalled from an information gathering trip to confer with Library Director Caldwell Patterson. A new government of the Galactic Union has been irritated by certain items in the random library broadcasts and is sending an official censor, who will also consider whether or not to close down or destroy the library entirely. Coogan is young and vigorous, and greatly disturbed by the much older Patterson's insistence on adhering to the Library Code, which mandates that the Library must first and foremost obey all rules and directives of the government in power. Another Library worker and friend of Coogan's, Toris Sil-Chan, is preparing a faction of Library personnel for armed resistance.

The new government's hatchetman and censor is Pchak, a chillingly brutal individual who immediately kills Patterson and installs Coogan as Director. Coogan finds his attitudes and priorities altered by the new situation. While fencing with Pchak and diverting him with Library records of weapons, gladiatorial combats, and histories and methods of warfare, Coogan outrages the Sil-Chan faction by insisting on compliance with the Library Code, even to the extent of suppressing Sil-Chan's rebellion before it comes to Pchak's notice. To this end Coogan rigs a switch that, if thrown, will cancel the gravitronic compensation and send every unattached item and person on Earth drifting into space. Coogan's hope is that the new Grand Regent, Leader Adams, may be unseated before he learns of Pchak's noncompliance with his orders and before harm comes to the Library.

This story forms Part I of the book DIRECT DESCENT.

a.   Astounding, December 1954.*

88.   "Passage For Piano" (6,000 words)
The Hatchells are a Seattle family preparing for transit to an as-yet-unnamed world as colonists. Walter Hatchell is the expedition's chief ecologist, expert in the delicate balances necessary to sustain human life on an alien world; his wife Margaret is a nurse-dietician and his two children are precocious and talented. Daughter Rita is a budding entomologist and 12-year-old David is a blind (from a disease brought back from another colony world--he "sees" when needed through a bat-eye radar box) piano prodigy with growing stature on Earth.

The 300-plus colonists must pack under strict weight limitations, 75 pounds of luggage for each adult and 40 pounds for each child. Walter and Rita are not particularly attached to any material things, but Margaret feels deeply the associations and auras of old and cherished possessions with their history and traditions. David has a still more difficult and deeply rooted problem; he has a tremendous psychic investment in his 1408-pound Steinway concert grand piano, a legacy from his grandfather who was also a famed pianist. Dr Lindquist, chief psychiatrist of the expedition, thinks that on a deep level David feels his own talents to be tied to this physical inheritance and that the 21-pound electronic piano built as a substitute will not satisfy David's emotional makeup in the new world; it is possible that David will lose his talents or even die if separated from the Steinway instrument.

When the expedition's departure date is suddenly moved up, Margaret Hatchell takes the unauthorized step of contacting other colonists and asking for donations of pounds and ounces, in the hope that enough can be collected to take David's piano. She meets both with sympathy and violent rejection. The Hatchells and the other colonists are forced to weigh the value that music and culture will have for the isolated new colony and for morale's sake they and David must look for a compromise that will blend Earthly traditions with the newness and unexplored potentials of the new world.

a.   THE BOOK OF FRANK HERBERT, DAW: 39, 1973, paper.*
b.   (as "Passage Pour Piano") [French], LE LIVRE D'OR DE LA SCIENCE-FICTION FRANK HERBERT, Ed by Gerard Klein, Presses Pocket: 5018, 1978, paper.*
c.   EYE, Berkley: 08398, 1985, paper.*

89. "Peking Goose"
    Non-Fiction.
    Recipe.
    a.   COOKING OUT OF THIS WORLD, Ed by Anne McCaffrey, Ballan-
         tine: 23413 ($1.50), 1973, paper.*

90. "Plywood For Boats"
    Non-Fiction.
    Advantages of constructing boats of plywood over other methods.
    a.   The Fisherman, June 1955, Vol 6 No 6.*

91. "Poetry"
    Non-Fiction.
    a.   California Living, San Francisco Sunday Examiner And Chronicle,
         31 August 1969.
    b.   THE MAKER OF DUNE: FRANK HERBERT, Ed by Timothy
         O'Reilly, Berkley: 09784, 1987, paper.*

92. "The Priests Of Psi" (22,300 words)
    Incorporated into THE GOD MAKERS.
    Lewis Orne #4.
    Lewis Orne's imminent marriage to Diana Bullone (who he met in
    "Operation Haystack") is officially postponed by the Investigation and
    Adjustment (I-A) agency for which they both work. Orne's name has
    inexplicably appeared on the list of religious students *summoned* to
    Amel, the "priest planet"--sanctuary of all religions in the Marakian
    League and a powerful focus of psychic forces. The matter is rendered
    notable in the extreme by reason of a motion pending in the League's
    Assembly, jointly sponsored by all the sects of Amel, to do away with
    the I-A department and reassign its functions.
         Orne is reluctant but enough of a "company man" to accept the
    charge. He receives orders from his superior Umbo Stetson and psi
    training from I-A specialist Ag Emolirdo; he is also equipped with
    extensive implants of psi-detection instruments. Emolirdo pronounces
    Orne a "psi focus" and attributes Orne's series of remarkable successes
    in the I-A's service to that fact or condition.
         Arriving on Amel, Orne is disconcerted by that world's con-
    centrations of psi-fields and its warrens of mysterious, quaintly
    atmospheric religious edifices and enclaves. He is met at the spaceport
    by the priest Bakrish and his implanted equipment immediately neutral-
    ized; Ag Emolirdo has passed on information about Orne to the
    priesthood. Bakrish initiates Orne into Amel's approach to religion as a
    "science of psi" and supervises his embarkation upon a series of tests
    and ordeals, via ancient and powerful psi machines. Orne confronts
    various parts and aspects of his own psyche as well as real-seeming
    manifestations from his past; during his third ordeal he escapes a
    pursuing mob and goes in search of the sinister Halmyrach Abbod,
    Amel's chief religious figure.
         The Abbod reveals that Amel's leaders regard their world as a
    school for prophets; by applying semi-scientific techniques and ap-
    proaches to religion they hope to avoid destructive upheavals in the
    League. The Abbod draws parallels between Orne's discovery of
    unknown and undealt-with things in himself, despite the best micro-
    surgical conditioning, and the possibility that the I-A is similarly
    overlooking factors and misusing its abilities in its functions as
    peacekeeper. Orne is a potential prophet, and has been brought to Amel
    to be trained in the nature and use of his very strong latent psi

abilities. Orne returns to the restructured I-A with a new mission, this
time from the Amel priesthood.
a. Fantastic, February 1960.
b. THE PRIESTS OF PSI, Gollancz, London, 1980.*

93. "The Primatives" (10,000 words)
Working titles "Solution Primitive", "Stonecutter".
Co-plotted with Jack Vance and Poul Anderson, however written alone.
Conrad "Swimmer" Rumel is a young man from a family of professional
specialists--mathematicians, physicists, biochemists and the like. Due
largely to his rather striking physical ugliness, Swimmer has decided on
a life of crime and has specialized in his own right, in aquatic or
underwater criminal enterprise, aided by gill masks and perma-dry
business suits. Though profit is a motive, Swimmer's thefts most often
embody a bizarre sense of humor and a spirit of challenge.

His latest exploit is the sinking, in Mexico, of a Soviet propaganda ship in order to facilitate the theft of the unique, cantaloupe-
sized Mars diamond. Swimmer hopes to fence the stone through a
criminal overlord and mobster, Bime Jepson. Unfortunately, Jepson is
considerably out-of-pocket because Swimmer induced him to clandestine-
ly furnish financial backing for a prototype time machine being built by
Swimmer's uncle, professor Amino Rumel. The machine required yet
more work before becoming functional (if ever) and Swimmer hopes to
mollify Jepson with the Mars diamond.

Jepson is outraged rather than pleased. The massive diamond is
famed as being uncuttable and is unfenceable in its present highly
recognizable condition. He is persuaded from violence only by Swimmer's revelation that his uncle's time machine is now operating and has
in fact brought back a prehistoric stonecutter who may be able to
reduce the diamond.

The stonecutter is Kiunlan-Ob, a young woman but Neanderthalish
and homely by modern standards; in addition she is a sport with four
breasts. She finds Swimmer appealing; his deformities make him appear
to her like another "human", while the rest of the men around her
seem some sort of demigods. Ob's stonecutting talent is a blend of
superb intuition and a natural empathy with the stones, plus craftsman's
"tricks of the trade" which appear to the modern humans to be
inexplicable rituals.

The arrangement becomes tense when Swimmer is identified by the
authorities as the culprit in the theft. Jepson kidnaps Ob and the
professor, removing them and Swimmer to a secret island hideaway.
When it is evident that Ob can cut the diamond, Jepson attempts to
dispose of the others. Ob demonstrates unexpected and frightening
physical and psychic strengths, however, and Swimmer escapes to seek
help from the people who are hoping to arrest him. Swimmer discovers
that he has developed strong feelings for Ob; he also learns, after
surrendering to law enforcement personnel, that his caper has created
an international incident and overwhelming forces have been set in
motion. Meanwhile, back at Jepson's hideout, Ob proceeds with the
cutting of the "uncuttable" stone, to a surprising end.

Though the story has humorous overtones, especially in the initial
scenes, it is also a serious speculative look at the roles of women and
a portrayal of the modern man's contact with the Cave-Mother magic
of "primitive" matriarchal women.

The plot of the story was developed by Herbert, Poul Anderson
and Jack Vance; they had planned to co-write it as well but work
pressures did not permit and Herbert wrote it alone. (The collaborative
story would have been published under the pseudonym "Noah Ark-

wright", referring to a houseboat the three were building together on the headwaters of San Francisco Bay.)
- a. Galaxy, April 1966.*
- b. THE TENTH GALAXY READER, Ed by Frederik Pohl, Doubleday, Garden City ($4.50), 1967.*
- c. (as "Les Primitifs") [French], Galaxie (New Series), sr2, August 1975, No 135, September 1975, No 136.
    Translator: Christian Meistermann.
- d. THE BEST OF FRANK HERBERT, Ed by Angus Wells, Sidgwick & Jackson, London, 1975.*
- e. (as "Les Primitifs") [French], LE LIVRE D'OR DE LA SCIENCE-FICTION FRANK HERBERT, Ed by Gerard Klein, Presses Pocket: 5018, 1978, paper.*

94. "Project 40"
Published as HELLSTROM'S HIVE.
- † a. Galaxy, sr3, November 1972*, January 1973*, March 1973*.
- b. (as "Projet 40") [French], Galaxie (New Series), sr5, October 1974, No 125, November 1974, No 126, December 1974, No 127, January 1975, No 128, February 1975, No 129.

95. "The Prophet Of Dune" (126,500 words)
Published as last part of DUNE.
In the wake of the combined Imperial/Harkonnen strike against House Atreides, Harkonnen and Sardaukar forces are proceeding with the mop-up of Atreides survivors who, like Mentat Thufir Hawat, are stunned by the magnitude of the coup. Hawat and the remnants of his troops have encountered Fremen and witnessed that the Dune natives are more than a match for the dread Sardaukar in combat, but before anything can come of this knowledge Hawat is captured by a Sardaukar force. Warmaster Gurney Halleck has escaped, linking up with a spice smuggler, Tuek.
Jessica and Paul, in the desert fleeing the Harkonnen searchers, rendezvous with Duncan Idaho. Idaho takes them to meet with Liet-Kynes, where Paul's maturity and command win Kynes' support and trust shortly before a Sardaukar raid breaks up the conference and Idaho is killed defending their escape. Liet-Kynes is captured and killed by the Harkonnens. In an ornithopter Paul pilots Jessica and himself deeper into the southern deserts, using his newly synthesized hyper-acute Mentat/prescient awarenesses to guide them through an immense coriolis storm. They survive the ornithopter crash and a desert crossing menaced by the largest sandworms they have yet seen. Even in these straights, Jessica maintains Paul's continuing instruction in Bene Gesserit disciplines.
Paul and Jessica encounter a Fremen band led by Stilgar, right hand of Liet-Kynes. Stilgar feels bound to save only Paul but is dissuaded from "taking Jessica's water" by her forcible demonstration that Bene Gesserit training in unarmed combat can master an armed Fremen. One Fremen, Jamis, still objects to the rescue of either of the fugitives. Among the group Paul encounters Chani, the daughter of Liet-Kynes; he has seen her face in numberless prescient visions.
Stilgar wishes Jessica to instruct the Fremen in the Bene Gesserit "weirding way" of combat; Jessica finds Stilgar a wise leader of unexpected stature. Jamis, grudging the acceptance of Jessica into the tribe, challenges her through Paul as her champion; Paul kills him in single combat, the first man he has so dueled. Paul takes the Fremen name Muad'dib, the kangaroo mouse, another presciently foreseen event. However, Paul is still learning the uses, extents and necessity for

caution in reliance on his prescience and "prescient memory"--knowledge of situations foreseen in such detail that he seems already to have lived them.

Baron Harkonnen acquires Hawat from the Sardaukar and, manipulating him through false information, coerces him into Harkonnen service as a replacement for the dead Piter de Vries. Hawat is convinced that Lady Jessica was the betrayer of House Atreides, perhaps acting from obscure Bene Gesserit motives. Hawat also perceives House Harkonnen as a tool that he may use and use up against the Emperor, whose involvement he sees as having been the final factor in laying low the Atreides.

The Baron has reinstated his brutish nephew Rabban as governor of Arrakis, this time with a completely free hand to squeeze the planet and earn back the Harkonnen losses and expenditures. The Baron anticipates eventually replacing Rabban with his younger nephew Feyd-Rautha who, compared to Rabban, will be received by the populace as a deliverer.

Feyd-Rautha's ambitions have been fanned; Hawat is playing him against the old Baron as he is playing the Harkonnens in total against the Emperor. On the Harkonnen homeworld Giedi Prime, Feyd-Rautha Harkonnen kills his hundredth slave-gladiator in the arena in an unexpectedly dramatic bout planned with Hawat's assistance. The event is attended by Imperial emissaries Count and Lady Fenring; Fenring is "the Emperor's errand boy", with messages and warnings for the Baron, and his wife is a Bene Gesserit who, before they depart, secures Feyd-Rautha's genes for her Order and conditions him with hypno-ligation.

Jessica replaces the Fremen tribe's aging Reverend Mother in a ceremony involving her manipulation of her internal biochemistry to transmute the Water of Life, the poisonous liquid exhalation of a drowned small sandworm. This becomes a mind-expanding narcotic facilitating the absorption of the memory-personalities of the old Reverend Mother and all her female ancestry. Because the ritual was begun in ignorance that Jessica was pregnant, her unborn daughter, Alia, is subjected to the awakening and memory-absorption process before she possesses a proper personality of her own to contain and ameliorate them. In the sharing of the drug, Paul and Chani recognize each other as lifemates.

Paul and Jessica adapt to the Fremen ways of deep-desert survival and to the crowded Fremen sietch communities, learning such things as that Fremen exist on Dune in unguessed-at numbers in many scattered communities, and that the tribespeople are able to traverse the forbidding deserts rapidly by luring the giant sandworms to be captured and ridden. Paul and Chani have a son. Alia is now old enough to make the Fremen uneasy by her strangely precocious meld of adult comprehension and mannerisms with a child's form and emotions.

Nearly three years pass before Paul feels ready to move against the Harkonnens and Imperium. He has fulfilled one after another of the Bene Gesserit-planted prophecies and their Arrakeen offshoots regarding the coming of a messiah and liberator, and has shaped and directed Fremen harassment of the Harkonnens. The omnipresent melange in the Fremen diet has fueled Paul's prescience and his sense of himself as an instrument able and thus perhaps obligated to shape the future of Arrakis and of all humanity.

Paul's single-handed capture of a sandworm is the last test to pass to achieve full acceptance into Fremen manhood, and thus leadership. This accomplished, he was expected to call out, kill and replace the naib Stilgar. Instead Paul seizes the opportunity to demonstrate that many of the old Fremen ways must change for his new order. He puts on his father's ducal signet ring and claims Arrakis as his fief.

Atreides warmaster Gurney Halleck has turned up in a captured band of spice smugglers. Sardaukar spies discovered among the band are bested by the Fedaykin of Paul's elite guard. Halleck, still believing that Jessica was the betrayer of Duke Leto, is narrowly prevented from killing her.

Paul, disturbed by failures of his prescience (Gurney's return, and the incident with Jessica, were not foreseen) along with the sense of tumultuous events moving toward a nexus, takes the test of the Water of Life and is thrown into a weeks-long catatonia. When Chani and Jessica succeed in awakening him, he proves himself to be the Kwisatz Haderach, the product of the Bene Gesserit's genetic manipulations achieved early and escaped from them.

Paul's name Muad'dib has become known to the Harkonnens and to the Emperor as the leader of Fremen resistance. The constant drain of Fremen raids and Fremen disruption of melange production finally grow so significant that the Emperor, accompanied by all of the Great Houses with CHOAM company holdings, mounts an expedition to Arrakis to stamp out Fremen interference with the only spice source. Paul is ready to grapple with the Imperium, but is also prepared to release a biological chain reaction destroying the sandworms and spice, and thus the foundations of Imperial, Guild and CHOAM power.

In a tremendous coriolis storm Paul, Gurney and Stilgar direct the use of the Atreides family atomics to open passage through the range of hills sheltering the Imperial and Harkonnen forces, just as a garbled message from the south informs Paul of a Sardaukar raid in which his son was killed and his sister captured. Paul proceeds with his attack in the face of this bitter personal loss. The Emperor's ships are immobilized, and the allied forces overwhelmed by Fremen and sandworms attacking through the breached Shield Wall. Alia has been brought to the attention of the Emperor's truthsayer, Gaius Helen Mohiam, who urges her death as an Abomination. Before escaping in the confusion, Alia kills Baron Harkonnen.

Paul Muad'dib interviews the captured Emperor and his entourage in the old Governor's Mansion, the residence where the Atreides began their occupancy of the planet. There Thufir Hawat refuses to cooperate in a scheme to poison Paul although he is dying himself; Feyd-Rautha Harkonnen, claiming vendetta, challenges Paul to a duel and is killed by him. Count Fenring, who might have achieved the task, declines to slay Paul for the Emperor. The Guild and other power centres must bow to Paul's control of Arrakis and the spice sources. The Emperor is constrained to abdication and an "alliance" setting Paul on the throne by his marriage to the Emperor's daughter Irulan. This is only for form's sake; like Jessica with Paul's father Leto, Chani remains Paul's true wife without official seals.

"Prophet of Dune" forms the latter portion of the novel DUNE; see the annotation of "Dune World", the first section serialized, for background. "Prophet's" serialization spanned *Analog's* transition from oversized to digest-sized format, the last episode appearing in the smaller size.

a.   Analog, sr5, January 1965*, February 1965,* March 1965*, April 1965*, May 1965*.

b.   (as "Dune"), THE GREAT DUNE TRILOGY, Gollancz, London, 1979.*

96.   "Randall Garrett"
       Non-Fiction.
       This roughly one-page piece is one of a dozen or so anecdotal accounts
       by SF writers and friends of Garrett, included in the collection and
       alternating with the stories. Herbert reminisces about Garrett as a
       ribald Friar Tuck at a 1968 Creative Anachronists picnic banquet in
       Marin.
       a.   THE BEST OF RANDALL GARRETT, Ed by Robert Silverberg,
             Pocket Books: 83574 ($2.95), 1982, paper.*
             "First Timescape Books printing January, 1982 //
             10 9 8 7 6 5 4 3 2 1" on the copyright page.

97.   "Rat Race" (10,400 words)
       Welby Lewis is chief of criminal investigation under Sheriff John
       Czernak in the moderate-sized city of Banbury. The town is the picture
       of ordinariness and the Sheriff's offices are the same: high ceilings,
       stained plaster walls, cast-iron radiators, cigarette-scarred vintage
       desks. It is hard to imagine an alien presence in this setting, but at
       the Johnson-Tule mortuary, where he has routine county business, Lewis
       is puzzled by the behavior of Mr Johnson, one of the owners. Johnson
       lies to keep Lewis from going out the back door, displays ignorance of
       such institutions as the Odd Fellows and has curious metal tanks, like
       the ones used in acetylene welding, stockpiled in a back hallway.
       Sheriff Czernak trusts Lewis' hunches and Lewis and Deputy Barney
       Keeler stake out the mortuary, noting more abnormalities.
            Johnson, confronted with Lewis' findings and intention to search
       the place thoroughly, holds Lewis at gunpoint, mimics Lewis' voice
       perfectly over the phone and then shoots him. Only an anatomical
       anomaly (Lewis' heart is on the wrong side of his body) saves the
       deputy. He awakens in the hospital to learn that Johnson committed
       suicide soon afterward. The Sheriff, Keeler, janitor Joe Welch, and
       autopsy surgeon Doc Bellarmine carry on the investigation, bringing
       their findings to share with Lewis: the dead Johnson's internal anatomy
       was not human and the mortuary has hidden chambers beneath it filled
       with curious machinery. Doc Bellarmine believes that one of the
       apparatuses was used to fractionate the proteins of cadaver blood;
       another, a silver grid, is possibly a matter transmitter.
            Bellarmine and Lewis thresh out the hypothesis that the mortuary
       was a test station for alien experimenters and that humans were being
       utilized as lab animals. Doc Bellarmine, tall, knobby, gray-haired, with
       cutting blue eyes, is especially concerned about what the reactions of
       the aliens might be now; what would human scientists do if their
       experimental animals attacked a lab worker? Bellarmine vanishes and
       the others suppose that he must have departed via the matter-trans-
       mitter to contact the alien scientists. A possibly symbolic clue to his
       fate, and that of humans in general, is found in return transit in the
       basement lab.
       a.   Astounding, July 1955.*
       b.   THE BOOK OF FRANK HERBERT, DAW: 39, 1973, paper.*
       c.   EYE, Berkley: 08398, 1985, paper.*

98.   "The Road To Dune"
       Non-Fiction.
       This piece is a sampling of excerpts from the (fictional) official
       Imperium guide for a pilgrim's walking tour visiting Arrakeen and the
       holy shrines of the religion which sprang up around Paul Muad'dib and
       was broadcast throughout the galaxy by his jihad. Included are portraits
       of various personages of Muad'dib's time and commentary on points of

interest, as well as on landmarks such as the Grand Palace and the Temple of St. Alia. (The guidebook appears to date to during, or shortly after, the time of CHILDREN OF DUNE.)

Eight black-and-white illustrations by Jim Burns (who also provided single illustrations for the rest of the stories in the collection EYE) are matched with around four pages of descriptive captions by Herbert.

  a.   EYE, Berkley: 08398, 1985, paper.*

99. "Sandworms Of Dune"
Sound Recording.
Herbert discusses the myth construction and mythological resonances that went into Dune's sandworms and their places, both ecological and symbological, in the novels. Their position (among other things) as guardians of treasure and of higher consciousness, both contained in the melange spice, are noted, as well as the prices to human adventurers of achieving higher states of consciousness and new awareness.

The readings on this recording consist of excerpts from DUNE, DUNE MESSIAH and CHILDREN OF DUNE, united by additional, connective text written especially for the record.

† a.   Caedmon: 1565, New York, 1978.*
Notes by Frank Herbert on liner. Episodes from the novels DUNE, CHILDREN OF DUNE and DUNE MESSIAH read by Frank Herbert and connected with new material. Record (TC-1565); duration 41 minutes, 10 seconds. Cover by John Schoenherr.

100. "Sandworms Of Dune"
Non-Fiction.
The liner notes from the recording "Sandworms Of Dune".
  a.   THE MAKER OF DUNE: FRANK HERBERT, Ed by Timothy O'Reilly, Berkley: 09784, 1987, paper.*

101. "The Santaroga Barrier"
Published as THE SANTAROGA BARRIER.
† a.   Amazing, sr3, October 1967*, December 1967, February 1968*.

102. "Science Fiction And A World In Crisis"
Non-Fiction.
Herbert opens this long (28 pages) essay by talking about the "straw man" crises set up to be solved in SF stories and their occasional interfacings with real life. This leads into a look at the novels 1984 and BRAVE NEW WORLD and their influences on our world since their writing. In contradiction to the general feeling that the dangers and grim scenarios featured in those works have been averted by the attention focused on the novels, Herbert points to numerous unremarked developments and trends in technology, and social and business institutions, whose practices and philosophies seem to be evolving as predicted in the two books. Examples are the increased freedoms in certain areas--safety valve, "soma" sorts of activities through which pacification functions as means of social control--such as sexual permissivity, television and drugs. These compensate for increased societal demands and restrictions in fields such as careers, social positions and all-around conforming behavior expected of the individual. Morality tends to function to maintain social stability and the "status quo".

Herbert sees dangers in the way our Western system believes in absolutes and refuses toleration, let alone perception of, the validities of other systems. Such linear social systems "create the conditions of crisis by failing to deal with change", and exacerbate many situations with attempts at control rather than at adaptation, most often one-point controls that will greatly aggravate future situations. Herbert uses as one example the heroin traffic and how the attendant crime and corruption of officials involved in the drug's international movement might be reduced by changes in the control methodology and the attitudes regarding it. Other examples of "one-point-control" mindsets at work are low-cost housing and a Pakistani malaria control program.

In a system that values stability and order above the change necessary for adaptation, too much individuality is perceived as a danger to the system. Herbert looks at the possible perceived threat of too much creativity (for example the "oddball-ism" typified by much SF writing) in a society such as ours that seems to be trying to avoid crises through increasingly more pervasive and sophisticated control and orchestration of all its members and processes, contrasted to the value of SF in indicating other avenues open to us by dealing with potential crises for story's sake.

Herbert discusses the "comfort in homogeneity" typical of Middle America and the control-oriented mindset's aggravation of problems through its stasis, using his novel THE SANTAROGA BARRIER as an example. Also touched on are the "programming" effects of any language system and its underlying assumptions and attitudes, which set limits on our perceptions of the universe. Herbert notes that a majority of utopian future scenarios seem to begin with a disaster that kills off 90% of humanity, from which something decent can be rebuilt. The avoidance of such a drastic happenstance lies not in planning to circumvent it, but in developing definitions of reality and assumptions of goals and needs that are applicable on a world-wide or a species-wide basis.

a.   SCIENCE FICTION, TODAY AND TOMORROW, Ed by Reginald Bretnor, Harper & Row, New York ($8.95), 1974.*
b.   THE MAKER OF DUNE: FRANK HERBERT, Ed by Timothy O'Reilly, Berkley: 09784, 1987, paper.*

103.   "Science Fiction And You"
Non-Fiction.
Introduction.
a.   TOMORROW, AND TOMORROW, AND TOMORROW, Ed by Bonnie L Heintz, Frank Herbert, Donald A Joos and Jane McGee, Holt Rinehart Winston, 1974, paper.

104.   "Seed Stock"
Working title "Follow The Falcons".
On a world with a purple ocean and an orange sun larger than Sol, a new colony is not flourishing. The world has no native land animals, only primitive sea creatures and some vegetation, but earthly trans-plants will not take but only die or grow scrawny and sickly. The colonists are hampered by the wasting "body burdens" imposed by the new world's differences from Earth's environments. Five years after their landing they are still living hand-to-mouth, most of their high-tech equipment exhausted or debilitated and their technology forced downscale by the unexpected difficulties of living on the still-unnamed world. Wood-burning steam engines provide most of their power; the colonists live in quonset huts built from the pieces of the spaceship that brought them.

The colony's organization has fallen into nearly feudal lines: a directing class of scientists, a technician cadre and a labor pool of workers who are practically peasants. The approach of the scientist directors of the colony has been basically antagonistic, directed at terraforming the world and establishing pure strains of Earthly plants and animals. Their stock consists of a few scrawny cattle and pigs. Insects, fish and plants distributed by the terraformers vanish or experience strange debilitations and attrition. The scientists cultivate the offspring of the most normal-looking, which suffer losses in their turn. Released gamebirds, songbirds and chickens have all died; only Terran falcons seem to be subsisting. They are never seen to eat, but periodically fly out to offshore islands and return. The colony does not have enough resources to study them adequately.

Kroudar is one of the labor pool "peasants", a scrawny individual whose stringy muscled frame, crooked nose and melon chin have earned him the nickname "Old Ugly". Kroudar's wife is Honida, a graceful Amerind woman with plaited hair and a genetics technician who chose Kroudar for a spouse rather than a member of her own class or even the scientific echelons from which she might have picked. Kroudar is slow and steady, not quick-witted but with a deep-seated empathetic "feel" for the new world and its systems, rhythms and cycles. He himself is unable to articulate what he senses, but sometimes Honida is able to act as a bridge, relaying Kroudar's hunches and intuitions upwards to the scientist ranks in a form acceptable to them. It was Kroudar who discovered the colony's chief food resource, the shrimplike *trodi*. (Even these must be processed to remove irritants, and the fishing boats often come in empty-handed, frustrated by the colonists' lack of understanding of the *trodis'* migrations and swarmings.)

The scientists are concerned with proving their methods right; Kroudar is concerned only with adapting and surviving by whatever means necessary, by attuning himself to the rhythms of the new world. Honida, in secret, has been experimenting along lines opposite to those pursued by the colony's leaders; she is following Kroudar's feeling that the warped, sickly, altered plants and animals may in fact be the ones adapting to the world, and the ones whose offspring will have the best chance of eventually flourishing. If Honida can produce a more viable strain of corn, the *trodi* boats can be freed to pursue Kroudar's long-standing urge to follow the falcons out to the sea islands and discover their food source.

† a.   Analog, April 1970.*
  b.   THE BOOK OF FRANK HERBERT, DAW: 39, 1973, paper.*
  c.   THE BEST OF FRANK HERBERT, Ed by Angus Wells, Sidgwick & Jackson, London, 1975.*
  d.   NIGHTMARE GARDEN, Ed by Vic Ghidalia, Manor: 12411, 1976, paper.
  e.   (as "Semence") [French], LE LIVRE D'OR DE LA SCIENCE-FICTION FRANK HERBERT, Ed by Gerard Klein, Presses Pocket: 5018, 1978, paper.*
  f.   Masterpieces Of Science Fiction, Ariel, May 1978.
  g.   EYE, Berkley: 08398, 1985, paper.*

105.   "Ships"
Non-Fiction.
An article written around 1968-1969.
  a.   THE MAKER OF DUNE: FRANK HERBERT, Ed by Timothy O'Reilly, Berkley: 09784, 1987, paper.*

106. "The Single Most Important Piece Of Advice"
     Non-Fiction.
     Herbert was one of the judges for the 1985 Writers of the Future
     Contest, from which the stories in this volume were selected. This
     brief (roughly 1-1/2 pages) piece was dictated by phone to Algis
     Budrys, the book's editor, shortly before Herbert's death. Herbert
     advises beginning writers to concentrate on story and gripping narrative
     quality and, when they have attained sufficient stature, to counsel and
     assist still newer writers.
     a.   L. RON HUBBARD PRESENTS WRITERS OF THE FUTURE II, Ed
          by Algis Budrys, Bridge Publications ($3.95), 1986, paper.*

"The Sky Is Going to Fall"
     See "Overview".

107. "The Small Worlds of UC Santa Cruz"
     Non-Fiction.
     The campus and innovations at the University of California, Santa
     Cruz.
     a.   California Living, San Francisco Sunday Examiner And Chronicle,
          22 September 1968.*

108. "Songs of A Sentient Flute"
     This story came about through Herbert's involvement with a 1975
     UCLA Extension course on science fiction, a series of evening
     presentations entitled "Ten Tuesdays Down A Rabbit Hole" conceptual-
     ized and hosted by Harlan Ellison. The April 15 "lecture" was a
     seminar in world-building and story germination. The specifics of a
     planet, Medea (planetary system, mass and gravity, weather, ecology,
     life forms, etc,) had previously been developed by Hal clement, Poul
     Anderson, Larry Niven and Frederic Pohl. These specs were assembled
     in booklet form and Kelly Freas executed a painting of the planet's
     surface, its major satellites and its inhabitants, which was on display.
     At a dinner prior to the seminar, and during the class itself, Thomas
     Disch, Frank Herbert, Robert Silverberg and Theodore Sturgeon
     brainstormed and plotted, with feedback from the audience, the stories
     that they would write about Medea.
          The book that resulted, after a 10-year hiatus (MEDEA: HAR-
     LAN'S WORLD), contains the original specs for Medea, a transcript of
     the "Concept Seminar" and "Extrapolation and Questions" (from the
     audience) featuring the above-listed panel, as well as a section for
     "Second Thoughts" from the authors involved (to which Herbert did not
     contribute), and the stories themselves, by Jack Williamson and Kate
     Wilhelm, as well as the spec-writers and seminar participants. Some of
     the stories, including "Songs", appeared in other places prior to
     publication in the Medea book.
          Frank Herbert set his Medea story into the continuity of his
     "Ship"series. Ship, the voidship Earthling transformed into a godlike
     entity at the conclusion of DESTINATION: VOID, is determined or
     compelled to induce its human charges to discover the proper form of
     WorShip--the manner of conduct that will constitute the most correct
     veneration of Ship. Ship's various essays in this direction have
     continued over an immense span of time and on many worlds in
     succession, in conditions ranging from paradisiacal to crisis-riven. In
     the current situation, Ship has gathered a selection of people from past
     experiments and transported them to Medea, which they are instructed
     to colonize.

Medea is a world of crisis, racked with storms, its twin suns sputtering with ultraviolet flares, and its menacing flora and fauna encompassing swarms of swift and deadly predators. Medea is a beautiful world as well. Its forbidding, vital landscapes--kelp-covered oceans and rocky continents--are tinted a blend of the sun colors: red, purple, silver, amber and orange.

Periodically the ocean's vast kelp beds bloom with thousands of brilliantly colored globes, airborne medusae filled with hydrogen, whose mass suicidal attacks on the colony have resulted in fire, death and mayhem. Attempts at study of the creatures from sensor-equipped floater nests carried by balloons have resulted in further loss of life, with little data collected. The medusae "sing", in a fluting, whistling set of tones that the colonists cannot positively identify as communication. There are much larger, evidently older medusae, but these are extremely quick and wary of investigation.

Nikki, 18 years old and specially coached by Ship since he was 12, is sent groundside to participate in the investigation of the medusae. He is not scientifically trained, but a poet. Ship's disciplines have hopefully instilled in him a oneness of body and mind and taught him to function on a strongly intuitive level. He is assigned to Tam Kapule, a woman twice his age and, like Nikki, of Polynesian genelines. Tam has nearly albino coloration resulting from her particular bodily reaction to Medea's conditions. Despite a latent rapport, Tam is made uneasy by Nikki's quick nonconformist insights and reactions, and Nikki senses confusion and discomfiture in Tam regarding both her work and himself.

Their superior on the medusae-study project is Tom Root, a cell surgeon, biochemist and meteorologist. Root is a wiry, weathered, middle-aged man with a harsh, penetrating manner and enormous reservoirs of confidence and energy. Nikki finds Root strangely familiar and vaguely repellent, as well as antagonizing; Root's lack of reverence for Ship leaves Nikki shocked and dismayed.

Nikki finds the colonists to have heightened reflexes and a greater intensity of being, compared to the humans still Shipboard. The colonists are hugely interested in Ship's purposes and influences, with Root in particular questioning the motives and goals of their deity/director. Briefings and debriefings of the medusae research team are fencing games; both Root and Tam are disturbed that Ship's direction to Nikki to join their team is a statement that logical approaches to the situation have failed. On the first foray of the new team, the trio witnesses a spectacular bloom of gasbags in a rocky-cliffed bay; the medusae appear to be thrown into a maelstrom of panic by the floater's presence. The "songs" and psychic emanations of the medusae induce an empathetic panic and disorientation in Nikki.

On their second mission, friction and hostility between Nikki and Root have approached dangerous levels; Nikki's impending comprehension of the medusae situation seems to turn in part on his achieving understanding of Root's inability to sense--or rejection of--the "magical spirit" that Tam and Nikki have touched in the globes' songs. The bloom of medusae occurs as a massive storm breaks; it appears that Root intends to crash the floater and once again be the lone survivor.

This story in MEDEA: HARLAN'S WORLD lacks a short explanatory preface which headed the magazine version, and may have other minor differences as well.

"Songs of a Sentient Flute" seems to take place before THE JESUS INCIDENT in the "Ship" chronology, although the explanatory foreword to the story (in the magazine version) is an excerpt from the

"Histories" of Kerro Panille, a character in THE JESUS INCIDENT. "Sentient Flute" is virtually THE JESUS INCIDENT in an alternate, miniature version, the novel treating the themes and settings on a larger scale and with a larger and more complex cast of characters (several of whom are equivalents to the characters of "Sentient Flute").

    a.   Analog, February 1979.*
    b.   MEDEA: HARLAN'S WORLD, Ed by Harlan Ellison, Phantasia Press, Huntington Woods (Michigan), 1985.*

109. **"The Sparks Have Flown"**
Non-Fiction.
Previously unpublished interviews by Willis McNelly in 1968 and by Timothy O'Reilly in approximately 1977.

    a.   THE MAKER OF DUNE: FRANK HERBERT, Ed by Timothy O'Reilly, Berkley: 09784, 1987, paper.*

110. **"Sukiyaki"**
Non-Fiction.
Recipe.

    a.   COOKING OUT OF THIS WORLD, Ed by Anne McCaffrey, Ballantine: 23413 ($1.50), 1973, paper.*

111. **"Survival Of The Cunning"** (2,000 words)
Working title "Victory Is Cold".
Herbert's first published story under his own name.
Mujik is an Eskimo guide accompanying Sergeant Kovacs on a mission to search out a Japanese weather and radio station near the Alaskan coast during World War II. Mujik knows little of and is not unduly interested in the war and broad questions of politics; he is more concerned with the fact that his traplines are being neglected and the sled dogs have gone unfed too long as the Sergeant pushes on in the face of a roaring blizzard. Stolid, practical and unemotional, Mujik considers disposing of the Sergeant and finding shelter to wait out the storm.

Before Mujik. has become too exasperated with Kovacs, the Japanese infiltrators' cabin is located; the wind and blowing snow make it impossible to see tracks around it. Inside a fire is burning and one Japanese soldier, dead of frostbite gangrene, lies in a bunk. Mujik and the Sergeant are surprised by a second Japanese returning from outside, who covers them with a machine pistol. The soldier announces his intention to take them prisoner and deliver them to a submarine that will be bringing replacements and supplies to the weather station. Before marching them to the cove where the sub is to appear, he warms himself by the fire. Outside the blizzard has given way to chill calm and the dogs and sled are buried by the new snow.

Once outside, after a brief interval has elapsed, Mujik attacks their Japanese captor with his knife, seemingly heedless of the machine pistol. Kovacs had supposed them to be well and truly caught, but the more weather-wise and practically experienced Eskimo knew that the gun, warmed by the cabin's moist atmosphere, would freeze up and be useless in the bitter open air.

    a.   Esquire, March 1945.*

112. **"The Tactful Saboteur"** (11,300 words)
The Bureau of Sabotage (BuSab) is an agency created to moderate a most unusual situation. For a period of time far in mankind's future, after the human race has colonized the stars and formed a Con-

sentiency with other intelligent races, red tape and government inefficiency were totally eliminated. The workings of government speeded up to a bewildering pitch; laws were passed, decisions made and resources assigned to one use or another at a juggernaut pace totally outrunning the public's ability to keep informed of government's doings and to moderate governmental actions through feedback. BuSab came into being as a safeguard of human rights, to act as the natural "predator" on government in place of the previous inefficiency. Its agents act to slow down and ridicule the various governing departments and agencies, never allowing them to become efficient enough to be overpowerful or secure enough to become pompously entrenched. The typical BuSab gambit is a daring, rather lighthearted and fanciful escapade that renders its victim ridiculous-looking but has much more serious and considered underlying purposes. Only a few governmental departments are protected from the antics of BuSab. A number are sanctioned against sabotage in certain degrees or at particular times; only the Bureau of Sabotage itself is *never* immune.

The BuSab agent is a highly trained, highly skilled and quick-witted individual, able to perceive and use to his advantage the self-imposed limitations of individuals and of whole species. Jorj X McKie is one of the Bureau's top agents, a squat and ugly little man with a mane of red hair whose bulk and features give him a gnomish or "grandfather toad" appearance. McKie deeply mistrusts power and those occupied in the exercising of it, extending his mistrust to his own department and himself. McKie has been trained for his position from a very early age when he first showed troublemaking tendencies; his energies were channeled through classes such as Applied Destruction and Advanced Irritation.

McKie appears to be furthering his own career by sabotaging the Secretary of Sabotage, pugnacious Clinton Watt (McKie, using an alien device, triggers the growth of a wriggling rainbow mass of tendrils on Watt's head); he is certainly in the line of succession once Watt is officially declared too bizarre-looking to function. But McKie has also engineered this exploit as the kickoff of an investigation into the Tax Watchers organization, about which both he and Watt are concerned. A Pan-Spechi BuSab agent, Bildoon, has vanished while on the same task. The Tax Watchers have been granted at least temporary immunity from the saboteurs and may be massing political clout to pose a threat to the Bureau of Sabotage itself.

On yet a deeper level, McKie's investigation is of the Pan-Spechi race, a five-gendered species whose creches of five individuals pass a single ego between them. Humans and Pan-Spechi have interacted within the Consentiency for years, but without any deep understanding of each other; relations of the two races are rendered sensitive and dangerous by each's ignorance of the more intimate and significant motivations and attitudes of the other.

McKie's conversation with Pan-Spechi Panthor Bolin is construed as attempted sabotage when Bolin is revealed to be the head of the Tax Watchers. The affair is played to its conclusion in a courtroom drama, with McKie defending himself in Magistrate Edwin Dooley's court. McKie is able to direct the proceedings into the touchy area of human/Pan-Spechi relations and to strive for real understanding between the races by the risky expedient of probing and exposing some of the more personal and private Pan-Spechi behaviors and rituals in the public forum, thereby risking his death at the hands of the morally outraged aliens.

†a.   Galaxy, October 1964.*

b.   SEVEN TRIPS THROUGH TIME AND SPACE, Ed   by   Groff
Conklin, Gold Medal: R 1924, 1968, paper.*
c.   THE WORLDS OF FRANK HERBERT, NEL: 2814, 1970, paper.*
d.   EYE, Berkley: 08938, 1985, paper.*

113. **"Test Tube Bay"**
Non-Fiction.
The ocean laboratory at Tomales Bay and the research there.
a.   California Living, San Francisco Sunday Examiner And Chronicle,
18 August 1968.

114. **"The Tillers"**
Non-Fiction.
Film.
A documentary film about land reform and agricultural development. It
was produced, directed, written and filmed by Frank Herbert. It was
filmed in Pakistan, Vietnam and Indonesia in June, July and August
1972. A few minutes of this film was incorporated into the widely
shown film "The Hungry Planet" by Keith Blume (1976).
a.   King Television, Channel 5, Seattle (Washington), 1972.
b.   PBS, Channel 9, Seattle (Washington), late 1972 or 1973.

115. **"The Tillers"**
Non-Fiction.
The script for the film "The Tillers".
a.   THE MAKER OF DUNE: FRANK HERBERT, Ed by Timothy
O'Reilly, Berkley: 09784, 1987, paper.*

116. **"Transcript: Mercury Program"**
In the year 2383, the human community encompasses numerous systems
and planets, but the premier media event of the year still takes place
in the Solar System. This is the annual Mercury-based "solar feeding",
originally begun as an aesthetic program to clean up space junk
scattered about the inner system. It has grown into a monumental
"experimental astrophysics" event in which millions of tons of heavy
nucleon residues and various detritus are packaged in dumpster craft
and piloted into incipient solar-flare spots on the sun's surface. The
resulting   spectacular   and   long-lived   coronal   displays--arches,
prominences and burning clouds--are the focus of both scientific
scrutiny and intense popular interest.
     The broadcast of this year's event is hosted by entertainment
personalities Murray Murray and Carol Bosier, providing somewhat
hype-laden commentary and background (including the historic role of
astronomer Pander Oulson, the originator of the project). (Much of the
story is presented in the form of transcripts of this broadcast.) At the
same time the current solar-feeding project head Ludmilla Santiana,
aging and fatally ill, has stolen a space tug and is accompanying the
feeding dumpsters into the sun, transmitting her final observations and
musings to a recording satellite.
     The volume THE PLANETS includes, for each major body of the
Solar System, a nonfiction "Essay" (often by a scientific authority) and
one or more "Speculations" (i.e. fiction) by an SF author, plus
illustrations by SF and futurist artists.
a.   THE PLANETS, Ed by Byron Preiss, Bantam Spectra: 05109, New
York ($24.95), 1985.*
Bound in a three-piece case with black paper front and rear
boards and with black cloth on the spine. Silver lettering on the
spine. No date on the title page. "A Bantam Book/December 1985"

on the copyright page. Also at the bottom of the copyright page is "WAK 0 p 8 7 6 5 4 3 2 1".

117. **"The Truths Of Dune 'Fear Is The Mind Killer'"**
Sound Recording.
Herbert talks about libraries and the stages of opening worlds in his own interest in books and reading, progression from wonder and enjoyment to stimulation and challenge and eventually to his own contributions to libraries.   The continuties of libraries, literary traditions and books are presented as the shaping influences on the excerpts from "the books of Dune" quoted in the novels and their changing tone and varied nature over the course of the series.   The writings of Dune include quotes and sayings from the majority of the major characters, also reflecting the different perspectives and attitudes of scholars and of individuals removed at various distances from the times and places, and sometimes the historical epochs of, the original events.
　　　The readings on this recording consist of excerpts from DUNE, DUNE MESSIAH AND CHILDREN OF DUNE, united by additional, connective text written especially for the record.
† a.　Caedmon: 1616, New York, 1979.*
　　　Record (TC-1616) or cassette (CDL-51616).   Read by Frank Herbert. Liner notes by Frank Herbert. Duration 45 minutes, 1 second. Cover by John Schoenherr.

118. **"Try to Remember!"** (14,400 words)
Working titles "Spiel Down", "Remember! Remember! Remember!".
The human race has been presented with a problem and an ultimatum by the alien Galactics. Every major government of Earth has received a copy of a statement, flawlessly phrased in its own language, to the effect that the people of Earth are set a task: they are to assemble their most gifted experts in communication and discover or develop a way to communicate with the Galactics' emissaries. Success will bring rewards; failure will result in the obliteration of the human race. The Galactics have given ample demonstration of their power to make good on all promises, including clearing Earth's sky of satellites and the disintegration of an uninhabited atoll.
　　　The aliens' huge paramecium-like spacecraft has landed in the desert country of eastern Oregon.   In the surrounding alkali flats a complex of hasty structures housing 30,000 people shares space with jackrabbits, tumbleweeds and omnipresent dust and grit.   Linguists, anthropologists, psychologists and experts of every shade from every nation are billeted in pre-fab buildings and tents.   Inevitably, the encampment is also well staffed with political and military personnel, and with spies and counter-spies. Along with the Galactic vessel, the camp is a target for terrorists, saboteurs and crackpots.
　　　The Galactic emissaries number only five.   They are of human stature, squat but graceful, broad-faced, built like powerfully muscled frog-men clad in black leotards.   Each day, from behind a forcefield barrier, one of the five presents a "lecture" in their own tongue--a fluid, fluting speech delivered with a broad array of ritualized motions, a swaying, undulating body, and many facial grimaces. The lectures can run up to 12 hours and are filmed and taped for exhaustive study by the human experts.
　　　The scientists of many countries have been formed into teams looking for correspondences with various Earthly language groups. American Francine Millar is assigned to the Indo-European Germanic-root team. Francine is middle-aged but alert, trim and wiry. She is

dealing with two levels of problem because the arrival of the Galactic ship came shortly after the death of her linguistics-genius husband in an airplane crash. Francine is battling her feelings of grief and displacement as well as struggling with the seemingly insoluble riddle of Galactic speech. She has been participating in brainstorming sessions with members of other national and linguistic groups, including Hikonojo Ohashi, a Japanese psychologist with a Princeton accent, and Zakheim, a burly, bearlike, uncouth and expansive Russian; these sessions are disapproved of but tolerated by the leaders of the various national delegations.

Most of the groups are headed by unimaginative administrators and military personnel, such as the USA's Dr. Langsmith, an organizer and politician with more drive than genius, and General Speidel. The officially sanctioned approaches preclude many spontaneous or unconventional tangents which Francine and Hiko Ohashi would like to try; the focus is instead on computer analysis and attempted understanding of the Galactics' fluid tongue by cataloging parts of speech and phonemes.

In their brainstorming sessions Francine and Ohashi have been trying a novel approach, the correlation of the Galactics' gestures and poses with those of dancers from primitive Earthly cultures. Francine is frustrated by Langsmith's opposition to the use of time and energy in this manner and by the military's certainty that the Galactics must surely be lying about the reasons for their presence. Her researches are hampered by the atmosphere of tension, paranoia, international intrigue and power politics.

Summoned to a secret conference of highly placed civilian and military leaders, Francine is presented with some unpalatable facts. These officials believe that the Galactics are not truly speaking any sort of language in their lectures, that the aliens were responsible for a spate of deaths of prominent linguists and thinkers--including Francine's husband--shortly before their appearance, and that the Galactics are the forerunners of an invasion force bent on colonization and cultural imperialism. The Russians are known to be plotting an attempt to seize the Galactic vessel; Speidel and Langsmith want Francine to aid them in smuggling a bomb aboard the ship to preempt the Russian strike. Francine discovers that her perceptions have altered and that the mens' true, underlying thoughts and meanings are obvious despite their practiced efforts at manipulation and intimidation.

Francine's personal crises, the arrival of a Galactic courier boat, and the impending elapse of the deadline and military moves against the aliens make Francine yet more intent on the problem at hand. She is more aware than ever of the ways in which every language conveys the worldviews and mental sets of its speakers and directs thought down premeditated channels through its lacks, assumptions and "givens"; there are hints of a unique feature setting the Galactic tongue apart from all human dialects. She is convinced that the modern concepts of language several times removed from the origins of human communication, must be set aside and that the human investigators must dig deeper and "remember" the earliest origins of language in basic emotions and in the genetic legacy from their primitive ancestors.

† a.   Amazing, October 1961.*
  b.   THE BEST OF AMAZING, Ed by Joseph Ross, Doubleday, Garden City, 1967.
  c.   THE PRIESTS OF PSI, Gollancz, London, 1980.*
  d.   EYE, Berkley: 08398, 1985, paper.*

119. **"Under Pressure"** (73,500 words)
Published as THE DRAGON IN THE SEA.
  † a.   Astounding, sr3, November 1955*, December 1955*, January 1956*.
    b.   (as "The Dragon In The Sea"), Excerpt, THE BEST OF FRANK HERBERT, Ed by Angus Wells, Sidgwick & Jackson, London, 1975.*
    c.   (as "Dragon In The Sea"), Excerpt, Eye, Berkley: 08398, 1985, paper.*

120. **"Underseas Riches For Everybody"**
Non-Fiction.
This 4,400-word article was originally sold to Colliers. However, Colliers ceased publication with its 4 January 1957 issue. This article was scheduled for the next issue. Timothy O'Reilly finally had it published in 1987.
    a.   THE MAKER OF DUNE: FRANK HERBERT, Ed by Timothy O'Reilly, Berkley: 09784, 1987, paper.*

121. **Untitled**
Non-Fiction.
A short foreword.
In a half-page frontispiece note, Herbert gives THE DUNE ENCYCLO-PEDIA his seal of approval and expresses delight at the range and depth of the topics covered, while reserving final word on certain issues of the Dune milieu, elucidated in the book or not, to himself.
    a.   THE DUNE ENCYCLOPEDIA, Compiled by Dr Willis E McNelly, Putnam, New York ($19.95), 1984.*
    A trade paperback was published simultaneously (Berkley: 06813 ($9.95)).

122. **Untitled**
(with Bonnie L Heintz, Donald A Joos and Jane McGee)
Non-Fiction.
Preface.
    a.   TOMORROW, AND TOMORROW, AND TOMORROW, Ed by Bonnie L Heintz, Frank Herbert, Donald A Joos, and Jane McGee, Holt Rinehart Winston, 1974, paper.

123. **"We're Losing The Smog War"**
Non-Fiction.
First part of a two-part article on the effects of smog and the small efforts being done to control it. The second part is "Lying To Ourselves About Air".
    a.   California Living, San Francisco Sunday Examiner And Chronicle, 1 December 1968.*
    b.   THE MAKER OF DUNE: FRANK HERBERT, Ed by Timothy O'Reilly, Berkley: 09784, 1987, paper.*

124. **"Whipping Star"**
Published as WHIPPING STAR.
  ††a.   If, sr4, January 1970*, February 1970*, March 1970*, April 1970*.

125. **"The White Plague"**
    a.   Excerpt, Omni, July/August 1986.

126. **"The White Plague"**
Sound Recording.

    a.   Listen For Pleasure: LFP 7168-7, Ontario (Canada), 1986.*
        Two Cassettes. About three hours duration. An abridgement of
        the novel read by Bradford Dillman.

127. **"Who Owns The Bay?"**
    Non-Fiction.
    A small amount of the San Francisco Bay is owned by private citizens.
    a.   California Living, San Francisco Sunday Examiner And Chronicle,
        19 January 1969.*

128. **"Without Me You're Nothing"**
    (with Max Barnard)
    Non-Fiction.
    a.   Excerpt, Computers 82, Vol 1 No 3, October 1981.*

129. **"Yellow Fire"**
    Two prospectors have been panning for gold in Alaska's remote
    Kenibuthet country: the tall, shaggy Frenchman Batiste and the little
    round Dutchman Hans Keller. Relations between the men have de-
    teriorated during their long stay in the wilderness; Batiste intends to
    kill Keller, both for the gold--four heavy pouches of dust--and
    because Keller's wife Lilah, waiting for him at one of the landings
    closer to civilization, is capping a series of unfaithfulnesses with a
    promise to Batiste. Keller is also ill, with bad lungs from a brush with
    the intense cold two winters past.
        Batiste is holding his hand because it will take two men to carry
    their food, gear and gold out to the river cache and canoe that will
    convey them south before winter grips the land too severely. In the
    meantime their conversations have become no more than a sly fencing.
    Batiste suffers Keller's companionship, wondering each day how much
    he suspects or knows, and feels goaded beyond endurance by the
    Dutchman's placid manner with its flashes of cunning.
        Eventually they break their streamside camp and head south,
    their way taking them through a wasteland of mire-rimmed hummocks,
    stunted tamaracks and a sun hanging low in the sky like a faint fog-
    ringed ball. A day from their goal Batiste kills Keller, and with his
    load lightened to the minimum races across the last stretch of swamp
    and tundra to the river in the season's first blizzard with 10-or-20-
    below-zero temperatures. But Keller, though unable to prevent his
    death at Batiste's hands, has played a trick that will ensure that
    Batiste does not survive to enjoy his gold and his unfaithful wife.
        Long afterward, via circuitous routes from Indians through the
    factors at several trading posts, the story of the inexplicable cir-
    cumstances of Batiste's death is related (in a brief preface to the
    story itself): a man found frozen to death, with no fire, in the midst
    of timber and plenty of firewood and even with waterproof matches in
    his pack.
    a.   Alaska Life, June 1947.*

130. **"You Can Go Home Again"**
    Non-Fiction.
    a.   California Living, San Francisco Sunday Examiner And Chronicle,
        29 March 1970.
    b.   THE MAKER OF DUNE: FRANK HERBERT, Ed by Timothy
        O'Reilly, Berkley: 09784, 1987, paper.*

131. **"You Take The High Road"** (5,500 words)
Incorporated into THE GOD MAKERS.
Lewis Orne #1.
Galactic civilization is rebuilding after a devastating series of Rim Wars 500 years in the past. Planets cut off in the turmoil are still being rediscovered. Two government departments are involved: R&R (the Rediscovery and Re-education Service) tries to integrate newly rediscovered worlds into the rebuilt interstellar community by giving them technological assistance and guidance; I-A (Investigation and Adjustment) guards against any repetition of the Rim War conflagration by scouting the new discoveries for any signs of militarism or belligerency, which are suppressed or rerouted immediately by overwhelming might. A rediscovered world that is too dangerous might be sterilized completely, rather than risking a re-ignition of galactic-scale conflict. The two bureaus exist in an uneasy cooperation, since each has somewhat the same field of operation and a good deal of opportunity to complicate matters for the other.
Lewis Orne's first field case as an investigative agent of the R&R is Chargon, an evidently peaceful, pastoral world inhabited by an almost over-serious people. The communities are scattered wooden towns built around cobblestone market squares; the populace dresses in medieval-type, archaic folk costumes; the landscapes are idyllic, with wood smoke from outlying homes rising over green forests.
Nevertheless, Orne pushes the "panic button" that will summon the I-A. Various clues and circumstances on Chargon unsettle him, from a practical joke played on him to a general feeling that the natives are hiding something. The planet was given a clean bill by the R&R first-contact man preceding Orne, but Orne suspects that the previous agent's unsubtle questions about military forces and fighting may have alerted the world's authorities. In the meantime, Chargon has been quickly taking to re-education and gearing up for industrialization and input of technology from the galactic league.
The I-A investigator who arrives in response to Orne's summons is Umbo Stetson; unfortunately, Orne's suspicions and hunches are not easily demonstrable and Stetson's air of haughty superciliousness does nothing to alleviate Orne's feelings of inexperience and insecurity. Orne and Stetson take an inspection tour while discussing the situation, examining Chargon's walled ridgetop roads, spyglass-carrying hunters and farmers pulling two-wheeled carts full of produce. Under Stetson's needling Orne is still unable to put his finger on the precise reasons for his disquiet; he is startled by Stetson's abrupt confirmation of his findings and announcement that Orne is going to be drafted into the I-A.
This story, rewritten slightly, was incorporated into THE GOD MAKERS.
a.   Astounding, May 1958*.

"2068 A.D."
See "One Hundred Years From Today: 2068 A.D.".

There was a story "Lawn Party" published in Atlantic, June 1954 by "Frank Herbert". However, an examination of that story, and the author biography included, shows that it was by a different author, although his name is indeed Frank Herbert.
Frank Herbert's first published work was a western, published under a pseudonym and sold in 1937 to a Street & Smith pulp. Although only the first story is certain, there is some reason to believe that there were more,

all under a pseudonym. They may have been written into the 1960's. Unfortunately, no further information is available to the compiler.

Frank Herbert has also ghost-written speeches for Mark Hatfield and S I Hayakawa.

Frank Herbert's book reviews, many in the San Francisco Examiner, have not been included.

At the least, Frank Herbert wrote articles for the Santa Rosa Press Democrat, The Seattle Post-Intelligencer, and the San Francisco Examiner. Twenty-one articles from the San Francisco Examiner and a book based on articles from the Santa Rosa Press Democrat are included here. However, the citation of most of Herbert's newspaper articles probably remains for the next bibliographer.

Manuscript Collection

A Frank Herbert manuscript collection exists at the University of California, Fullerton in the Special Collections Section. The collection consists of both published and unpublished manuscripts, some letters and miscellaneous documents and a small number of published books. Although a detailed description of the collection did not seem appropriate, it was thought that a brief description indicating the scope of the collection should be presented.

PUBLISHED MATERIAL

Novels

1. DESTINATION: VOID--Correspondence, outline, working notes, three drafts, setting copy, page proof.
2. THE DRAGON IN THE SEA--Correspondence, working notes, manuscript.
3. DUNE--Correspondence, working papers (extensive), parts of various drafts, page proof.
4. DUNE MESSIAH--Working notes, two drafts.
5. THE EYES OF HEISENBERG--Correspondence, working papers, manuscript, setting copy.
6. THE GREEN BRAIN--Correspondence, synopses, working notes, setting copy.
7. THE HEAVEN MAKERS--Correspondence, working notes, three drafts.
8. THE SANTAROGA BARRIER--Correspondence, outline, working notes.
9. WHIPPING STAR--Working notes, two drafts.

Shorter Works

All of the following have one or more manuscripts, most have correspondence and some have working notes.

1. "A-W-F Unlimited"
2. "Accidental Ferosslk"
3. "The Being Machine"
4. "By The Book"
5. "Cease Fire"
6. "Committee Of The Whole"
7. "Direct Descent"
8. "Egg And Ashes"
9. "Encounter In A Lonely Place"
10. "Escape Felicity"
11. "The Featherbedders"
12. "The GM Effect"
13. "Gambling Device"
14. "The Gone Dogs"
15. "Looking For Something?"
16. "The Mary Celeste Move"
17. "Mating Call"
18. "A Matter Of Traces"
19. "Mindfield"
20. "Missing Link"
21. "Murder Will In"
22. "The Nothing"
23. "Occupation Force"
24. "Old Rambling House"

25. "Operation Haystack"
26. "Operation Syndrome"
27. "Pack Rat Planet"
28. "Passage For Piano"
29. "Plywood For Boats"
30. "The Priests Of Psi"
31. "The Primatives"
32. "Rat Race"
33. "Seed Stock"
34. "Survival Of The Cunning"
35. "Try To Remember!"
36. "Yellow Fire"
37. "You Take The High Road"

UNPUBLISHED MANUSCRIPTS

Novels

1. "Angels Fall" (Part of this was used in THE GREEN BRAIN)
2. "A Game Of Authors" (160 pages)
3. "High-Opp" (183 pages)

Shorter Works

It is probable that some of these were published as articles in the San Francisco Examiner.

1. "Ashby" (Article)
2. "The Cage" (13 pages)
3. "Columbia" (Article)
4. "The Illegitimate Stage" (12,000 words)
5. "In This Corner...The Challenger, California Wine" (Article)
6. "Iron Maiden" (Farce, 5,000 words)
7. "Little Window" (Suspense, 12,500 words)
8. "Oregon" (Article)
9. "The Pinata That Talked" (Juvenile, illustrated by Howard Hansen)
10. "Skindive" (Article)
11. "Slug-Ross" (Article)
12. "So Many Years" (Very short story)
13. "Survival Is Their Business" (Article)
14. "They Stopped The Moving Sands" (Article)
15. "A Thorn In The Bush" (Straight fiction)
16. "US Of California" (Article)
17. "The Waters Of Kan-e" (18 pages)
18. "Weekender" (Article)
19. "What Did He Really Mean By That?" (40 pages, Jorj X McKie story) (This may be "The Tactful Saboteur".)
20. "The Wrong Cat" (Very short story)
21. "Yanko" (Article)
22. "The Year That Was" (Article)
23. "The Yellow Coat" (Straight Fiction, 4,636 words)

Series and Connected Stories

Dune:
  "Dune World"
  "The Prophet Of Dune"
  DUNE
  "Dune Messiah"
  DUNE MESSIAH
  "Children Of Dune"
  CHILDREN OF DUNE
  GOD EMPEROR OF DUNE
  HERETICS OF DUNE
  CHAPTER HOUSE DUNE

Earth Week:
  "Don't Buy Death!!!"
  "NEW WORLD OR NO WORLD

Fables And Fairy Tales Of The Future:
  "Frogs And Scientists"
  "Feathered Pigs"

Jorj X McKie:
  "A Matter Of Traces"
  "The Tactful Saboteur"
  WHIPPING STAR
  "The ConSentiency--And How It Got That Way"
  THE DOSADI EXPERIMENT

Lewis Orne:
  "You Take The High Road"
  "Missing Link"
  "Operation Haystack"
  "The Priests Of Psi"
  THE GOD MAKERS

Ship Series:
  "Do I Wake Or Dream?"
  DESTINATION: VOID
  "Songs Of A Sentient Flute"
  THE JESUS INCIDENT
  THE LAZARUS EFFECT

Unnamed:
  "Carthage: Reflections Of A Martian"
  THE HEAVEN MAKERS

Pseudonyms

F.P.H.

"Haiku" (October 1960)
"Haiku" (November 1960)
"Haiku" (November 1960)
"Haiku" (November 1960)
"Haiku" (December 1960)

In 1937, at the age of 17, Frank Herbert sold his first story. It was a western, sold to a Street & Smith pulp, and it was published under a pseudonym. There is some reason to believe that there were others, under the same or other pseudonyms, written possibly as late as the 1960's. Unfortunately, no further information is available.

Collaborations

With Max Barnard
  "First Word"
  "Without Me You're Nothing"
  WITHOUT ME YOU'RE NOTHING

With F M Busby
  "Come To The Party"

With Bonnie L Heintz, Donald A Joos, and Jane McGee
  Untitled (TOMORROW, AND TOMORROW, AND TOMORROW)

With Brian Herbert
  MAN OF TWO WORLDS

With Bill Ransom
  THE JESUS INCIDENT
  THE LAZARUS EFFECT

Chronological Order of Publication of Frank Herbert's Work

1937
Western in a Street & Smith pulp
(Details unknown)

1945
"Survival Of The Cunning"

1946
"The Jonah And The Jap"

1947
"Yellow Fire"

1952
"Looking For Something?"
SURVIVAL AND THE ATOM

1954
"Operation Syndrome"
"The Gone Dogs"
"Pack Rat Planet"

1955
"Plywood For Boats"
"Rat Race"
"Occupation Force"
"Under Pressure"

1956
"The Nothing"
THE DRAGON IN THE SEA

1958
"Cease Fire"
"Old Rambling House"
"You Take The High Road"
"A Matter Of Traces"

1959
"Missing Link"
"Operation Haystack"

1960
"The Priests Of Psi"
"Egg And Ashes"
"Haiku" (October)
"Haiku" (November)
"Haiku" (November)
"Haiku" (November)
"Haiku" (December)

1961
"A-W-F Unlimited"
"Mating Call"
"Try To Remember!"

1962
"Mindfield!"

1963
"Chinatown: A Changing World"
"Flying Saucers--Fact Or
Farce?"
"Dune World"

1964
"The Mary Celeste Move"
"The Tactful Saboteur"

1965
"The Prophet Of Dune"
"Greenslaves"
"Committee Of The Whole"
"The GM Effect"
"Do I Wake Or Dream?"
DUNE

1966
"The Primatives"
"Escape Felicity"
"Heisenberg's Eyes"
"By The Book"
DESTINATION: VOID
THE EYES OF HEISENBERG
THE GREEN BRAIN

1967
"The Heaven Makers"
"The Featherbedders"
"The Santaroga Barrier"
"The Gift of Time"

1968
"Bullit"
"A First Look At Our Galaxy"
"One Hundred Years From Today:
2068 A.D."
"Adventures In Movement"
"Mud Sandwiches And Healthy
Teeth"
"Test Tube Bay"
"Knighthood Re-Flowers In
Medieval Marin"
"The Small Worlds Of UC Santa
Cruz"
"Is Your English Well Bread?
Don't Be Mizled"
"Market Day, Mexico's Vanishing
Bargain Game"
"Fancy Feathers"
"We're Losing The Smog War"
"Lying To Ourselves About Air"

1968 (continued)
THE HEAVEN MAKERS
THE SANTAROGA BARRIER

1969
"Who Owns The Bay?"
"Dune Messiah"
"The Mind Bomb"
"Poetry"
DUNE MESSIAH

1970
"Whipping Star"
"You Can Go Home Again"
"Seed Stock"
"Murder Will In"
"Don't Buy Death!!!"
WHIPPING STAR
NEW WORLD OR NO WORLD
(Edited)
THE WORLDS OF FRANK
HERBERT (Collection)

1971
Carthage: Reflections Of A
Martian"

1972
"Project 40"
"The Tillers" (Film)
THE GOD MAKERS
SOUL CATCHER

1973
"Beef In Oyster Sauce"
"Death Of A City"
"Encounter In A Lonely Place"
"Gambling Device"
"Introduction" (SAVING WORLDS)
"Passage For Piano"
"Peking Goose"
"Sukiyaki"
"Introduction: Tomorrow's
Alternatives?"
"Listening To The Left Hand"
THE BOOK OF FRANK HERBERT
(Collection)
HELLSTROM'S HIVE
THRESHOLD: THE BLUE ANGELS
EXPERIENCE

1974
Untitled (TOMORROW, AND
TOMORROW, AND TOMORROW)
"Science Fiction And A World In
Crisis"
"Science Fiction And You"
"The Godmakers"

1974 (continued)
TOMORROW, AND TOMORROW,
AND TOMORROW (Edited)

1975
"Men On Other Planets"
"Introduction" (THE BEST OF
FRANK HERBERT)
THE BEST OF FRANK HERBERT
(Collection)

1976
"Children of Dune"
"The Future of Ecotopia"
"Overview"
CHILDREN OF DUNE

1977
"New Lifestyle To Fit A World of
Shortages"
"The ConSentiency--And How It
Got That Way"
"The Dosadi Experiment"
"Dune: The   Banquet   Scene"
(Sound Recording)
THE DOSADI EXPERIMENT

1978
"Come To The Party"
"Sandworms Of Dune (Sound
Recording)
LE LIVRE D'OR DE LA
SCIENCE-FICTION FRANK
HERBERT (Collection)

1979
"Songs Of A Sentient Flue"
"On The Tenth Of Apollo 11"
"Frogs and Scientists"
"Feathered Pigs"
"The   Battles   of   Dune"   (Sound
Recording)
"The Truths of Dune 'Fear Is
The   Mind   Killer'"   (Sound
Recording)
THE GREAT DUNE TRILOGY
(Collection)
THE JESUS INCIDENT

1980
"First Word"
"Dune Genesis"
THE PRIESTS OF PSI (Collection)
DIRECT DESCENT

1981
"Introduction" (NEBULA WINNERS
FIFTEEN)

1981 (continued)
"Introduction" (THE BEST OF
THOMAS N SCORTIA)
"Without Me You're Nothing"
NEBULA WINNERS FIFTEEN
(Edited)
GOD EMPEROR OF DUNE
WITHOUT ME YOU'RE NOTHING

1982
"Randall Garrett"
"God Emperor Of Dune" (Sound
Recording)
THE WHITE PLAGUE

1983
THE LAZARUS EFFECT

1984
"Heretics Of Dune"
"Heretics Of Dune" (Sound
Recording)
Untitled (THE DUNE
ENCYCLOPEDIA)
HERETICS OF DUNE

1985
"Introduction" (EYE)
"The Road To Dune"
"The Concept Seminar"
"Transcript: Mercury Program"
CHAPTER HOUSE DUNE
EYE (Collection)

1986
"The Single Most Important Piece
Of Advice"
"The White Plague"
"The White Plague" (Sound
Recording)
MAN OF TWO WORLDS

1987
"The Campbell Correspondence"
"Conversations In Port Townsend"
"Country Boy"
"Dangers Of The Superhero"
"Natural Man, Natural Predator"
"New World Or No World"
"Sandworms Of Dune"
"Ships"
"The Sparks Have Flown"
"The Tillers"
"Undersea Riches For Everybody"
THE MAKER OF DUNE: FRANK
HERBERT (Non-Fiction
Collection)

Forthcoming
"Accidental Ferrosslk"

Fiction Checklist

"A-W-F Unlimited"
"Accidental Ferrosslk"
"The Battles Of Dune" (Sound Recording)
THE BEST OF FRANK HERBERT (Collection)
THE BOOK OF FRANK HERBERT (Collection)
"By The Book"
"Cease Fire"
CHAPTER HOUSE DUNE
"Children Of Dune"
CHILDREN OF DUNE
"Come To The Party"
"Committee Of The Whole"
"Death Of A City"
DESTINATION: VOID
DIRECT DESCENT
"Do I Wake Or Dream?"
"The Dosadi Experiment"
THE DOSADI EXPERIMENT
THE DRAGON IN THE SEA
DUNE
"Dune: The Banquet Scene" (Sound Recording)
"Dune Messiah"
DUNE MESSIAH
"Dune World"
"Egg And Ashes"
"Encounter In A Lonely Place"
"Escape Felicity"
EYE (Collection)
THE EYES OF HEISENBERG
"The Featherbedders"
"The Feathered Pigs"
"Frogs And Scientists"
"The GM Effect"
"Gambling Device"
"God Emperor Of Dune" (Sound Recording)
GOD EMPEROR OF DUNE
"The God Makers"
THE GOD MAKERS
"The Gone Dogs"
THE GREAT DUNE TRILOGY (Collection)
THE GREEN BRAIN
"Greenslaves"
"The Heaven Makers"
THE HEAVEN MAKERS
HELLSTROM'S HIVE
"Heisenberg's Eyes"
"Heretics Of Dune"
"Heretics Of Dune" (Sound Recording)
HERETICS OF DUNE
THE JESUS INCIDENT
"The Jonah And The Jap"
THE LAZARUS EFFECT
LE LIVRE D'OR DE LA SCIENCE-FICTION FRANK HERBERT (Collection)
"Looking For Something?"
MAN OF TWO WORLDS
"The Mary Celeste Move"

"Mating Call"
"A Matter Of Traces"
"The Mind Bomb"
"Mindfield!"
"Missing Link"
"Murder Will In"
"The Nothing"
"Occupation Force"
"Old Rambling House"
"Operation Haystack"
"Operation Syndrome"
"Pack Rat Planet"
"Passage For Piano"
"The Priests of Psi"
THE PRIESTS OF PSI (Collection)
"The Primatives"
"Project 40"
"The Prophet Of Dune"
"Rat Race"
"Sandworms of Dune" (Sound Recording)
"The Santaroga Barrier"
THE SANTAROGA BARRIER
"Seed Stock"
"Songs Of A Sentient Flute"
SOUL CATCHER
"Survival Of The Cunning"
"The Tactful Saboteur"
"Transcript: Mercury Program"
"Truths of Dune 'Fear Is The Mind Killer'" (Sound Recording)
"Try To Remember!"
"Under Pressure"
"Whipping Star"
WHIPPING STAR
"The White Plague"
"The White Plague" (Sound Recording)
THE WHITE PLAGUE
THE WORLDS OF FRANK HERBERT (Collection)
"Yellow Fire"
"You Take The High Road"

Non-Fiction Checklist

"Adventures In Movement"
"Beef In Oyster Sauce" (Recipe)
"Bullit"
"The Campbell Correspondence"
"Chinatown: A Changing World"
"The Concept Seminar"
"The ConSentiency--And How It Got That Way"
"Conversations In Port Townsend"
"Country Boy"
"Dangers Of The Superhero"
"Don't Buy Death!!!!"
"Dune Genesis"
"Fancy Feathers"
"A First Look At Our Galaxy"
"First Word"
"Flying Saucers--Fact Or Farce?"
"The Gift Of Time"
"Introduction" (THE BEST OF FRANK HERBERT)
"Introduction" (THE BEST OF THOMAS N SCORTIA)
"Introduction" (EYE)
"Introduction" (NEBULA WINNERS FIFTEEN)
"Introduction" (SAVING WORLDS)
"Introduction: Tomorrow's Alternatives?"
"Is Your English Well Bread? Don't Be Mizled"
"Knighthood Re-Flowers In Medieval Marin"
"Listening To The Left Hand"
"Lying To Ourselves About Air"
THE MAKER OF DUNE: FRANK HERBERT (Collection)
"Market Day, Mexico's Vanishing Bargain Game"
"Men On Other Planets"
"Mud Sandwiches And Healthy Teeth"
"Natural Man, Natural Predator"
"New Lifestyle To Fit A World Of Shortages"
"New World Or No World"
"On The Tenth Of Apollo 11"
"One Hundred Years From Today: 2068 A.D."
"Overview"
"Peking Goose" (Recipe)
"Plywood For Boats"
"Poetry"
"Randall Garrett"
"The Road To Dune"
"Sandworms Of Dune"
"Science Fiction And A World In Crisis"
"Science Fiction And You"
"Ships"
"The Single Most Important Piece Of Advice"
"The Small Worlds Of UC Santa Cruz"
"The Sparks Have Flown"
"Sukiyaki" (Recipe)
SURVIVAL AND THE ATOM
"Test Tube Bay"
THRESHOLD: THE BLUE ANGELS EXPERIENCE
"The Tillers" (Film)
"The Tillers"
"Undersea Riches For Everybody"

Untitled (THE DUNE ENCYCLOPEDIA)
Untitled (TOMORROW, AND TOMORROW, AND TOMORROW)
"We're Losing The Smog War"
"Who Owns The Bay?"
"Without Me You're Nothing"
WITHOUT ME YOU'RE NOTHING
"You Can Go Home Again"

Verse Checklist

"Carthage: Reflections Of A Martian"
"Haiku" (October 1960)
"Haiku" (November 1960)
"Haiku" (November 1960)
"Haiku" (November 1960)
"Haiku" (December 1960)

Other Media Checklist

FILMS
DUNE (Film version in 1984)
"The Tillers"

SOUND RECORDINGS
"The Battles Of Dune"
"Dune: The Banquet Scene"
"God Emperor Of Dune"
"Heretics Of Dune"
"Sandworms of Dune"
"The Truths Of Dune 'Fear Is The Mind Killer'"
"White Plague"

Magazine Checklist

Magazines that have material by Frank Herbert are listed in this section. The term magazine is used somewhat loosely to include periodicals of all kinds, including newspapers, but not quite loosely enough to include yearly compilations. The number in parentheses following each issue is the number of the work as given in the NON-BOOK APPEARANCES section of this bibliography.

Alaska Life
June 1947 (129).

Amazing
Nov 1954 (43); Oct 1961 (118): March 1962 (72); March 1965 (44); Aug 1966 (43); April 1967 (50); June 1967 (50); Oct 1967 (101); Dec 1967 (101); Feb 1968 (101).

Amazing (British)--Third Series
Vol 1 No 8, Jan 1955 (43).

Astounding/Analog
June 1954 (85); Dec 1954 (87); July 1955 (97); Nov 1955 (119); Dec 1955 (119); Jan 1956 (119); Jan 1958 (10); May 1958 (131); Feb 1959 (73); May 1959 (84); Dec 1963 (27); Jan 1964 (27); Feb 1964 (27); Oct 1964 (67); Jan 1965 (95); Feb 1965 (95); March 1965 (95); April 1965 (95); May 1965 (95); June 1965 (38); June 1966 (30); Aug 1966 (7); Aug 1967 (32); April 1970 (104); Jan 1976 (11); Feb 1976 (11); March 1976 (11); April 1976 (11); Dec 1978 (13); Feb 1979 (108).

Computer 82
Oct 1981, Vol 1 No 3 (128).

Destinies
Aug-Sept 1979 (37); Oct-Dec 1979 (33).

Doc Savage
April 1946 (61).

Esquire
March 1945 (111).

Fantastic
Aug 1955 (80); Feb 1960 (92).

Fantastic Universe
Jan 1956 (79); Nov 1958 (69).

Fantasy & Science Fiction
May 1970 (75).

Fiction (French)
June 1971, No 210 (75).

The Fisherman
June 1955, Vol 6 No 6 (90).

Galaxie (French)
Old Series: July 1958, No 56 (81).

New Series: Jan 1971, No 80 (71); March 1973, No 106 (1); Oct 1974, No 125 (94); Nov 1974, No 126 (94); Dec 1974, No 127 (94); Jan 1975, No 128 (94); Feb 1975, No 129 (94); Aug 1975, No 135 (93); Sept 1975, No 136 (93).

Galaxy
April 1958 (81); June 1961 (1); Oct 1961 (68); Oct 1964 (112); April 1965 (14); Aug 1965 (21); April 1966 (93); June 1966 (51); Aug 1966 (51); July 1969 (26); Aug 1969 (26); Sept 1969 (26); Oct 1969 (26); Nov 1969 (26); Nov 1972 (94); Jan 1973 (94); March 1973 (94); May 1977 (16, 23); June 1977 (23); July 1977 (23); Aug 1977 (23).

Galaxy (Italian)
Dec 1962, No 55 (1); April 1963, No 59 (68).

Galileo
July 1979, No 13 (83).

Harpers
Dec 1973 (63).

If
Nov 1960 (28); Oct 1969 (71); Jan 1970 (124); Feb 1970 (124); March 1970 (124); April 1970 (124).

The Most Thrilling Science Fiction Ever Told
Aug 1972 (44); Dec 1973 (80).

Omni
April 1980 (35); July 1980 (25); March 1984 (52); July/Aug 1986 (125).

San Francisco Examiner And Chronicle
Examiner: 6 Feb 1963 (12) (Wed).
People: 20 Oct 1963 (36) (Sun).
California Living: 10 Dec 1967 (40); 2 June 1968 (6); 14 July 1968 (34); 28 July 1968 (83); 11 Aug 1968 (3); 18 Aug 1968 (74, 113); 8 Sept 1968 (62); 22 Sept 1968 (107); 20 Oct 1968 (60); 3 Nov 1968 (66); 10 Nov 1968 (31); 1 Dec 1968 (123); 8 Dec 1968 (65); 19 Jan 1969 (127); 31 Aug 1969 (91); 29 March 1970 (130); 4 July 1976 (86); 25 March 1977 (77).

San Francisco Star
29 Oct 1960, No 4 (45); 9 Nov-2 Dec 1960, No 5 (46, 47, 48); 1-15 Dec, No 6 (49).

Science Fiction Greats
Spring 1971 (44).

Science Fiction Monthly (British)
Vol 1 No 2, 1974 (42).

Science Fiction Yearbook
No 4, 1970 (64).

Seriatim: Journal Of Ecotopia
Spring 1977, No 2 (86).

Startling Stories
April 1952 (64).

Startling Stories (British)
No 16, Jan 1954 (64).

The Stranger
June 1970(?), No 9 (22).

Unknown Worlds Of Science Fiction
May 1975, No 3 (81).

Urania (Italian)
Sept 1965, No 400 (14).

Works about Frank Herbert

This section is merely intended to list some representative works about Frank Herbert for the interested reader. It is not intended to be a complete secondary bibliography.

1. CLIFFS NOTES ON HERBERT'S DUNE & OTHER WORKS, David Allen, Cliffs Notes, $1.50, 1975, paper.*
    Contains biographical notes and background on Herbert and individual discussions of Herbert's novels up to HELLSTROM'S HIVE (1973) (except for THE HEAVEN MAKERS and SOUL CATCHER, which are not discussed). There is a long section on "The Unity and Continuity of DUNE and DUNE MESSIAH" (CHILDREN OF DUNE had not yet appeared). This work discusses THE GOD MAKERS at considerably more length than other critical works on Herbert, finding it a more single-focused exploration of some of the major themes of DUNE. It also pays the most individual attention to Herbert's short fiction, though only to the stories anthologized in THE BOOK OF FRANK HERBERT and THE WORLDS OF FRANK HERBERT.

2. "*Dune*--An Unfinished Tetralogy", Robert C Parkinson, Extrapolation, Dec 1971, No 13.

3. THE DUNE ENCYCLOPEDIA, Compiled by Dr Willis E McNelly, Putnam, New York ($19.95), 1984.*
    This is the work of McNelly and more than 40 other contributors, presented as an assemblage of the records unearthed in God Emperor Leto II's secret no-room repository, as ordered and with commentary by scholars and historians of the following era. Entries relate to the DUNE series through GOD EMPEROR (with gaps in regard to that book since Leto II was moved by whim as much as anything else in his selection of data to be preserved and particularly did not preserve a great deal concerning himself).
    The entries range from informational to scholastically dry to myth, folktale and convincingly presented historical misconceptions (an interesting look, using the DUNE books, at how events may be interpreted, reinterpreted, distorted or dismissed with the passage of time). As well as being a careful compilation of facts from Herbert's novels, the volume contains considerable extrapolation and outright invention. The book has Herbert's stamp of approval but nothing in it can be taken as binding on future works nor even as absolutely definitive regarding the first four books. It is probably best viewed not so much as a guide or a concordance but as a rather monumental work of associational fiction in its own right.

4. FRANK HERBERT, David M Miller, Starmont House, 1980, paper.*
    Starmont Reader's Guide 5.
    Concentrates on Herbert's novels, discussing each individually (including all the science fiction novels and SOUL CATCHER) up to THE JESUS INCIDENT (1979), the most recent work dealt with. There is little attention to Herbert's short fiction, although the stories collected in THE BOOK OF FRANK HERBERT and THE WORLDS OF FRANK HERBERT are en masse allotted a couple of pages of commentary. Includes annotated primary and secondary bibliographies.

5. FRANK HERBERT, Timothy O'Reilly, Frederick Ungar, New York, 1981.*
    The most in-depth and comprehensive critical/evaluative work on Herbert. O'Reilly's approach is to look at the development of Herbert's major themes and philosophical concepts and the variations and evolutions in their treatment, discussing individual books and

stories where they become pertinent. (Many of the short stories discussed are ones not covered in other reviews of Herbert's short fiction.) All Herbert's novels through THE JESUS INCIDENT (1979) receive attention, with perhaps a quarter of the book devoted to the DUNE trilogy. This book was prepared with the cooperation and input of Herbert, and O'Reilly was able to draw on unpublished materials and correspondence as well as background from Herbert's family and friends.

6. "From Concept To Fable: The Evolution Of Frank Herbert's *Dune"*, Timothy O'Reilly, CRITICAL ENCOUNTERS, Ed by Dick Riley, Frederick Ungar, New York, 1978.

7. "Future Grok", R Z Sheppard, Time, 29 March 1971.

8. "Idea And Imagery In Herbert's *Dune"*, J Ower, Extrapolation, May 1974, No 15.

9. "Is Jaspers Beer Good For You? Mass Society And Counter Culture In Herbert's *Santaroga Barrier"*, L E Stover, Extrapolation, May 1976, No 17.

10. "Science Fiction As Mythology", Thomas C Sutton and Marilyn Sutton, Western Folklore, Oct 1969, No 28.

11. "The Societal Quest", Steven E Kagle, Extrapolation, May 1971, No 12.

Appendix: Illustrations of Covers

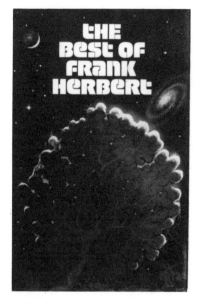

B 1. a.

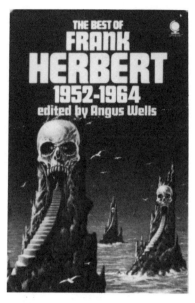

B 1. b.

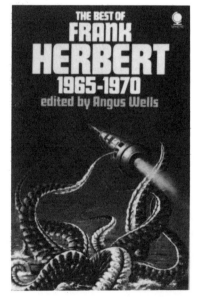

B 1. c.

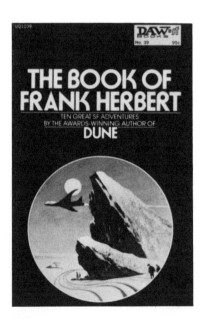

B 2. a.

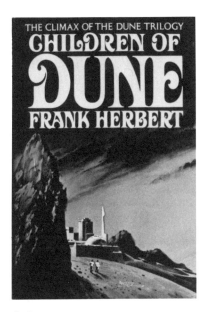

B 4. a.

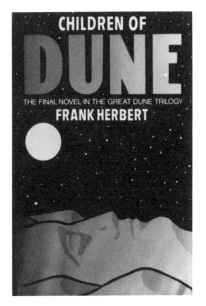

B 4. c.

B 4. e.

B 5. a.

B 5. h.

B 5. j.

B 7. a.

B 7. e.

B 8. a.

B 8. j.

B 9. a.

B 9. a

B 9. s.

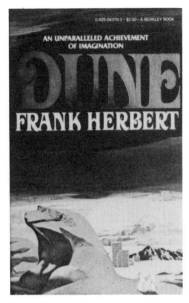

B 9. ac.

B 9. ad.

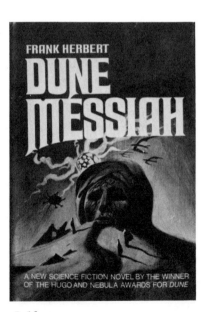

B 10. a.

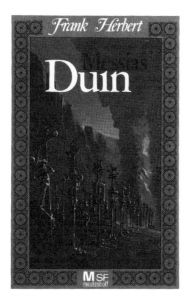

B 10. m.

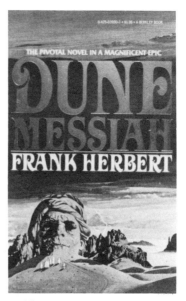

B 10. q.

B 12. a.

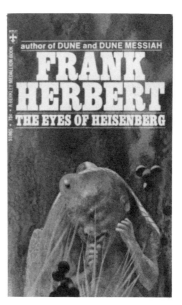

B 12. e.

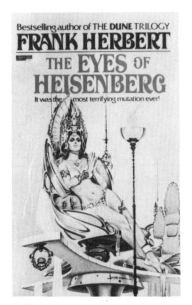

B 12. o.

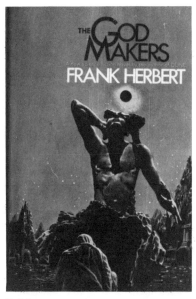

B 14. a.

B 14. c.

B 14. l.

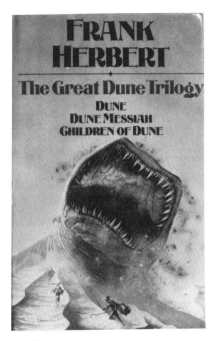

B 15. a

B 16. a.

B 16. i

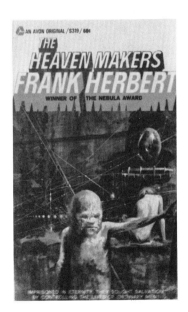

B 17. a.

B 17. f.

B 18. a.

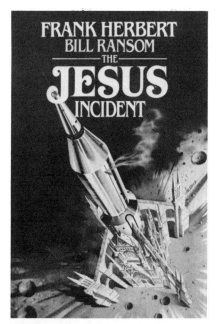

B 20. a.

B 26. a.

B 26. c.

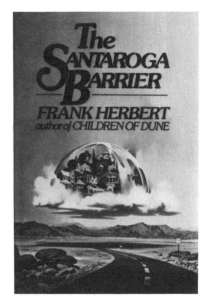

B 26. i.

B 27. a.

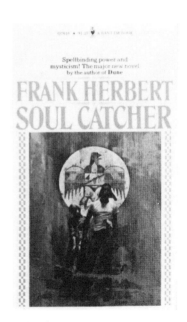

B 27. b.

B 27. f.

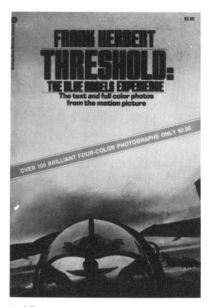

B 29. a.

B 30. a.

B 30. k.

B 30. n.

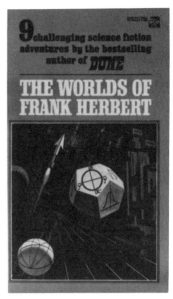

B 33. b.

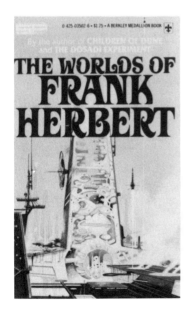

B 33. h.

NBA 1. a.

NBA 4. a.

NBA 13. a.

NBA 14. a.

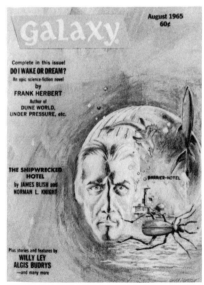

NBA 21. a.

NBA 23. a.

NBA 23. a.

NBA 24. a.

NBA 38. a.

NBA 43. a.

NBA 43. c.

NBA 44. a.

NBA 50. a.

NBA 51. a.

NBA 64. a.

NBA 68. a.

NBA 69. a.

NBA 71. a.

NBA 72. a.

NBA 73. a.

NBA 75. a.

NBA 84. a.

NBA 85. a.

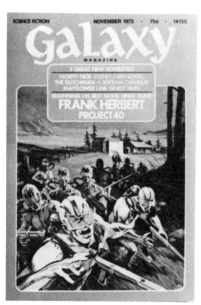

NBA 94. a.

NBA 99. a.

NBA 101. a.

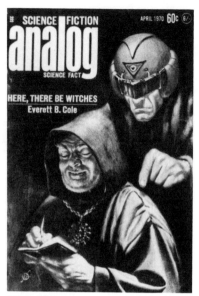

NBA 104. a.

NBA 112. a.

NBA 117. a.

NBA 118. a.

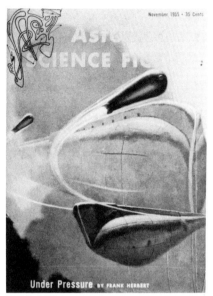

NBA 119. a.

NBA 124. a.

NBA 124. a.

Dune Calendar. One example of the many Dune associational items.

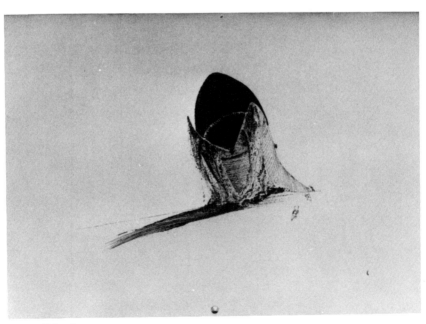

Dune Calendar.